Jeanne Unbottled

Adventures in High Style

Jeanne Beker

A Peter Goddard Book

Published in 2000 by Stoddart Publishing Co. Limited
34 Lesmill Road, Toronto, Canada M3B 2T6
180 Varick Street, 9th Floor, New York, New York 10014

Distributed by:
General Distribution Services Ltd.
325 Humber College Blvd., Toronto, Ontario M9W 7C3
Tel. (416) 213-1919   Fax (416) 213-1917
Email cservice@genpub.com

04   03   02   01   00 1   2   3   4   5

Canadian Cataloguing in Publication Data

Beker, Jeanne
Jeanne unbottled: adventures in high style
"A Peter Goddard book"
Includes index.
ISBN 0-7737-3266-7

1. Beker, Jeanne. 2. Fashion — Biography. 3. Journalists — Canada — Biography. I. Title.
TT505.B45A3 2000   746.9'2'092   C00-931364-8

Text and jacket art direction and design: *Bill Douglas at The Bang*

THE CANADA COUNCIL | LE CONSEIL DES ARTS
FOR THE ARTS | DU CANADA
SINCE 1957 | DEPUIS 1957

We acknowledge for their financial support of our publishing program the Canada Council, the Ontario Arts Council, and the Government of Canada through the Book Publishing Industry Development Program (BPIDP).

Printed and bound in Canada

Contents

Part 3   Fashion Forward

Part 4   The Good, the Bad, and the Beautiful

Part 5   After a Fashion

Acknowledgments

So many have helped me tell my stories: Thanks to Peter Goddard, who, as a rock reporter in 1969, saw an enthusiastic fan dancing her heart out on stage and decided to put her in the paper. Thirty years later, he got her to write a book. Also thanks to Rita Zekas, Matthew Kudelka, and Bill Douglas, along with Marnie Kramarich and Don Bastian at Stoddart, for all their talent and insight; my agent, Tony Gardner, for his wisdom and support; Jennifer Randall and Alisa Kerr, for going through all that tape and finding the moments; Gregory Parvatan, for always trying to make me feel beautiful; Nieva Debuque, for taking care of things when I can't; my *Fashion Television* family — especially Mary Benadiba, Jay Levine, and Marcia Martin; the Waters, CHUM, and Citytv, and Moses Znaimer for his extraordinary vision; Bonnie Brooks, Suzanne Boyd, and *Flare* magazine, who gave me a voice; Brian McDermid, who taught me to see; my parents, who taught me to dream; my sister, Marilyn, who taught me how; my gorgeous daughters, Becky and Joey, who teach me why; and all my precious friends, who share the tears and laughter. Special thanks, too, to Todd Oldham, for taking me to Oz . . . and to Jack, for showing me the way home.

I dedicate this book to the memory of my father.
"Don't be afraid. And never give up."

Becoming Jeanne

Baby Chanel

Spring 1985. There's a cattle call in the lobby of the old Citytv building. About a hundred models of every description are clustered around the front reception desk when I arrive at the studio, all of them eager for the chance to host a new TV show about fashion, which will act as a vehicle for the many fashion videos that are being produced.

As a baby, I was content and quiet — and apparently opted for the "classics" in fashion. Evidently, my style changed over the years . . .

The station is looking for a kind of fashion veejay — a gorgeous babe who will introduce the material. I may be the last person they have in mind, but a six-year diet of rock reporting is getting to me. I've ridden the crest of punk and New Wave and got to meet most of my old rock idols, and I've had my share of seedy clubs and smoky tour buses. It's time to move on, and the fashion scene has struck me as the next big arena: it's just as laden with egos and glitz as the rock world but allows a wider choice of wardrobe beyond the black vinyl jeans that are starting to feel a bit snug. I see the fashion scene as one I can grow gracefully older in. I take the elevator directly to the third floor and knock on the station manager's door, eager to plead my case.

Summer 1989. A sweltering day in Paris, and I'm seven months' pregnant. Karl Lagerfeld has already kept us waiting over three hours in his rue Cambon couture studio. That's bad enough, and the fact that I'm wearing a drab, olive-green maternity suit from a dowdy Toronto maternity boutique is making matters worse.

While my cameraman and I wait, a half-dozen thin, young female assistants scurry about, each turned out impeccably in coordinated black-and-white outfits. They look like senior girls at a swank prep school: some are wearing tunics with starched white shirts, others sport simple pleated black skirts with delicate little white sweaters. They all wear black stockings and identical shiny black loafers, and the ones with long hair have it tied back neatly with black grosgrain ribbons.

I feel as though I'm trapped in the pages of a fashion editorial. Every so often, studio director Gilles Dufour, Lagerfeld's right-hand man, pops in to reassure us that the boss is on his way. The elegant Dufour, also clad in black and white, his eyes hidden behind impenetrably dark sunglasses, looks as though he'd be more at home in a Monte Carlo casino than in a Paris dress salon. I make sure to tell him I have a baby brewing, fearing he might just mistake me for plain old fat.

Continuous cups of water see me through the long hot wait as Dufour and I make small talk. He explains that Lagerfeld has been delayed coming from the airport. He's returning from opening an exhibition of his photographs in Washington, D.C., and is due at the studio any minute for some couture fittings.

"Would you care to wear something from the collection for your interview with Mr. Lagerfeld?" he asks.

Qui, moi? I think, feeling a little like a beached whale by that point. "*Est-que c'est possible?* I don't think you'd have anything that would fit me now," I respond hopelessly.

"*Ah, bien sûr, il y aura quelque chose. Viens avec moi.*"

And he leads me down the hall to an amazing room crammed with racks laden with creations from dozens of past collections: original samples to die for.

"Choose something, anything. There must be something to fit."

What a situation! The most incredible clothes in the world are on offer, and I probably won't be able to squeeze into a single one. Suddenly a divine number in black crêpe and white satin, with signature pearl-and-gold Chanel buttons, catches my eye. It looks loose enough to work. I try it on *et voila!* — a runway wannabe is born.

Karl finally arrives, a mass of photo-lab envelopes under his arm. In his black suit, white shirt and tie, and trademark silver-white ponytail and dark sunglasses, he exudes intrigue and importance. His assistants gather around and he rattles on, a mile a minute, about how wonderfully his photos were received in Washington. Dufour interrupts and introduces me. Lagerfeld immediately recognizes his dress and comments on how well it suits me.

"And I'm seven months' pregnant," I boast.

"*Ah, vraiment?*" he exclaims, as he peers over his thick, smoky glasses.

"Have you ever designed maternity clothes?" I ask half-jokingly. "It would be a real service to women, you know."

And he smiles modestly. "I only designed some maternity clothes once. For Jerry Hall."

Our interview goes very well indeed. He reminds me of Ludwig Von Drake — a lovable cartoon caught up in his own genius, with a German edge for order and excitement.

He keeps me on my toes for the duration of our conversation, as I scramble to keep up with his brilliant thought patterns and keep those provocative questions coming. At the end of the interview, Lagerfeld tells Dufour I must be given the dress to keep.

"*Un petit cadeau, ah?*" he says, and then to Dufour, "*Elle est charmante.*"

I grin like the Cheshire cat, as I groove on the fabulousness of fashion.

I've never found my soul in my closet. Clothes are there to enhance our appearance and delight us with their creativity, but as Bill Blass once confided to me, "Nothing bores me more than a woman who shops all day." People who obsess about clothes drive me crazy. They're like actors worrying more about the costumes they're wearing than the lines they're delivering. Clothes are a prop, they're not the drama itself.

Don't get me wrong: I adore great clothes. I believe in the power of fashion to instill confidence and well-being. But whenever I catch myself agonizing over what to put on my back, I try to snap out of it. "This is not what it's supposed to be about," I tell myself.

I didn't wind up hosting *Fashion Television* for fifteen years out of a love of *schmattes*. It's the people that excite me: not what they wear, but how they wear it. It's attitude, not attire, that inspires me and that drives every creative aspect of the fashion scene today. I've met countless stylish people over the years, but the ones who really stand out are those who dress with attitude, with a sense of who they are and what they're trying to tell the world. People who have lots of money and access to designer clothes aren't necessarily the ones with great personal style. Those who impress me know how to put things together with apparently effortless grace.

I used to think that fashion sense was something certain people were born with. Now I realize that anyone can cultivate it. Honesty in front of the mirror is the first prerequisite, and learning to love your image whatever your shortcomings and insecurities. This is something we all struggle with constantly, and some days or weeks or months are better than others. But dressing up should be adding pleasure to our lives, not grief. With all the options available to us these days, there are smart solutions to every figure problem and fashion crisis. I still don't have all the answers, but I have had the chance to pick many of the world's most image-conscious brains.

Throughout my career in the fashion media I've tried to hold on to a real woman's perspective. My concerns have seldom been those of a typical fashion journalist. I rarely focus on cut or color or silhouette: I'd much rather explore the spirit and fantasy underlying a designer's work and quiz him or her about everything from creative drive to the viability of the clothes.

I've learned a considerable amount by sheer osmosis. I hope, as I share some of my own vulnerabilities, fashionable adventures, and stylish encounters, that you too will see the light at the end of your closet. And by the way, much to my regret, I didn't end up getting much use out of that Chanel dress. A couple of weeks after Lagerfeld gave it to me, I grew too large to fit into it. Then, once I had the baby and lost the weight, it never did look right — it just felt too much like maternity wear.

Sorry, Karl. Still, it was a great fashion moment.

Mitzi

My first fashion memories are of paper dolls, or "cut-outs" as we called them. I was only about four years old, and my eleven-year-old sister, Marilyn, did the scissoring. Her imagination and worldly ways made the flat '50s drawings come to life, opening doors to exotic style realms that were a constant delight to me. Gail Storm and Donna Reed were our favorites. Marilyn always had the final say on which outfits were appropriate for which occasions. My mother found these cut-outs the perfect distraction while she pulled a comb through my waist-length hair.

I loved the way my cut-outs launched grand fantasies. For the glamorous adventure to begin, all I had to do was choose the right outfit, put it on the doll, and fold back the tabs. Our cut-out books usually came with a couple of dolls and enough elegant ensembles to take us anywhere. From swank restaurants, exciting movie premieres, swishy dinner parties, and ritzy luncheons, to fun shopping sprees and important job interviews, our paper gals were always dressed to the nines. We sometimes fought over the accessories — chic little hats and furry muffs and luxurious stoles and killer shoes: the perfect complements that said we, and our dolls, took this business of dressing up very seriously. Delight was often in the details, and nothing felt better than coming up with the appropriate pulled-together look that would carry us through to our next big appointment . . . and wardrobe change.

I lived vicariously through my cut-outs when I was growing up. Now I look back at all my old photographs and press clippings and letters and journal entries and magazine stories and videotapes, and I'm amazed that I've managed to lead such a rich, extraordinary life, surrounded by exquisite friends and so much love, with two precious children and the most incredible gig anyone could imagine. Yet as weary and incredulous as I usually am, I always look forward to the time I can change outfits one more time, fold back the tabs, and go off on still more exciting and glamorous adventures.

Like most North American girls who grew up in the 1950s, my earliest fashion fantasies were fueled by the impossibly perfect Barbie. It was 1959, the year we'd moved into the suburbs. I was seven and Barbie was being advertised everywhere. Pretty soon, all my friends owned one. The concept was too alluring to resist: a glamorous little gal pal through whom you could play out your dreams and whom you could dress in all kinds of nifty outfits. I wanted a Barbie more than anything, and my parents promised that if I could wait until Chanukah, she would be mine.

I was patient, but when Chanukah finally rolled around, my mother told me that Barbie was simply too expensive. She tried to convince me that I'd be just as happy with a Mitzi doll that looked just as good but was only half the price. I was disappointed that the real thing was beyond my grasp, but I resigned myself to falling in love with this knock-off version of my ideal.

The night I got Mitzi, I examined her intently. The most obvious difference was that Mitzi's plastic limbs weren't of as high quality as Barbie's. And her hair was nowhere near as blonde. Mitzi's facial expression was more detached than Barbie's, not really engaging at all. Maybe it had something to do with her thinner lips, or darker eyebrows, or more sleazily applied eye-liner. My sister reasoned that this was an admirable, snobby look that gave Mitzi a certain classy air; I was persuaded that Barbie was too darned common. Mitzi was destined for the world of high fashion, even though she came from the wrong side of the toy racks.

I started thinking that because Mitzi was so different, she needed a new hairstyle. Not having the nerve to take scissors to it, I started

While she may have come from the wrong side of the toy racks, my Mitzi exuded a *je ne sais quoi* quality that gave her a couture edge. (Photo: Bill Douglas)

playing around with her ponytail, flipping it up over her forehead. With another rubber band and a straight pin out of Mom's sewing box, I anchored the ponytail in place. Hey, if those "earring" pins could be stuck way into her head like that, why not let Mitzi suffer just a bit more for the sake of exceptional beauty!

The new look was secured with several spritzes of Final Net hairspray. Now Mitzi even *smelled* as if she'd just been to the hairdresser! My mom and sister were impressed: this sophisticated up-do was just the lift

my new doll needed. I decided that Mitzi was clearly destined to be more than a mere Barbie knock-off; my Mitzi was special, and in my care she was going to be the most unique fashion doll the world had ever seen.

Everywhere I took Mitzi, adults commented on what an unusually pretty hairstyle she had and how they'd never seen a doll quite like her before. So what if my friends pointed out that she had a "Reliable" logo on her back with "Made in Canada" stamped in teeny words underneath?

Mitzi was far too original to wear those commercial, prepackaged Barbie outfits — they were way too expensive anyway — so Mom, ever the eager seamstress, promised to provide her with the most extraordinary wardrobe any doll could dream of.

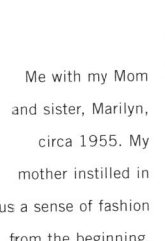

Me with my Mom and sister, Marilyn, circa 1955. My mother instilled in us a sense of fashion from the beginning.

Unlike New York designer Anna Sui, who once told me she made her Barbie's clothes out of Kleenex, my doll's wardrobe was created from precious leftover sewing scraps. My mom made nearly all of our clothes in those days and for every new outfit my sister and I got, there would be a matching one for Mitzi. The fabrics were always top notch: great ginghams and corduroys and Viyellas. Mom had her own formal wear made by a local dressmaker out of the finest velvets, satins, brocades, and laces, and Mitzi was fortunate enough to inherit those leftovers.

7

Dad, who worked in the garment district alongside several furriers, also contributed to Mitzi's burgeoning closet by providing us with scraps of luxurious pelts and skins. The mink stole we made for Mitzi was divine, and her gray Persian lamb coat was *to die for!*

Still, what ultimately worked so well about my cheapo doll and her luxe couture collection was that arrogant, almost bitchy look on Mitzi's face. Man, that chick had attitude! Barbie would have been too wholesome and squeaky clean to wear any of those over-the-top, high-fashion creations we custom-made for Mitzi. I learned that to pull off wearing fabulous clothes, you have to have attitude. Of course she also had a killer figure. I didn't realize it at the time, but the fact that Mitzi really did look good in everything was probably due to her impeccable proportions.

A lot of feminists today blame those classic fashion dolls like Barbie and Mitzi for women's low self-esteem and poor personal body images, but I never aspired to look like my Mitzi. I just fantasized about exuding the same *je ne sais quoi* when it came to wearing clothes — as if they had been made especially for me. That ideal is the essence of what we call "couture," but it would be years before I came to experience it in reality.

The Hebrew parochial school where I attended first grade in 1958 enforced a uniform: a pleated navy tunic, white shirt, and white socks. I was proud to wear my little uniform, which surprisingly accentuated my classmates' differences rather than obliterating them. Some girls wore long-sleeved shirts, some short-sleeved. Some wore shirts with button-down collars, others had slightly frilly collars. Some girls wore ankle socks, some wore knee socks. I always wore the latter, because my legs were so skinny and I wanted to expose them as little as possible. Wearing a uniform, yet being able to make it my own, heightened my awareness of the subtleties of individual expression. Suddenly I was more aware of body types: those tunics looked so different on the chubby girls from the way they appeared on the thin girls.

My parents were determined to give me a religious education. Most of our relatives had died in the Holocaust, and Mom and Dad felt obligated to pass on their Jewish traditions and heritage. During my six years at parochial school, I learned to read and write Hebrew at the same time I learned to read and write English. Talmud Torah (aka the Associated Hebrew Day School) promoted stringent work habits, and the teachers piled on the homework. I was very earnest about my education and never failed to earn straight "E's" for "Excellent." My father always called me "Your Excellency" for days after I brought home my report cards.

By the end of grade six, I was tired of having religion drummed into me, and I begged my parents to let me go to a public junior high school for grade seven. I excelled my first year there and made the honor roll because of good work habits. But in grade eight I discovered boys, and my marks plummeted. By then I was having so much fun that I couldn't have cared less.

War and Peace

My parents emigrated to Canada from Poland in 1948. Penniless Holocaust survivors, they maintained the courage to dream and slowly rebuilt their shattered lives despite the devastation of war.

My dad, Josio Beker, circa 1945. A true survivor, my dad's motto was always "Don't be afraid. And never give up."

I grew up hearing stories about the war and of my relatives' horrible experiences in "the old country." I came to think of Europe as a terrible, ugly place, until one day I discovered a weathered brown-leather purse at the back of my parents' closet. Sitting in the closet and going through that purse became one of my secret pastimes. The purse was filled with old black-and-white photographs of my mother and father from the postwar years before they came to Canada. It was a treasure trove of European style. My mom wore a series of hats with elegant brims, and chic tailored suits and fur-trimmed coats that she'd got second-hand.

Dad cut a dashing figure: he was tall and handsome, with a little mustache. There were shots of him in smart pinstripe suits and long, flowing overcoats. There was even a picture of him wearing jodhpurs!

Dad always used to say that people's first impressions were based on what you wore and the way you looked. That's how they'd judge you, so you must always pay close attention to your clothes. Mom once told me she fell in love with my dad the first time she saw him in his Polish soldier's uniform — he was that striking.

During the war years my parents succeeded in staying alive, but only just, through their own wits and the kindness of strangers. They were often on the run, hiding in abandoned barns and underground bunkers.

After the war ended, my parents' main mission was to reclaim their humanity. My father's first postwar gift to my mother was an exquisitely delicate gold bracelet set with three tiny diamonds. This wild extravagance was a celebration of their survival, a tribute to their love, and a manifestation of their undying sense of style.

My father, Josio Beker, was born in Kozowa, Poland, in 1913 and came from the other side of the tracks. He lived in a humble, earth-floored wooden house with his father, Beryl, a shoemaker; his mother, Genia (whom I'm named after); a younger sister Esther; and two brothers, Shmuel and Israel (or "Srul Hersh," as my dad always called him). My grandfather died of a stroke at the age of forty-five, leaving his wife and children to fend for themselves. Dad was forced to quit school at fourteen and earn a living to take care of his family. Charismatic by nature, he became a salesman, flogging everything from honeybees to workhorses to flints. He was fiercely responsible and always prided himself on being able to take care of people. As he became more worldly, he grew into quite the entrepreneur and began throwing money-making parties for all his friends, complete with live Big Band music.

In 1937, my parents started their clandestine romance, knowing that their relationship would have been strictly forbidden by my mother's father. Josio was from a poor family, was not orthodox, had little schooling, and was seven years older than Bronia Rohatiner. They were from two different worlds, so all their rendezvous had to be kept top secret.

When the war broke out, my parents' lives were shattered. In

My mom and dad, in Austria, just after the war. They were always deeply in love.

11

1941, Dad was mobilized into the Russian army and subsequently captured by the Germans. He escaped, returned to the Jewish ghetto, and spent the next two years living there, continuing secretly to romance my mother.

My maternal grandmother Rohatiner died of typhoid fever in the ghetto two months before the rest of my mother's family (except for four of my mother's step-siblings: my aunts Lena and Rose and my uncles Harry and Sam, who had all moved to New York in 1918). My mother was the sole survivor in her family.

My mother's family hid in the cellar of their home when the Nazis came to town. Ten people: my mother's father, her brother and his two daughters, a sister-in-law and her three children, my mother's beautiful sister, Sarah. Six family members had already been taken to a camp or had been killed. The Germans must have caught wind of the family's whereabouts, because they sealed off the family's air vents, suffocating everyone except my mother. She used to tell the story of how her family's corpses were being loaded onto wagons to be taken away and someone noticed she was still breathing. Even though she'd always been the frailest and skinniest, she was miraculously revived.

She had lived through the first round of terror, only to wake up and realize she was all alone, her family decimated. It was then that my father came to her rescue, taking her to live with his family. In June 1943, the ghetto was liquidated, and those who could went into hiding.

When I was growing up, my parents continually retold stories about how they survived. I hated those terrifying accounts and remember hiding under my bed when I was little in an effort not to listen to them. Even when I was five, I knew that my beloved parents had lived through a thousand hellish adventures. While their survival made me very proud of them, I secretly wished they'd been born in Canada and had nice normal lives, like most of my friends' parents.

Slippers

Work hard and be honest: those were two of the most important things my parents taught me. Dad always set the hard work example: he went into his slipper-making shop seven days a week, and on weekdays he'd be gone from seven in the morning until seven at night. He was adamant about being his own boss and enjoyed calling the shots in his business. But aside from the glories of deal-making, he had little respect for the nature of his business and always reminded us that he'd never be working at "the shop" if he had been born in Canada and enjoyed the opportunities available to the native born.

My father started a small manufacturing business called Quality Slippers in Toronto in the early '50s. He produced children's novelty slippers, the kind with little bunny-rabbit heads and clown faces. He worked on the first samples in the basement of our house, and he'd come up periodically to ask our opinion.

I realize now that he was actually playing the part of designer! He was so proud of his new ideas. Thrilled to find tiger-striped plush, he quickly came up with tiger heads. Leopard plush naturally led to leopard heads. As his business grew, he was taxed to think of more original designs. One year he started putting "squeakers" in the heads of his slippers. I felt lucky to be privy to the inner workings of these squeakers. Just to see the way the little cardboard and paper cylinders came packed in their boxes, before they were inserted in the clown or bunny or tiger heads, was intriguing. But soon the squeakers started giving my dad more grief than they were worth: kids would overplay with them until they finally stopped squeaking. This meant returns, which did not please the stores.

Dad abandoned the squeakers and started looking for the next big thing. In the early '60s, an Inuit handicraft creation called the "ookpik" emerged. Made of sealskin, this big-eyed owl was hugely popular. My father got the bright idea to make ookpik slippers. The first batch was a hit, but soon someone threatened to sue him for ripping off the idea, so my dad quickly changed the name to "ook-kik." We all thought that was brilliant.

He branched out into other novelties, including Davy Crockett coonskin hats. He brought home the reject raccoon tails and I played with them for hours. Still later, he started manufacturing sheepskin vests for hunters and construction workers. The sheepskin had a soft, dusty, leather smell, which along with the distinct odor of stamp pads (used for stamping sizes on the bottoms of soles), permeated the shop floor.

13

I never thought of Quality Slippers as a fashion-related business, but I suppose it was. Each season, Dad had to come up with new styles, convince buyers that they were just what the consumer wanted, and then fill those important orders on time. As for all designers, his biggest challenge was to bring out an attractive, quality product at an affordable price point. And in those days, competing with the Japanese was next to impossible. I learned a lot about the stresses of the *schmatte* business from my dad, and I respect anyone who has managed to succeed in such an insecure and highly competitive industry.

Every Saturday my mother would take me to my father's factory. The shop was a decrepit place, three floors up on Adelaide Street in downtown Toronto. Because of all the plush that was being worked with, little fibers were always flying around in the air. It was sweltering in the summer, and I remember seeing the sweat on Dad's brow and feeling sorry that he had to work so hard to give the four of us a good life. But I adored him for it and knew he loved us all deeply and unconditionally.

All my dad's workers were Italian, and they always greeted me effusively. I don't think it was just because I was the boss's daughter — it was because they all loved and respected him so much. I'd go around to each of their sewing machines and they'd all comment on my clothes and how big I was getting.

Dad was always sitting at his machine, too, and he'd never be ready to leave just yet, so I'd kill time in his office, playing with the stamps and checking out the new samples. I was also interested in seeing competitors' products, slippers from the U.S.A. and Japan that never seemed as familiar and cozy and charming as our own "Quality Slippers." Naively, I figured these slick foreign slippers were just there for inspiration. I knew how concerned my father was about what the competition was doing — I never guessed that he might actually be trying to knock them off.

After work on Saturdays, Dad loved to shop in Kensington Market, a few blocks from his factory. The sights and sounds and smells of that open-air, European-style market were so colorful. Everyone seemed to know him from his rounds flogging slippers and vests to the dry-goods merchants. I'd follow behind as he made his rounds, greeting everyone, making little deals, forever joking around.

The fish store was always our last stop. There, we would buy a huge live carp for my mom to make gefilte fish with a few days later. Because I was never allowed to have a pet (except for boring guppies), I was happy these big, interesting creatures came into our lives on a regular basis. We'd take the heavy fish home, wrapped in newspaper, and plop him into our bathtub, where he'd swim around for a couple of days until Dad was ready to do him in. I'd kneel by the tub late into the evening, watching short-lived pets swim around and petting their iridescent scales. It was a little traumatic when their time was up. Dad would lift the slippery fish out of the tub and carry it into the kitchen. I'd watch from a distance as he chopped off its head with the big knife, and shiver as the head would jump around on the counter for a few seconds.

Though I felt a little lonelier each time I lost a fish, I was still happy that my parents were actually bringing pets into the house!

Mom, the Neighborhood, and Marilyn

While both my parents were honest by nature, Mom often felt she was honest to a fault. She always spoke her mind and sometimes thought she got into trouble because of it. But she was such a highly emotional person that wearing her heart on her sleeve came naturally, and she instilled in me the belief that as long as you tell the truth, nothing can ever hurt you. In the end, all we have is ourselves, and it was imperative to face that.

Mom was an ultra-feminine, dedicated wife, totally devoted to my father. Because he'd rescued her during the war, she felt indebted to him. He was her hero, and she'd do anything to please him.

She had earned a diploma as an aesthetician in Austria after the war, but worked for the first three years after she came to Canada at a pants factory for $12 a week. She quit just before I was born and became a full-time housewife. She'd take long baths late in the afternoon and dress up in one of the dirndls or hostess gowns she'd made herself, looking fresh and pretty for my father's return. Every night, she waited at the window for him, worrying if he was even five minutes late. She described herself as a "professional worrier," a trait she claimed came with the territory if you were a Jewish mother. Years later, she'd always wait at the window when I came home from dates. We'd pull into the driveway, and I'd see this little crack in the front window curtains quickly close. She'd never go to bed until I was home.

Mom's sense of style demanded that she be frequently coiffed. She went to a salon over a store on Bathurst Street owned by a hairdresser named Toby. Toby was a tough, bleached blonde who wore lots of makeup and called everybody "honey" and "baby doll" with a slight Yiddish accent. Because there were so many weddings and bar mitzvahs on Sundays, Toby also saw clients in the basement of her home when the salon was closed. I often went to the salon with my mother. The place was filled with big, silver industrial hair dryers and packed with the neighborhood *yentas* and *prietzas*. Toby's clients always left with unnaturally big hair, either bouffants or up-dos, teased and sprayed to resemble helmets.

After she got her hair done, Mom always slept on a satin pillowcase and either wrapped toilet paper around her hair or wore a pair of silk underpants on her head to protect her new do. She assured me that her best friend, Mrs. Jaskolka, did the same thing. I always thought this was totally creepy, until my cool sister Marilyn started doing it, too. Then I just looked at it as another fashion statement, a necessary part of being a grown-up.

At Toby's, I never failed to get my cheeks pinched and be told I was a natural beauty. For my sister's Sweet Sixteen luncheon, when I was nine, Toby styled my waist-length hair into a bun and told me I looked exactly like Audrey Hepburn. I was terribly proud, but I couldn't bring myself to protect this new look with either toilet paper or silk underpants.

We had subscriptions to *Vogue* and *Harper's Bazaar* when I was growing up and my mother, sister, and I spent a lot of time poring over them, dreaming up ways to knock off those outrageous creations. We could never afford designer clothes, but we had wealthy cousins in Passaic, New Jersey, who regularly sent us their cast-offs. These clothes sported exotic labels from stores like Bergdorf's and Saks. There were smart little tailored woolen suits and crisp cotton pique outfits, delicate cashmere twin sets, and even the odd taffeta party dress. Sometimes accessories were thrown in, like little white gloves and lacy collars you could attach

My mom's dressmaker custom-made the creations we wore to my sister Marilyn's Sweet Sixteen luncheon. My dress was a pink organza fantasy, with a little matching purse that I found especially charming.

to your own sweaters. Even though many of these things weren't really appropriate, we wore them eagerly; we were proud that we didn't really look like the rest of the kids at school.

Until I was seven, we lived in a three-storey red brick house on Delaware Avenue, in the west end of downtown Toronto. Backyards were filled with rhubarb and lilies of the valley. Lilac trees grew in front yards, and gardens were bursting with peonies, snapdragons, and tiger lilies.

Families from all kinds of backgrounds — Italian, Chinese, British, Polish, and plain old Canadian WASP — lived in the neighborhood. We shared our house with boarders to help make ends meet, and I have fond memories of living with this extended family.

We got our first TV set when I was five years old, a huge eye set in a mahogany cabinet that matched our *faux* mahogany coffee table.

My favorite show was *Howdy Doody*. I especially adored Flub-A-Dub but could never figure out exactly what kind of critter he was. My parents loved Sid Caesar, Jack Benny, Gary Moore, and Dinah Shore. My mother still tells the story about the time we were watching Dinah Shore with some company when one of the ladies commented, "That Dinah Shore stinks!" I went over to the TV set, sniffed the screen, and said, "Yeah, she sorta does." To my puzzlement everyone started laughing. I remember thinking that maybe the people on TV could see into our living room, so occasionally when I was alone watching *I've Got a Secret* or *To Tell the Truth*, I'd pull my pants down to see if anyone noticed!

I always thought of our tiny family as a very tight unit. It was the four of us against the world.

We moved to the suburbs in 1959, when I was seven. My parents chose Downsview, mostly because of its Jewish ghetto quality: here, they felt, their daughters would be able to mingle with other kids who had a similar cultural background. They were terrified that we might lose our religious identity. It was exciting to be moving into a brand new house that would be our own — except for some tenants in the basement apartment — but I remember thinking the new neighborhood was a little sterile, not nearly as charming as our old haunts. Still, there were lots of new kids around to play with who ate the same food as we did and regularly attended synagogue. Somehow I felt a strange sense of belonging. There was also more of a "country" quality to this new suburban lifestyle. We spent hours playing in the big fields across the street from our house, catching tadpoles in swamps and exploring mysterious ditches along the road. I missed the sidewalks and gardens of the old neighborhood, but learned to enjoy the rugged nature of my new suburban existence.

While my fantasy life was filled with sending Mitzi off on dates, my big sister Marilyn, as a teenager, was starting to have her own real-life dates. Marilyn wore lots of black, read poetry, listened to Bob Dylan, and carried a clipboard to school that had "1-2-cha-cha-cha" written on the back of it. If she deemed somebody a creep, he definitely fit the bill. And most of the guys she went out with fell into that category. Usually, it was something subtle that gave the guy away, like wearing white socks. I always knew exactly what my sister meant. My father was fascinated by what determined a creep in my sister's book. He constantly asked, "Can you please explain me, what means a 'creep'?" Only to get the stock answer: "Oh, you know, Daddy. Just plain creepy!"

I never had a problem understanding — or accepting — anything my sister said or did. She was a goddess to me and I would spend hours watching her get ready to go out or secretly listening in on her phone conversations or going through her stuff whenever she left the house.

Besides having superb personal style, Marilyn also had great spirit and became active in all kinds of extra-curricular activities. Her passion for writing led her to write for *The Varsity*, the campus newspaper. And she was quite the peacenik, always taking part in ban-the-bomb rallies and other peace demonstrations. One of her more controversial activities included an annual parade led by the University of Toronto engineering department, the Lady Godiva Parade. I wasn't sure exactly what Marilyn did in that parade, but I eventually found out she played a memorable, starring role! She was determined to be a journalist one day. She was also buddies with cool people like the future filmmaker David Cronenberg.

Before Marilyn graduated from university, she got a job writing for the *Toronto Star* and later wrote for *The Globe and Mail*. Soon she was getting me free tickets to all the groovy concerts, from Herman's Hermits to The Doors. She also brought home lots of freebie albums, which I listened to religiously on the living-room hi-fi. Before long, I'd been exposed to a lot of great blues artists, developing a pretty sophisticated music palate for a fourteen-year-old.

My sister paved the way for a lot of my liberal, artistic thoughts and softened the blows I eventually dealt my parents with my unconventional dreams and aspirations. She constantly inspired me and taught me about magic and mysticism in everyday life. To this day, I consider Marilyn to be one of the hippest, most brilliant, creative, and spiritual people I have ever known. I'll forever be grateful for having her in my life.

"The Undershirt Kids"

Ever since I found some clear, plastic stencils of eyebrows and lips in one of my mother's drawers, the paraphernalia and procedures used to enhance feminine beauty have always fascinated me.

Except for scarlet red lipstick and nail polish, my mother wore little or no makeup. Nevertheless she had a collection of aids stashed away, teeny little lipstick samples that she kept in the same drawer as the tweezers and the Maybelline Cake Mascara, which came in a bright red plastic case. There were also some fine little hairnets and strangely shaped hair clips for making Marcel waves. I equated the oddments in my mother's makeup drawer with bras and girdles and garter belts — things that were beyond my experience but were getting closer.

My best friend, Penny Chikofsky, and I were the only girls left in our grade seven class who didn't wear bras. A jerky guy named Howie

Greenwood noticed that we were still wearing undershirts under our white blouses and, to our mortification, started calling us "The Undershirt Kids."

Mom thought the idea of a flat-chested twelve-year-old wearing a brassiere was preposterous, but I assured her I was in dire need of a "training" bra, and on Saturday, we went to the mall in search of one. At a store called Teen Canada, I raced over to the brassiere rack, and with the help of a sympathetic saleslady, found the right training bra for me: size 28 AAA. Actually, it was just a flat piece of stretchy fabric, but it had real bra straps and, most important, a back closure that would be highly visible under a white shirt.

The next day I proudly wore my new bra under a white shirt and made sure to bend down when Howie Greenwood was behind me, so that he'd see I had finally joined the club.

There's no question that lingerie separates the girls from the women. Over the next three or four years, I traded in my Ladybird undershirts for a whole new collection of teen bras. My faves were the ones that were padded with a stiff foam rubber that could be deftly stuffed with Kleenex. In those days I needed all the help I could get.

Seeing Stars

By the time I was twelve, I knew I wanted a life on stage, or in television. I can remember wishing on my birthday candles every year for my own TV show. I worshipped Michelle Finney, the fourteen-year-old Toronto girl who co-hosted the CBC show *Razzle Dazzle*.

My mother allowed me to take acting lessons when I was twelve. I enrolled at the Toronto School of Drama, where under the direction of Marjorie Purvey I learned elocution and articulation. (This was around the time that I dropped the "i" in my first name. "Jeanne" seemed classier than "Jeannie." That was how the actress Jeanne Crain spelled her name, and besides, it looked French, exotic.)

Miss Purvey was a tall, no-nonsense woman with permed hair and tortoiseshell glasses. She always wore long straight skirts and twin sweater sets. She was old — at least forty — and unmarried, for which I pitied her.

I craved Miss Purvey's approval. I wanted her to believe in my talent. I worked hard to memorize the soliloquies she assigned us and took great pride and delight in reciting them in front of the class. The piece I worked hardest on was a poem called "The Fan," which I delivered very demurely with the aid of a prop:

> If you want to learn a lesson with the fan,
> I'm quite prepared to teach you all I can.
> So ladies, every one, please observe how it is done;
> This simple little lesson with the fan.
> . . . .
> With your fan just idly play,
> And look at him as if to say,
> It's a matter of indifference to you.

I always thought it was strange that a spinster like Miss Purvey would be trying to teach us how to seduce a man. Evidently, "The Fan" hadn't worked for her.

One of my biggest beauty influences during my teens was the pop singer Cher. I had long, stick-straight hair, but because I read somewhere that Cher ironed hers, so did I. And I used to try to wear my eye makeup just the way she did. Cher had extremely long fingernails, always painted white. Her lips, too, were always pale — pearlized white or light, light pink. And her eyes looked like she had brushes around them: thick black false eyelashes, with black eye-liner turned up at the end, cat style. She also wore a thick line of black just above her eyelid, on her brow bone. This had a kind of Cleopatra Egyptian effect, and certainly made her eyes look very big and very dramatic. I spent hours experimenting, trying to get the look just right.

When I was almost sixteen, a short, dark-haired, skinny girl around the corner named Eva tried to convince me that I could benefit from modeling lessons. Eva had a jaunty sense of style: she always wore berets and lacy stockings and carried purses, giving the impression that she was wearing perfectly coordinated outfits. She did her utmost to conceal her flaws with layers of makeup, whose mysteries she had been taught at Eleanor Fulcher's modeling school.

Eva made an appointment for me at Fulcher's, and I went downtown to Yonge and Bloor for my interview. The place didn't feel very glamorous to me and I wasn't prepared to dish out the hundreds of dollars in course fees. I decided to learn about makeup from magazines instead. Eva's Sweet Sixteen gift to me was a pair of false eyelashes, complete with a personal lesson in their application. She came over with these ultra-long, feathery lashes and a tube of glue and taught me how to trim them and put them on. I was dazzled by the effect, and from then on false eyelashes and I were inseparable.

I read that Cher sometimes wore more than one pair: two on the top and a disassembled pair on the bottom. The lashes could be picked apart and glued individually under your natural lashes to really give you a wide-eyed effect. I tried the three-pair approach and it was a knockout. But I reserved the look for only the biggest parties: Sweet Sixteens, Shy Seventeens, proms, weddings, and bar mitzvahs. The minute I got home from my dates, I couldn't wait to rip all those heavy lashes off!

Years later, as a radio entertainment reporter, I found myself in Cher's hotel room for a post-show interview. As I started up my tape recorder, she plopped right down on the bed and started to peel off her big false eyelashes. It was one of the most endearing gestures I've ever seen a celebrity make.

Toby's Best Friend

I always thought I deserved the leading roles in school plays, but I rarely got them because the plays were usually always musicals and I couldn't sing on key. I was dying to break into "the business" but didn't have a clue how to go about getting discovered. Then one day, my friend Marsha Rocket called with what sounded like a golden opportunity.

"Hey, Jeanne, the CBC is holding open auditions for a new show," she said breathlessly. "You should go down and try out."

Marsha had read the notice in the Saturday paper. The sitcom was going to be called *Toby*, about the trials of a teenage girl and her French-Canadian boyfriend.

"You mean anyone can go down and audition?" I asked.

"That's what it says: Tuesday, between 5 and 7."

Three days later I was standing in front of my bedroom mirror deciding whether to wear my long hair up or down. I went for two pony-

tails on either side of my head — just the right do for the Canadian Gidget I aspired to be. I painted on some Twiggy-style lashes and a few faint freckles and donned a shiny, purple turtleneck jersey and matching flower-power kilt. I felt cute and confident.

I arrived at the CBC's downtown studios on Jarvis Street ready to take on the world, toting my Sweet Sixteen photo and a flimsy resumé boasting such questionable credits as Fruma Sarah in *Fiddler on the Roof* (I didn't dare mention it was a Camp New Moon production) and training at the Toronto School of Drama. A bespectacled production secretary handed me a couple of script pages and pointed me down a corridor. My heart sank when I walked through the door: about fifty teenage girls of every size, shape, and hair color were laughing, giggling, and talking among themselves as if they'd all been friends for ages. And they didn't just have a lousy one-sheet resume and snapshot with them: they had binders filled with tear sheets from magazines and catalogs and I could tell from the snippets of their conversations that most had been professional models and

As a starry-eyed young teen, I was passionate about pursuing a career as an actress.

actresses since they were two and had starred in all kinds of commercials and campaigns and kids' series. Some of them had even worked in movies.

I felt like a complete amateur — a hack, a groupie. Who did I think I was, daring to come downtown to the CBC to audition for a national TV show? What if they asked me to talk about my experience? What would I do? Recite "The Fan"? I was dying to leave but this was the closest I'd come to show biz and I wanted to see more.

I stared down at the dialogue on the script pages in my hand and took a deep breath. I knew I was a good reader. Maybe I'd just wow them with my delivery. My name was called, and I was escorted down the hall into a large, dark room with about eight people in it. There was a video camera and a bank of monitors behind a glass wall. A woman in a severe dark suit with black-and-gray hair introduced herself. Her name was Gloria White, the producer, and I knew she was the one I'd have to impress.

"So, Jean, tell us what professional acting experience you've had."

"Well, actually I haven't had that much," I offered, "but I've been in plays at summer camp and I've taken drama lessons."

I must have been insane. There were dozens of girls out there with real credentials — I even recognized one from *The Forest Rangers*. They'd done important work like Cheerios commercials and the Eaton's catalog; I'd heard them talking about their jobs, their agents, and their callbacks. Some of them were there with their mothers: young, groovy, Canadian-born mothers. These girls were pros with turned-up noses who went to auditions as a way of life.

"Okay, Jean. Let's hear you read the part of Toby," said Ms. White, almost sympathetically.

I knew I was good; Toby's words rolled off my tongue simply, naturally. And even though I felt uncomfortable acting against Ms. White in the role of Toby's boyfriend, Pierre, I felt I pulled it off. After my read, the group in the room put their heads together for a minute.

"That was just fine, Jean. We'll be in touch."

I walked past the room of giggling pros and took the long subway and bus ride home, still clutching my two pages of Toby dialogue and thinking of all the ways I could have read the part even better.

Two days later when I got home from school my mother told me someone from the CBC had called. A Ms. White wanted me to call her back. When I did, she seemed delighted.

"Jean, do you think you can make it down here tomorrow after

school? We're having some of the girls read for us again."

The next day, I decided to go the same route with the hairdo, but this time opted for a hot-pink knit outfit: a little pleated skirt and a V-neck top that I'd purchased in Miami. I was excited, buzzing, eager to prove my first read wasn't just a fluke. This role had my name written on it. Look out, Michelle Finney!

But when I got to the CBC studio again, I realized I was just one of many who were getting a second chance. I took the additional pages of dialogue that were being handed out and decided to learn my lines off by heart this time. There were only two people to hear me, Gloria White and her director. They nodded with satisfaction when I'd finished, and Ms. White told me she thought I was really a very talented little actress.

"Thank you, Jean. We should be making our decision in the next couple of weeks."

I thanked them both and floated out of the building and down the street.

When I heard nothing after three weeks, I was devastated and decided that a dramatic gesture was in order. I went down to Bloor Street with Marsha and walked into Gus Caruso's hair salon, Toronto's best, and I told the stylist I wanted to chop off my hair — all of it. I wanted to do what Mia Farrow's character, Alison, had just done on *Peyton Place*. I wanted the shortest haircut possible. I had to somehow demonstrate my loss of innocence.

Marsha stood by as each long section of my hair was lopped off. She placed each handful of hair gingerly in a bright pink cardboard box, laying it to rest with my dreams of landing that part. That pink cardboard box filled with my long, silky hair is still tucked away in a closet at my mother's house, an eternal reminder of the first sacrifice I made as a tormented young artist.

My first professional photo shoot was for my "comp" card; evidently, it brought out the moody artist in me.

(Photo: Mike Gluss)

As I left the salon, I felt more grown up and sophisticated than ever before. My hair was no more than an inch long on top, with longer, spiky bits at the back and ears. I couldn't wait to get home and start experimenting with eye makeup to accentuate my glamorous new image.

A few days later, Ms. White phoned back. Her voice was warm and friendly.

"We really agonized a lot over this, Jean. The director and I were both so impressed with your audition, but because of your lack of professional experience, we just couldn't cast you as Toby."

I accepted the bad news stoically but I was close to tears at the disappointment.

Then she went on: "But we think you're so talented and so right for the show. How would you like to play Toby's best friend, Phyllis? It's a recurring role with lots of comedic potential — the character's got an edge. We think you'd be perfect."

I couldn't believe what I was hearing! My dream was coming true. I was to become a real actress after all. And then I remembered my new hair.

"But I've done something stupid, Miss White. I've cut off all my hair."

I braced myself for rejection once again, convinced that it was probably my ponytails that had won me the role. Instead, she sounded delighted.

"Oh, don't worry, I'm sure you look great. We'll call you in a couple of days and give you rehearsal times for your first episode."

Toby lasted only one season, but I appeared in about eight episodes and the credit was enough to get me a union card and an agent. Before long, auditions became a way of life for me, too. I started getting commercial work, parts in other TV shows, and even a supporting role in a full-scale feature, *Class of '44*, the sequel to the hit movie *Summer of '42*.

Teen Fashion Essentials

By my mid-teens, clothes were no longer for mere comfort or convenience — or even for the simple and innocent purpose of looking pretty. For me, certain garments were status symbols — flags that marked my coming of age and the beginning of an exciting new identity that I had secretly been cultivating for months, for years. These were essential garments that would see me grasp the first rungs of womanhood — that would help me feel strong and sexy and closer to whom I thought I wanted to be:

Striped denim Tee-Kay bell bottoms. I bought these at Thrifty's, the biggest jeans store in town. They were light blue and lime green and it

This contact sheet, circa 1969, features me in a very "Austin Powers" dress, with the letters L-O-V-E printed all over it. What a poseur! (Photo by Mike Gluss)

took me forever to decide on them. When I got home, I put them on and sat in a tub of hot water, hoping they'd shrink to fit me tighter after a good soaking.

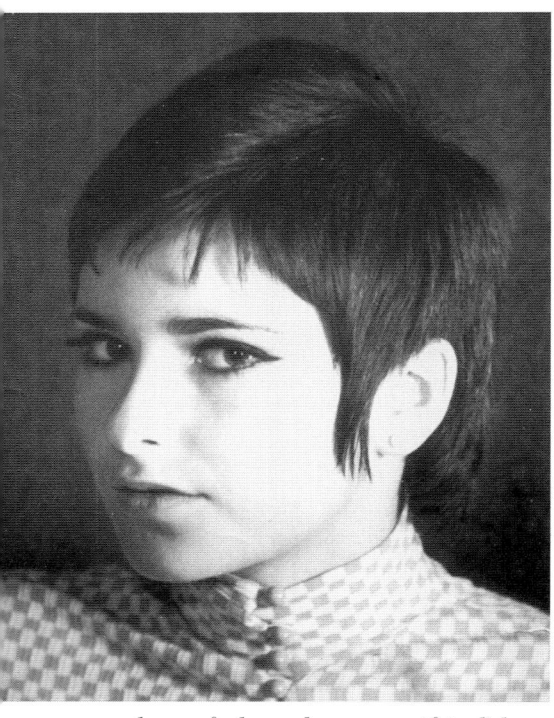

A zippered black leather jacket. Our mild-mannered next-door neighbor Tibor Berk was a traveling coat salesman who always had racks of coats and jackets in the back of his blue-and-white Chevy wagon. But these were all ordinary, conservative things made out of nylon or polyester. One day, he told my mother he had a one-of-a-kind leather sample he thought I might be interested in. It was a small, tight-fitting zippered jacket that was the coolest thing I'd ever seen. It fit me perfectly, and I wore it everywhere. It was especially right for hanging out at the Dairy Queen, when I first started smoking. This jacket made me feel tough — even if it did come from Mr. Berk, a devout Jew who took me to synagogue with his own kids.

The "mod look" was my style mantra back in 1969. The pink-and-white jersey dress I'm wearing in this shot came from a fab Toronto boutique called The Unicorn. (Photo by Victor Jacobs)

An "I Dream of Jeannie" outfit. I was one of the nominees for Prom Queen at my high school. I knew my wild reputation would prevent me from winning, but I still wanted to wear something unforgettable. I decided an *I Dream of Jeannie* outfit was the way to go. Mom and I found a pattern for a fancy jumpsuit with harem pants. She made it for me out of bright yellow raw silk. She then made a small black velvet vest and trimmed it with gold-sequined ribbon. I wore the outfit with gold-beaded sandals, and it looked divine even though a beautiful girl named Gina won the crown. Her conventional gown wasn't nearly as memorable as mine.

Landlubber, hip-hugger blue jeans. In Florida with my parents at Christmas, I befriended a tall, lanky hippy from New York named Lief Erickson (he was actually a Jewish guy from the Bronx, whose real name was Eric Liefer, but he had a thing for Vikings), and he had the grooviest blue jeans I'd ever seen. They were faded just right and made of great lightweight denim, but it was the cut that drove me wild: extremely low-riding, well below the belly button, tight on the thighs and flaring out generously below the knee. I asked Lief if I could try them on and they fit fabulously. The bottoms were too long, but it was cool to have them dragging on the ground.

Lief gave me his "Landlubbers" as a going-away present, and I wore them to every rock concert, patching them up and rubbing cigarette ashes into the thighs once in a while to give them an even more weathered look. Eventually, I embroidered flowers on the back pocket and a daisy coming out of one of the front pockets. One hot summer day, I turned them into ultra-sexy short shorts, which I wore for another few years. I had those cut-offs on the first night my husband Denny and I made love — over a decade after Lief gave them to me.

Yellow bikini with pompoms. This flashy swimsuit might have been tacky, but it never failed to spark the attention I craved. It went down in rock history the day I wore it to the first Toronto Pop Festival in the summer of '69.

I was sitting up front, on the field at Varsity Stadium, grooving to the music with a group of kids, when one tune in particular got me up on my feet. It was Ronnie Hawkins's "Bo Diddley," and I just started dancing my heart out. Ronnie, wearing a purple suit, must have spotted my shaking pom poms, because suddenly I saw him pointing at me from the stage. My friend Esther Goldfluss started screaming and pushing me forward, encouraging me to get on up there. Before I knew it, I was on stage, boogying it up alongside Ronnie and the boys. When the song ended, the crowd roared and I scooted down off the stage and back to my

Dancing my heart out at the Toronto Pop Festival in the summer of '69 was a total thrill. (Courtesy Sun Media Corporation)

spot, glowing from my moment of glory. A photographer even asked me for my name and address!

The next day, my mother was shocked to get a call from her friend, Mrs. Kreinick, with the news that a shot of her little Jeanne, wearing something very skimpy, had made the front page of the *Telegram*'s entertainment section. The caption read: "Fan Jeanne Beker, 17, [. . .] Blvd., couldn't resist the Ronnie Hawkins' beat and was invited on stage for an impromptu dance." My parents were outraged. It *was* a little creepy that the paper actually printed the name of my street. Now the weirdos would know where to find me!

A day later, I got a call from Hawkins's manager, a guy named Heavy Andrews, who asked me to come downtown because he and Ronnie wanted to meet the chick who had given them all this publicity. I heard Hollywood calling, so I put on a tight little dress and my high-heeled sandals and headed down to their Yonge Street address, above The Hawk's Nest, a popular rock 'n' roll bar. There Heavy, an old guy with a snow-white beard and twinkling blue eyes who called everybody "Baby Blue," introduced me to Ronnie. Then he started telling me about another really cool rock concert that was going to take place later that summer in upstate New York. They were trying to get Ronnie on the bill and if they could, would I be interested in doing another "impromptu" dance on stage with the band? They had fancy plans to drop me out of a helicopter just as Ronnie started singing "Bo Diddley." "Only this time, Baby Blue," Heavy went on to say, "we want you to take off your bikini top!"

I was tempted, especially after Ronnie promised to take me to see his old pal Elvis Presley in Memphis if I'd accept the gig. But I knew my mother would have a bird, and I had to turn him down.

Of course, the concert ended up being the legendary Woodstock, and Ronnie never did get the gig.

Years later, as a rock reporter, I went to Memphis with Ronnie to do a story, and he confessed he'd never even met Elvis. I visited the legendary Sun Recording Studio with Ronnie, arranged a private tour of Graceland for him, and interviewed him in Elvis's famous TV room. Ronnie was thrilled, and I was happy to be able to repay the fantasy he'd given me so many years before.

It must have been the *Vogue* cover for December '67: there was a glitzy holiday dress featured that I thought would be perfect for my Sweet Sixteen. Naturally, I'd try to get my mom's German dressmaker to copy it. The dress was a turtle-neck, skin-tight, long-sleeved, sparkling mini, complete with matching knee socks. My mom and I rushed out and bought a turquoise and silver lamé fabric — which had no stretch whatsoever. We didn't realize that the *Vogue* dress was a knit.

Regardless, we took the fabric to the dressmaker and presented her with the challenge. In order to make it fit tight, she had to sew little zippers up the arms. As for the matching knee socks, well, she ingeniously sewed the fabric into a pair of booties that zipped up the shin. I then went out and found a pair of turquoise patent leather pumps — on sale — that were two sizes too big for me, but fit beautifully over the knee socks. It was the hottest outfit imaginable.

I only wore it one other time after my Sweet Sixteen, on a big date with a very rich fellow whose brother was getting married at a swishy country club. I was invited to the reception and I borrowed my sister's white fox stole and silver plastic evening bag for the occasion.

Some older men must have thought I looked pretty hot, because shortly after I arrived, they started plying me with rum and Cokes. It was the first time I ever had hard liquor and by about the third drink, I started feeling queasy. I disappeared into the ladies' room and everything started spinning.

I quickly made it into a stall and threw up all over my sparkly knee socks. Not missing a beat, I removed them, quickly rinsed them out, rolled them up and crunched them into my evening bag. I wonder if anyone noticed I was sockless for the rest of the night.

I think my cool about that fashion crisis kicked in because of an old Miss America Pageant I watched once. For her savvy-testing, on-the-spot question, the eventual winner was asked what she would do if she was walking down the street and her heel broke off. She promptly replied that she'd take off both shoes and continue on her way, barefoot.

The audience loved her response, and evidently it helped her win the pageant. So I always thought that would be the best thing to do in those emergency conditions. Yeah, me and Miss America: never afraid to take it off.

Bad Trips

At sixteen I said to myself that there were two things I'd never do: drop acid and lose my virginity before I got married. By seventeen I'd done both.

The acid had been slipped to me at an outdoor concert, the Toronto Rock and Roll Revival at Toronto's Varsity Stadium, in early September of 1969. It turned into a bad trip, with faces melting and me on the verge of freaking out just as Chuck Berry took the stage. By the time John Lennon and Yoko Ono started performing, I'd started to come down and felt exhausted but somehow proud that I'd been catapulted into adulthood.

Since I'd experienced losing my mind, I thought I might as well lose my virginity. Unfortunately, that was a bad trip too. It was with the wrong person — a spoiled rich kid I'd been dating for a few months. He was an arrogant, pretentious guy whose parents had bought him a groovy clothing store which was basically a cool hang-out for a bratty crowd that spent their time traveling to exotic destinations, dealing hashish, and bragging about meeting rock stars.

I thought these were the most glamorous people I'd ever met. I'd regularly skip school with my wild and gorgeous girlfriend, Jackie Feldman, and head downtown to hang at the boutique, where a cast of exciting characters would drop by, wearing the best clothes I could imagine: snakeskin boots and Afghani Mongolian lamb coats and tight velvet pants. They all had long, silky hair, smelled like patchouli oil, and invariably had big chunks of black Nepalese hash in their back pockets.

My boyfriend was at the center of this social milieu and, although he was only a couple of years older than I was, he seemed like one of the wisest and most worldly guys I'd ever known. Sometimes he'd encourage me to "look around the store and pick out some clothes." One time, he gave me one of those embroidered Mongolian lamb coats to wear "for as long as I wanted." It was purple and it made me feel hipper than I'd ever felt in my life. Sometimes he loaned me his muscle car to drive home. I had to park it around the block because I wouldn't have known how to explain it to my parents.

One weekend he was staying at his parents' place in a classy

Toronto apartment. He'd been telling me he wanted an "adult" relationship with me and that if I didn't comply, he'd have to call it quits. I decided to take the plunge. We met at his parents' place and shortly after I got there, he told me to take a Quaalude — a potent tranquilizer that was popular among the cool set at the time. I was reluctant but complied. He turned the lights down in the bedroom and we started making out. I was feeling increasingly relaxed as the effects of the pill set in. But as things heated up and it looked like the "big act" was inevitable, I got cold feet.

I told him I'd changed my mind, but he wouldn't hear of it. I struggled to get up; I just wanted to get my clothes on and get out of there. But he held me down and I couldn't muster the strength to push him off me. I started yelling. "No. Don't. Please. No!" But he was determined. When it was over, I started crying. He told me I was nothing but a screwed-up little girl and that I should take some lessons from my friend Jackie.

I stayed over at the apartment, with the creep sleeping on the far side of the bed. I couldn't leave right away because I'd told my parents I was sleeping at a friend's. I lay awake all night reliving the nasty episode. I had never felt so rejected and lonely and stupid.

Sleazoid Talent Inc.

As I got older, I realized the stage was the perfect place to strut my stuff. I began to see clothes as costumes and delighted in the effect some of my wild outfits had on observers. Not to belittle my own talent, I'm sure I landed my first dramatic TV role in the early '70s NBC series *Dr. Simon Locke* because the director loved my outfit: Mom had crocheted hot-pants overalls for me out of bright orange wool. And not only did I have the gall to sew a big yellow star on the bib, I was nervy enough to wear this tasteless get-up to the audition — teamed with white, skin-tight, knee-high vinyl boots.

Another one of my questionable acting credits was for an episode of a short-lived dramatic series called *Mahoney's Estate*, starring Patrick McGoohan of *The Prisoner* fame. I was cast as a "special business extra"

— which meant I didn't have any lines but had to do something other than just stand around.

I was called for the part by a casting agent. I showed up wearing a black-and-white African print dress with a black gaucho hat. My "special business" was being a chick who is making out in the back seat of a car with a low life who is suddenly recognized and has to jump into the front seat and quickly drive away. I assumed that this "making out" business was going to be faked, but the guy playing opposite me wasn't a professional actor — he was a stunt driver! During the scene, he took advantage of the situation by sticking his tongue down my throat and grabbing my boobs.

I was mortified, and complained to the director, but when questioned if all that was really necessary the jerk simply shrugged and said, "Well, yeah, man. I wanted it to look as real as possible." I warned the guy to "cool it" for the second take. And though he calmed down considerably, he made me feel like a loser for not going for authenticity.

This wasn't the first time someone had tried to take advantage of me as an aspiring actress. In the late '60s there was a Toronto talent agent who was well connected and well respected — at least as far as I knew. Someone at a modeling agency suggested I contact him for movie work, and I called for an appointment. I dressed in a tight, toffee-colored jersey dress and brown high-heeled sandals. I felt very grown-up and professional taking the subway to his office, a stack of resumés and composite pictures in a brown manila envelope tucked under my arm.

The agent was short, with greasy black hair, and he was wearing a grotesque plaid jacket. He focused his eyes on my chest right off the bat.

"So . . . you've done a little TV. And now you want to do some movie work," he said knowingly. "How would you feel about doing a nude scene?"

I was flabbergasted. "Well, uh, I'm not sure, really. I guess it depends on the movie. Like, if the director thought it was really important to the script, well, maybe I might, but I'm not sure really . . ."

My mother would kill me if I even considered taking my clothes off in a movie. But if the part was great and if this is what you had to do to make it, I might have to abandon my mother's moral code.

He didn't seem to hear what I was saying — or care for that matter. "Are your breasts firm?" he asked, nonchalantly.

"Uh, well, I guess so," I replied stupidly.

"Okay, we've got to get some video on you. Can you make it to my office one night next week? It's much better to tape this sort of screen test without too many people around. Anytime after 5 p.m. would be great."

"Okay," I said. "I'll check and see when I can do it."

"Yeah, you're cute. I'll probably be able to get something going for you. Just give me a shout and let me know when you can make it."

I said thanks and goodbye, without the slightest intention of ever calling this sleaze-bag again. If this was the route to success, I'd just have to draw my own map.

Media
Maverick

Aspiring Actress

In 1971, at the age of nineteen, I tried out for the National Theatre School in Montreal. Applicants were required to prove their abilities with one classical piece and one contemporary piece. I picked a soliloquy from *Romeo and Juliet* and a scene from *The Fantastiks*.

Getting through the Juliet piece was a struggle — I was too hung up on the language to portray the character. But the reading from *The Fantastiks* impressed the panel.

"You're really very good," one woman told me, "but obviously you had a hard time with the Shakespeare material. Why would you want to study at the National Theatre School? The emphasis is on the classics here, you know." She went on to tell me that if I was really gung-ho on acting, I might want to check out a school in New York called the Herbert Berghoff Studio, which offered a wide assortment of acting, dance, and voice classes and was far less strict and structured than the National.

Most of the teachers at HB were working performers, doing shows off-Broadway and giving classes between gigs, she said. Best of all, it was in New York, right in the heart of the West Village.

By the end of that summer, I had saved $500 from a camp job. As much as my mother believed in me, she was freaked at the thought of her baby moving to the wilds of New York City all by herself. She begged me to think about staying with my cousin Charles in Brooklyn, but I craved total independence.

Days before I left, Mom played Cat Stevens's "Wild World" over and over again on the stereo, a song about a young girl going off into the world by herself, and the person saying goodbye to her is telling her to beware, because it's "hard to get by just upon a smile." The words were so appropriate, she might have written them herself.

As worried as she was, Mom put on a brave front and along with Dad encouraged me to follow my dreams. She didn't realize that New York in 1971 was a very different place from Tarnopol, Poland, in 1937. She was convinced the best way to protect my cold, hard cash was to sew it into my underpants, as her mother had done for her when she'd gone to the big city.

I had a pair of bright orange panties with a picture of the Parliament Buildings and the infamous words of Prime Minister Pierre Trudeau, "Fuddle Duddle," emblazoned over the crotch. I had bought them at Kresge's for a multimedia university project I'd done, entitled "The Sacred and the Profane." Mom sewed a little cotton pocket in the back and proudly inserted my $500. "See how nice this is? They'll never get the money in there."

I took a bus to New York City wearing the loaded panties. Dad had driven me down to the bus station and given me a teddy bear in a plaid jacket as a going-away present. "Don't be afraid," he told me. "And never give up." That was his motto and unquestionably it was that mindset that saw him through the war and helped him survive the Holocaust.

A friend I'd made at camp made good on her offer to introduce me to her New York friends. The Aldens were a wonderfully bohemian family, eager to help young artists. They lived in a rambling old apartment on the Upper West Side with tapestries on the walls and Oriental rugs on the floors. They took me in warmly for my first few nights in New York.

They suggested I go down to Actors Equity to hook up with some other young actress for accommodation. Inside the union's office was a big bulletin board where notices were posted. I knew God was talking to me when I came across this one: "Young actress looking for another young actress to share rent-controlled apartment. $75 a month. Call Jeannie." Wow. Somebody else with my name! It was too good to be true.

Even more uncanny was that this other Jeannie was also taking classes at the HB Studio.

The apartment was a fifth-floor walk-up on Riverside Drive, between 77th and 78th. I moved in right away. The building had been used as the location for John Cassavetes's film *Rosemary's Baby*, and every time I came home, the doorman would tell another anecdote about the memorable shoot.

Walking to and from the subway every day, I soon realized that the hot pants I'd brought to New York were all wrong — I was getting too many catcalls from construction workers. I discovered a funky vintage shop on Columbus Avenue called Like a Rolling Stone that sold old overalls. I bought an oversized pair. The next stop was an army surplus store for a pair of trusty combat boots. Tucking my super-long hair into a tattered houndstooth salt-and-pepper cap, I walked the sidewalks and rode the subways a new woman: completely liberated. No one whistled at me anymore and if my butch appearance put off the guys, all the better. I didn't want attention on the street anymore. I wanted it on the stage.

My New York experience gave me an "earthier" style sense, which helped me avoid the catcalls of construction workers! (Photo by Struan Campbell-Smith)

The First Time I Saw Paris

Ever since my sister turned me on to Gigi, I fancied myself running off to Paris, preferably in pursuit of some great artistic challenge. I wanted to wear berets and drink Pernod at corner bistros and smoke Gitanes and listen to Edith Piaf. It was a romantic notion most artistic young adults would embrace. But I knew I didn't have what it took to study at the Sorbonne. Then, one day, I fell in love with the art of pantomime.

In 1972, just back from acting studies in New York, I enrolled in the theater department of Toronto's York University. I guess I thought I needed more of a rounded education, a dose of academia in the mix. I was appalled on the first day of performance classes at York when the teacher began handing out copies of 5BX and 10BX army exercise pamphlets, primers for our creative movement course. I guess the message here was "First, we get in shape."

But after being exposed to all those months of modern and jazz dance classes at the HB Studio in New York, I craved a more meaningful approach. When somebody told me there was a great mime class going on downtown, I was intrigued: corporal expression was an interesting concept to me. Besides, I never really liked the sound of my voice. It would be interesting not to have to rely on the spoken word.

Mime was an art form that was theatrical and larger than life. It sounded like fun. So I talked my best friend, Penny, into signing up with me and we began our studies in silent expression. Our teacher was a tall, skinny, gentle guy with wiry black hair and a long French nose. His name was Paul Gaulin and he'd just come back from Paris after studying for years with Etienne Decroux, an actor known as "The Father of Modern Mime." Gaulin had come back to Toronto and had opened a little mime studio, over a furniture store on Yonge Street.

Then in the fall of 1973, determined to learn an exacting technique that would set me apart from other young aspiring actresses who seemed to be getting roles based on the shape of their nose I took off for Paris.

I had heard that Etienne Decroux ran a small school out of his home. Many famous people had studied there, including David Bowie and Jessica Lange. In fact, Decroux himself had played a role in the classic

With mime, I felt as though I'd found my new calling. It was liberating, and taught me new discipline as a performing artist. (Photo by Andrée Gagné)

44

French film *Les Enfants du Paradis* and had taught mime to the legendary actor Jean-Louis Barreault. I figured that while the old man was still alive and welcoming young students, it would be a privilege to study with him. So I wrote Decroux a letter, asking if I might enroll at his tiny school. A couple of weeks later, I received a letter telling me that all classes were full and to try again next spring. They were sorry but they couldn't accommodate me.

I went anyway.

For my big trip to Paris, the first time I'd ever gone to Europe, I bought a new, brown suede, wraparound jacket and a brown fedora complete with huge pheasant feather. I was determined to go to the world's fashion capital in style. At twenty-one, it seemed I was doing the most exciting, romantic thing possible: off to Paris to study art. I felt like Audrey Hepburn in *Sabrina*.

Leaving Toronto was bittersweet, because I was in love and would have to leave my boyfriend behind. Marty Laba was a cute, brainy, romantic poet. I'd known him from high school, but we'd been together since meeting up again at summer camp in 1971, just before I took off to study acting in New York. Our relationship had already survived that separation, and we felt destined to be together. Besides being a talented singer-songwriter, Marty was studying folklore at York University. He encouraged me to follow my artistic dream, but said he wouldn't be able to accompany me. I promised him I'd come back.

Marty, forever the sensitive poet, always inspired the artist in me.

Paris Diary

October 29, 1973. I feel as though I've been drugged.

Here I am in Paris and it's everything I'd imagined it to be. It's almost as though I've taken a trip to some forgotten, dusty corner of my mind. This place is so strangely familiar to me.

The bus pulls up in front of Place d'Italie, a multitude of criss-crossed cobblestone roads. In the center of it all is a small parkette and there, under a tree, sits a woman artist in front of an easel.

I just can't explain what is going through me. I just can't believe I'm here. There's something magical about the pigeons and the old people and the cobblestones and tiny, antiquated shops.

My room is grotesque/charming/grungy/cozy. It's all so strange. There's a bidet in the center of the room, which is pretty funny, since my room is about 2 by 4.

I want to run out and dance down the streets.

My first night in Paris, I went to a corner bistro, Le Nemrod, with a Berlitz dictionary in my hand. I wanted to feel elegant so I wore a full-length, hunter-green maxi-skirt that my mother had made for me. There was a cool guy sitting at the next table wearing a faded denim jacket. He reminded me of Peter Fonda, and we struck up a conversation, me struggling along with my Berlitz French. His name was Patrick (Pa-*treek*) and he said I reminded him of Ali McGraw, probably because of my long, dark, parted-in-the-middle hair.

When Patrick learned it was my first time in Paris, he asked if I wanted to go to the Eiffel Tower. We hopped into his burgundy Austin Mini. I guess the tower was closed, because we didn't go up — we just stood under it. But that was enough for me.

Patrick dropped me off at my hotel and said goodnight. The next morning, there was a knock on my door. The chambermaid stood on the threshold with a vase of gorgeous red roses. She seemed to be telling me they were from a young man who was waiting outside. I opened my window and stuck my head out, and there was denim-clad Patrick, smiling, waving, and wishing me a "bon matin."

October 30. C'est fantastique. C'est romantique. C'est incroyable. I only arrived yesterday morning, and already I desire to write this entire diary in French.

Paris goes beyond my dreams. At times I feel as though I am retracing Anaïs Nin's footsteps. And then, suddenly, I am partaking in a scene directly out of a Truffaut film. Every action, every word, every bit of my existence here seems so vital.

I am in love with Paris.

October 31. Went to the Louvre today. Magnificent. I spent a long time gazing at the *Mona Lisa* and she at me before I was moved to tears. I was that inspired.

Soon afterwards, I dropped by Decroux's studio. He lived and worked in a small house just outside the Bois de Boulogne. I was confronted by an ancient, motherly-type woman — Madame Decroux *naturellement*.

She was in her kitchen preparing some roast beef and toting these fantastic tomatoes. Madame Decroux, the wife of a *maître*, standing there in her oh-so-humble kitchen in her little apron, beside her old-fashioned stove, cooking tomorrow night's dinner. She immediately took a liking to me when she found out my name was "Jeanne" — *Jahhnn* — just like hers. At the top of the stairs, which led down to the basement where a class was going on, were ten pairs of shoes belonging to the students. Decroux's secretary informed me that I could start classes the next morning.

November 1. My first day at Decroux's. The basement studio was crowded and sweaty. Monsieur Decroux enters the class grandly, wearing sport trunks. He is a cute old man, *un petit peu comme* Ed Wynn. His manner seems rather blasé. He rhymes off his philosophies on dramatic art, he sings now and then. It's all quite amusing.

Afterwards, I go to a *salon du thé* and write letters home.

November 2. My first Decroux lecture. He talks of will, of having a goal that always sucks you forward. Obstacles may get in the way, sometimes making it necessary to go back and find a way to bypass them. He compares the artist to a river, constantly flowing, yet sometimes having to by-pass rocks.

Decroux speaks of writers. He sees their frustration, the desire for physical action. Mime must equal the word, not try to replace it. He also says plays should be written after they have been rehearsed.

Later that night, I take a boat ride down the Seine. Placid, I float through Paris.

Late November. Possibly because of my inability to relate to anyone about art in this foreign place, I have begun to develop a new awareness. I hold lengthy dissertations about art and life in my head. I am discovering myself as an artist.

Sitting in the corner bistro, watching the people glide by through glass walls, I begin to notice movement. I see my art in life. For me, this is an important step. I am starting to understand mime a little bit better.

Decroux says that it is not objects we are interested in, it is man. How a man deals with the object is what we must focus on. I realize the truth of this statement. It is not the fact that the man is smoking the cigarette that gives him his character, it is how he smokes the cigarette. It is not the clothes that give us style, but how we wear them. It is not the espresso cup in my hand that I love, it is the way it feels when I delicately balance it with two careful fingers.

To the Rock

By the end of my first Paris winter, I was too lonely to go on. I was missing Marty. I decided that maybe starving in a garret for your art wasn't all it was cracked up to be. I didn't want to burn any bridges with Monsieur and Madame Decroux, so I told them I was being called away on a family emergency and would likely return by the end of the spring.

I couldn't bear the thought of leaving Paris forever — the city had entered my soul. But I felt I had to get back home to quell my romantic anxiety. If I stayed away any longer, I was certain I'd lose Marty to some hot young waitress at the Old Spaghetti Factory, where he'd taken a job to help pay his tuition.

To keep my eye on the situation I landed a job at the same restaurant, as a hostess. I got to wear long dresses and announce "Biernblatt, party of six" in an authoritarian way. It wasn't exactly art, but the actor in me used the opportunity to perfect my vocal technique after months of silence as a mime. Within a couple of months I'd been promoted to waitress, where the money was better. Tips were pretty generous, especially because I seemed to know just how to schmooze parties like the Biernblatts. I prided myself on being able to carry six plates of pasta on a single tray overhead with one hand, while holding a jug of beer in the other. I considered myself one of the restaurant's best waitresses: I never screwed up orders and I got along famously with the regular clientele. Waitressing was one of the best gigs around — I made lots of extra cash. Of course, you could never let all those flirtations amount to anything, so it all felt very safe.

Marty proposed marriage, asking me to join him on the East Coast. He'd received a fellowship to do postgraduate work at Memorial University's folklore department in St. John's. I'd been biding my time slinging beer and pasta at Toronto's Old Spaghetti Factory, taking theater and TV courses at York, and going to auditions, waiting for the next big moment. The prospect of marriage at a time when I was feeling directionless and insecure was the kind of grown-up opportunity I craved.

Besides, I'd just come back from a trip to Israel with my mother, where I'd prayed at the Western Wall for just such a miracle. Onto a tiny scrap of paper I'd written my innermost desire: that Marty, my heartthrob since the age of nineteen, would ask me to marry him. I scrunched up the paper and faithfully pushed it into a crack in the wall, which was already overflowing with countless secret messages to God.

The night I returned from Israel, I discovered Marty had been having an affair with a girl in his gestalt therapy group. When I questioned him about it, he admitted everything but swore it was me he really loved. And then, probably afraid I would be reluctant to move to Newfoundland with him or might even break up with him, he asked me to marry him. It wasn't the ideal, romantic proposal I'd been dreaming of, but I said yes anyway. The Lord works in strange ways.

I designed my wedding dress, and my mother's German dressmaker made it for me: a white jersey, Empire-cut gown with spaghetti straps and a full skirt topped with a little hooded, satin-lined jacket. It was chic, simple, and elegant. I wore it with a tiny ivory heart and a bangle from a small French accessories boutique that I bought as a special present to myself.

The night before the wedding, my sister gave me a manicure and we watched a Marx Brothers movie. I was nervous as hell and needed to be distracted.

The afternoon of the wedding, Marilyn and I had a big fight over the use of the bathroom, or something stupid like that. The photographer was due at the house. I was determined not to be a wreck, so I popped one of my mother's tranquilizers. It really did a number on me and I remember feeling as if I was floating down the aisle of the temple.

About 150 guests were there and I felt a great outpouring of love and support for the two of us. But I also remember wondering whether I'd made the right decision, whether I was ready for marriage, and whether this was what I really wanted after all. Marty must have sensed my doubts, because just before we took our vows, he whispered in my ear that everything was going to be all right. I decided to stop second-guessing myself.

My best friend, Penny Chikofsky Fiskel, has always been there for me. Here we are at my 1975 wedding.

The day after our wedding, we left for Newfoundland. St. John's in the '70s seemed frozen in time — a small town oblivious to the dictates of fashion and adamant about hanging on to its heritage, which included fiddle fests in outport kitchens and all the screech and flipper pie you could swallow.

Marty and I found it invigorating to escape the neon of Yonge Street and the pretension of Yorkville. It would be a good three years before we started missing the gritty big-city sensibility that downtown Toronto offered. Meanwhile, buying codfish at Caine's Grocery on Duckworth Street and knocking back pints at Bridget's while our friends played the blues provided all the exoticism we needed. We spent lazy

Sunday afternoons hiking up Signal Hill and whale-watching from rugged cliffs. We roamed around tiny outports with names like Heart's Content and Joe Batt's Arm.

We found the most fabulous apartment, a furnished upstairs flat in a historic home on Forest Road, complete with plush cranberry carpeting, antique furniture, a cozy fireplace, and a gymnasium-sized bed. We threw some amazing dinner parties there. There were no great restaurants to speak of in St. John's at the time, so I took up cooking with a vengeance and read *Gourmet* magazine religiously. It was a joy preparing vichyssoise and coq au vin for twenty, despite our minuscule pantry kitchen. We relished our evenings entertaining friends, usually capping things off with cognac, after-dinner cigars, and living-room dancing to the beat of Stevie Wonder deep into the night.

Needless to say, there wasn't much work available for mimes in St. John's, so I knew I'd have to be resourceful. And I was. As the province's only mime, I ended up as a radio broadcaster — the ultimate Newfie joke!

St. John's was an unlikely place for someone with my drive and energy. But I soon discovered the passion that brewed beneath its charming exterior, and by the time I left the island three years later, I'd grown into the doer I'd always dreamed about being.

Living in St. John's, Nfld., from 1975 to 1978 was one of the best and happiest experiences of my life.

My first job was with a small radio station called CJON, where I worked as promotions director. I was encouraged to be as bold and creative as I pleased, so chutzpah became my operative word. As much as I thought I understood and appreciated Newfoundland's unique culture, I was oblivious to the subtle nuances of the place and must have appeared pretty brash to anyone watching me fly.

One of my more memorable promotions was a Kiss-a-Thon staged at an unassuming little shopping mall in downtown St. John's. The occasion was Valentine's Day. I had heard about a previous Kiss-a-Thon in Toronto to help promote the release of a new album by the rock group KISS. The event got TV coverage and looked like a hoot — just slightly sexy but certainly innocent enough not to offend. I figured a contest of this sort — seeing which couple could lock lips the longest — would be perfect for those warm, fun-loving Newfoundlanders.

My boss thought the concept was a tad outrageous, but he was confident I could pull it off. I scored a highly seductive prize package for the winners: a free vacation, romantic dinners, dozens of roses, and a cash prize. Entry forms were posted at the mall, and by the end of the week there were about a dozen couples eager to take the plunge: locking lips for the amusement of fellow shoppers in an abandoned store in the city's only downtown mall.

I became nervous when some of the couples showed up with sleeping bags and blankets. We gave them tubes of Chap Stick and packages of mint chewing gum to help them through the day. They were allowed to take one five-minute break each hour.

It was one of the most outrageous events ever to take place in St. John's, and the local media had a field day. By noon, my couples were lying on the floor, making out in earnest, much to the delight of the watching crowd. Children were especially intrigued. This was not what I'd envisioned. Somehow I had managed to orchestrate a public orgy in this God-fearing little town!

By two o'clock, the clergy had arrived. A couple of nuns and an elderly priest were quick to let me know this was a bad influence on the youngsters and teens who had turned up to cheer their friends on. By about nine o'clock that night, we had to call it a tie: two couples persevered in puckering up to the very end, determined to claim the big prize pack. Finally, afraid that this could turn into an all-nighter, my boss coughed up some cash and the prizes were split between the couples.

I eventually knocked on CBC Radio's door, with no experience as an on-air reporter or interviewer, but with enough chutzpah and creative ideas to get me a meeting with John Dalton, the newly appointed producer of St. John's *Radio Noon*. This was a daily, consumer-oriented program that was trying to break new ground in the province by focusing on lifestyles.

I didn't know anything about consumer issues and barely understood the concept of "lifestyle," but I figured I knew a lot about the arts. Since St. John's had such a lively arts community, perhaps reviews and interviews with these artists would be possible. Of course, I could always put a "consumer" spin on these stories and profiles: Was it really worth $20 to go and see a particular performance? Did the movie deliver enough bang for your buck?

Dalton bought my pitch, and I came on board his show as a writer/performer, responsible for contributing interviews and features. Happily for me, some of my stories got national airplay. But as much as I was enjoying my new broadcasting career, I was still perceived by some as from away. My style wasn't appreciated. Newfoundlanders, as warm and friendly as they can be, are leery of anyone who might exploit their experience. I understood their suspicions, but it hurt every time I felt their distrust. I vowed that I'd continue my broadcasting career and work harder than ever to prove to doubters that I really did know what I was doing.

Rock 'n' Radio

Immediately on our return to Toronto in August of 1978, armed with several impressive demo reels, I started calling every station programmer in town. All were impressed with my experience. Although they all said they had no openings, they agreed to meet with me and hear my tapes. They were encouraging and told me to stand by.

One programmer, J. Robert Wood at CHUM, was especially enthusiastic about my energetic, "young-sounding" voice. He told me he'd seriously consider trying to fit me into his format.

Patience has never been one of my virtues. I began calling J. R. Wood every day, five times a day. I was determined to land a job at CHUM. I'd read in the paper that the station had just acquired Citytv, a small, hip, downtown, independent TV station. Instinctively, I felt this mini-multimedia empire was my destiny. I'd always perceived the CHUM deejays as the coolest — I'd even been an official preteen "CHUM Bug" — and had spent countless nights under the covers with my orange transistor radio glued to every song and contest that station played.

After a couple of weeks of being hounded, J. R. told me to come down to the station for an audition. I was to do a few minutes with their morning announcer, "Jungle Jay" Nelson. I was thrilled — I'd listened to his silly upbeat show religiously throughout the late '60s.

The morning of my audition, I donned a fabulous navy-and-white batik outfit I'd made myself and headed over to the station with stars in my eyes. This was the big time, I told myself. I was going to *make it*.

For my audition I read a traffic report and kibitzed with Jay. He was kind and encouraging and constantly cracking corny jokes. I was nervous, but we chatted a bit to warm up, and then the operator rolled tape. The first question Jay asked me was: "If you could meet anyone who ever lived, who would it be?"

I knew I couldn't stop to think, so I just blurted out the first name that popped into my mind. "Picasso," I answered.

Yeesh. Why did I say that? It was too high-brow for a Top Ten radio station, and I immediately wished I could go back and come up with a name that was more relevant to the pop/rock world, like Elvis or something.

I'm Jeanne Beker.

Sometimes Jeanne gets in hot water to get a story, but whether it's a new craze like hot-tubbing, an interview with Rod Stewart or checking out the newest club in town, Jeanne takes to the street looking for things that might be fun for you.

1050 chum

News that matters for the way you live.

CHUM radio helped build my image as its "Good News Girl," and encouraged my energetic, unconventional style.

But we proceeded to discuss why I'd chosen Picasso. I babbled earnestly about the importance of art in my life, and Jay must have been sympathetic because a couple of months later, after I got the gig, he invited me to *Swan Lake* and took me backstage to meet his friend, ballerina Vanessa Harwood.

Later that night, I showed him a picture of me performing mime, and he asked if he could borrow it. A few days later, he brought the picture into the station, blown up to huge poster size and beautifully framed. He told me to hang it on my wall as a constant reminder of my true passion.

I was moved by Jay's sensitivity and always held him in high esteem, knowing that a lot of the frivolous, mindless banter he engaged in morning in and morning out for all those years had little to do with who he really was.

J. R. Wood wasn't sure what to do with me at first; the station already had a traffic girl and female disc jockeys were still rare. Even though I'd never worked in news, let alone read a newscast, he said I could start working in the newsroom, reading the 5 a.m. newscast. But I was game for anything, even getting up at 3:30 in the morning.

It was pretty grim the first night when I rang the front door buzzer to come in for my first shift. The only two people in the station at that ungodly hour were the operator — or "op," as he was called — and the deejay on duty. That first morning, it was Bob Magee, a gorgeous guy from Vancouver who was still paying his dues on the all-night shift. He came to open the door for me dressed in a vintage white navy surplus outfit. CHUM had had a staff cruise earlier that night and Bob had bought this get-up especially for the party. Bob had the most beautiful sky-blue eyes imaginable, and was the cutest guy I'd ever seen, and one of the most charming.

"I've got to get back into the studio, I'm on the air for another hour," he said. "You can make yourself at home in the newsroom. Or you can come in and sit with me for a bit."

I didn't hesitate in accepting his offer. Before you knew it, he was pouring me a cup of tea out of his Thermos and impressing the hell out of me with his amazing knowledge of rock 'n' roll.

I was smitten.

I didn't start dating "Bob Magee" until a year later, after I'd learned his real name was Denny O'Neil, and after Marty and I separated.

Marty and I had grown apart shortly after moving back to Toronto. Though we still loved each other, we seemed to be leading separate lives. While Marty was at home diligently working on his pop culture thesis, I was off living the life: covering concerts, meeting rock stars, falling in love with the excitement of broadcasting. Within a few months, even though he hadn't yet completed his thesis, he was offered a wonderful job teaching back at Memorial University. He was eager to go. I wasn't.

There were new professional opportunities for me on the horizon with Citytv, the station that had recently been acquired by CHUM. It was an extremely painful decision, but we realized we'd have to split and agreed we would start to see other people.

By 1983, when I was working at Citytv, Denny and I were living together. By 1985, we had bought a house. In 1986, we were married. Denny was wildly romantic and imaginative. He

proposed to me on Christmas morning through an ad in the personal columns. Madonna's hit movie *Desperately Seeking Susan* had come out that year. I had a small production company called M Face, named after our beloved orange cat, Moochie. Denny's ad read: DESPERATELY SEEKING M FACE: Let's run away to Switzerland and get married. We won't tell anyone until we're there. Well? Will you marry me?

Reading that ad and looking up to see Denny on his knees, saying "Well?" was the happiest moment of my life. I said yes immediately.

My heart melted when I came across Denny's ad. His Christmas card came with a pair of tickets to Switzerland.

Six weeks later, we were married in a judge's office in Toronto's west end, with only our two close friends, Clint and Melanie, there as witnesses. I wore a royal blue '40s-style suit with very '80s pearl earrings I'd bought in Paris. I carried a small bouquet of orchids that Marilyn had sent to me.

The next morning we took off for Switzerland and honeymooned in Zermatt. Life had never seemed so perfect.

As soon as I got back, I announced our marriage on Citytv's six o'clock news, the perfect ending to a romance that got its start behind the CHUM microphone.

Citytv and Me

In 1979, less than a year into my gig at CHUM, I was told to go down to Citytv and see Fred Klinkhammer about doing TV work. The station thought it would be a great cross-promotion to have some of its radio personalities appear on TV. I was thrilled to have a shot at being on camera again because I always felt I was a visual performer at heart.

When I finally made it to Klinkhammer's office, he told me to talk to the news director, Ivan Fecan, about doing feature stories for the news. He also told me about a music magazine show that City was launching called *The New Music*, which they might be interested in having me co-host.

First I'd have to pass the news test: go out with a cameraman and shoot a lifestyle story — something light, with a consumer angle, something that would lend itself to reporter involvement. This was a new trend in reporting and the people at Citytv, under orders from the station's visionary leader Moses Znaimer, were committed to perfecting it.

My first story was about a sailing school on Toronto's Harbourfront. I thought the subject would lend itself to pretty pictures, offer lots of movement, and present me with a challenge as a reporter: I would be going out on the water and trying my hand at the tiller. Besides, I had this sexy little navy surplus jacket that I thought would be perfect in front of the camera.

My cameraman was Al Macpherson, a tall, skinny guy with a big mustache who was kind, patient, and sympathetic to my not knowing what I was doing. At first, he was expecting me to call the shots, direct him, and get exactly what I needed to put my piece together. But I didn't even know what a "cutaway" was (it's a shot that can be used to cover an edit point in an interview or as visuals over the audio track), and I had no idea how to structure a story. Al helped as best he could and then dropped me off at the station, tape in hand. I was left to the mercy of a weekend editor who had no interest in helping me make my story make sense.

My sailing school feature eventually got edited, but it wasn't any great shakes. My navy surplus jacket, on the other hand, made a considerable

Honeymooning in Zermatt was the epitome of romantic adventure.

impression. A few days later, I got a call from Klinkhammer telling me that I was going to be a co-host on City's *The New Music*, alongside a cute, self-involved CHUM deejay named J. D. Roberts.

"Just like that?" I asked. "Don't you want me to do a screen test for you or anything?"

"No, that's okay," Klinkhammer assured me. "We saw you in that

sailing school story. You looked fine. Now you've got to meet the show's producer — he'll fill you in."

It was miraculous how the whole thing fell into my lap. Sure, I'd worked my ass off doing everything from community theater to cocktail waitressing, and my experience on radio was invaluable. I always knew I was a natural performer, and had relentlessly pursued my passion. Still, nothing ever comes that easy. The dues-paying process had only just begun.

It was in a dark downtown bar called the Montreal Bistro that I first met John Martin, the producer of *The New Music* and the man who invented rock 'n' roll TV. John was a brilliant, enigmatic, and witty character with a thick Manchester accent, bad teeth, and wiry blond hair that he joked had been styled by Ontario Hydro. When I arrived at the bar, he was sitting at a small table, chain-smoking the strongest cigarettes known to man and knocking back several glasses

J. D. Roberts and I were sometimes intimidated by the cocky and irreverent rock stars we interviewed on *The New Music*. But we were always up for the ride. (Courtesy Citytv)

60

of beer, or "pints" as he called them. My co-host, J. D., an earnest, straight-laced, smooth-as-silk jock with Ken-doll good looks, was at the table with him, trying to make sense of John's quirky rantings.

John was cordial to me, but I learned later that he'd wanted his girlfriend to co-host the show. The idea was an off-beat magazine show that went behind the scenes: on tour, in the studio, backstage with the who's who of the popular music world. It would be an eclectic mix of rock, pop, and blues icons and any other luminaries that might be good for a laugh, from Timothy Leary to Liberace.

John wanted *The New Music* to reflect his irreverent attitude. He wanted to make a TV show like no other: one that was ballsy, brash, in-your-face. Until that time, people's idea of music on TV was *American Bandstand*, *Hullabaloo*, *Lloyd Thaxton*, and *Shindig*. None of these shows had tried to expose the personalities behind the music in any context outside a television studio. It was time to meet musicians where they lived and capture their wild and crazy times on video for their fans to see. I listened wide-eyed to everything John was saying, thrilled that I was going to help pioneer this new form of entertainment.

And I asked that all-important question: "What should I wear?"

"Just go through old copies of *Rolling Stone*," John suggested, "and look at what the rock stars' girlfriends are wearing. That's how you should dress. Think Anita Pallenberg, Marianne Faithfull, Patti Boyd. You've got to look cool, sexy — like you hang with these people normally. And one more thing — I see you as this older, wiser, downtown chick. J. D. is the good-looking young stud. I don't care what you have to do between now and the time we have to tape in a couple of weeks. Get to know each other, have sex, whatever. Just get some chemistry going."

And with that, he exited the bar, leaving me and J. D. in the dust, two naive kids from the suburbs who would have to reinvent ourselves for the new challenge ahead.

"What do you suppose he wants us to do?" asked J. D. earnestly.

"Who the hell knows," I answered. "But this could be fun."

New Music

Our first *New Music* shoot was with The Good Brothers, a Canadian country rock group, at their farm outside Toronto. I wore extremely tight jeans and a pair of wooden stiletto sandals — totally inappropriate for walking across muddy fields.

I knew nothing about The Goods going into the interview, but by the end of the day we were old buddies, proof that getting a great rock 'n' roll TV interview had more to do with personal rapport than painstaking research.

John was impressed with my work in the field, but screening the raw tape was less satisfying. I walked into the edit bay, eager to see how I came across on camera.

"Do I look okay?" I asked eagerly.

John turned to me, and with an air of resignation, half-jokingly quipped, "Well, they learned to love Streisand . . ."

I've hated my profile ever since. This was TV: cold, brutal, honest, revealing. What you saw was what you got. When you were capturing fleeting moments, there were no second takes. You had to think on your feet, be spontaneous and smart — and deal with lots of assholes.

Meeting Keith Richards in Antigua was a fantasy come true. He was sweet, sensitive, humble, and shy — so unlike the tough rock image he projected.

Joe Strummer of The Clash was an angry young man who had a lot to say. Interviewing him in his dressing room was an unnerving experience. (Courtesy Citytv)

The year 1979 was a tough but exciting time to be covering pop music. The punk scene had started to stir things up in the U.K. and was quickly infiltrating North America. New Wave was gaining steam and suddenly our perception of conventional pop music was changing. Ska, reggae, and rockabilly were creeping into the musical fray, and the new unstructured, rough-around-theedges, angry tone of punk was quickly becoming the rebel yell of a generation fed up with the glammy, big-money concert performers of the '70s.

Many of the young upstart musicians coming over to North America for the first time were cocky, rude, egotistical, and unsophisticated. They were preoccupied with image, yet most had never been on TV and had no idea how to act in front of a camera. J. D. and I ("video virgins" ourselves) had to hold their hands and see them through it.

Some musicians treated us like shit, no doubt out of their own insecurities. And then there were bands like The Clash, who made *us* feel insecure in the light of their notorious reputation. The Clash, fronted by Joe Strummer, a tough, wiry guy with a permanent scowl, was one of England's premiere punk bands. The Clash encouraged their fans to go nuts at their gigs. They were booked to play Toronto's O'Keefe Centre, one of the country's most conservative venues. I showed up with J. D. and our cameraman, John Grierson, just after the group's gig, apprehensive about meeting these boys, who had attitude up the wazoo.

Before we could talk to the band, we had to deal with their road manager, a slick young cockney in an iridescent blue suit improbably named Cosmo Vinyl. Cosmo reminded me of Edd "Kookie" Byrnes on *77 Sunset Strip* as he combed his bleached blond pompadour. He was eager to point out what some of The Clash's devoted fans had been up to during the concert. He took us onto the stage, and started counting the slashed red velvet seats in the auditorium.

"One, two, three, four, five, six, seven, eight, nine, ten, eleven, twelve . . . only thirteen real rock 'n' roll fans in Toronto," he said disappointedly, tucking his comb in his back pocket. "Pity, that." J. D. and I winced at each other.

In his wisdom about what it took to produce great TV, John Martin encouraged his cameramen to start rolling moments before the first encounter. If the interview was going to take place in a hotel room or a dressing room, we'd make sure we were rolling before the door opened. It was probably rude not to warn our subjects that they were already being taped, but the approach always made for great candid moments. I still subscribe to this technique most of the time. (How else could I later have gotten Karl Lagerfeld without his trademark sunglasses on? He was mortified when he realized he'd been caught off guard and quickly ran to find them.) When I already have good rapport with my subject, capturing our initial warm greeting makes for intimate television.

So, true to our style, our cameraman was rolling when The Clash's dressing room door opened. A couple of the guys were running around with toy machine guns, shooting pretend bullets at each other. Joe Strummer was leaning on a counter in front of a mirror, looking as if he was already regretting his decision to be interviewed. We were intimidated as hell and didn't dare ask Joe to reposition, so we shot him where he stood. A haunting image in the mirror of the cameraman at work made the shoot unusual and funky.

Joe never looked J. D. or me in the eye. He obviously thought that media types were whores and was determined to get more than mere exposure of the experience. He ranted about shaking people out of their complacency and about fighting "the system." It was refreshing to see a punky young musician from a lower-class background talk about what was wrong with society. I applauded Joe's using his fifteen minutes of fame to make a difference in the world even though it was clear he thought we were just a couple of wankers.

Being subjected to the arrogance and self-importance of various rock personalities was some of the best training I could have ever received. I learned to deal with delicate, overblown egos — and I'd encounter too many of those over the years. It taught me how to ignore rudeness, walk on eggshells, and stroke like nobody's business. During twenty-five years of schmoozing celebrities and interviewing some of the biggest names in popular culture, there was only one person who pissed me off to the point that I walked out of the interview: hard-core rock star Iggy Pop. A native of Detroit, Iggy Pop is a tough, kinda mean, wiry little demon who wears lots of denim and leather and performs with an edgy kind of verve and reckless energy to spare. He's an angry young man who's not really young at all anymore, and he's the apotheosis of rebellious raunchiness. He is anti– just about everything, and he used to drink a lot, making his unfocused rage even scarier.

I met Iggy in the summer of 1980 at a festival outside Toronto called Heat Wave. I was wearing vinyl jeans and he actually hit on me. I couldn't bring myself to get into anything with Iggy, other than a quick interview.

A couple of years later, Iggy came to Toronto to perform at the Danforth Music Hall. I was having dinner at my parents' home when John called to ask if I'd go down to the Music Hall after dinner for an interview with Iggy.

I was wearing a red fox coat, leather pants, and a Cartier tank watch — the trappings of a middle-class Jewish American Princess who'd just been having a Friday-night meal with her parents. It was after midnight by the time I made it to the venue. When I arrived, Iggy was in the green room, chugging a bottle of Jack Daniel's, surrounded by a motley entourage of adoring hangers-on. Iggy was certainly feeling no pain and agreed to be interviewed, despite the fact that his speech was a bit slurred. I don't think he remembered me, even though I reminded him about the Heat Wave festival.

The interview was going along uneventfully when out of the blue, Iggy started commenting on how I was dressed, and attacking my credibility as a rock interviewer. He soon became downright insulting, making cracks about my "bourgeois" outfit. For the first and only time in my entire career, I got up from my seat and said, "Okay, that's it. I'm outta here."

Iggy was dumbfounded that I'd cut him off so abruptly. The camera continued to roll even though I split immediately. The tape I viewed the next day revealed Iggy playing dumb, asking everyone in the room what he'd done to offend me.

Frank Zappa

Many of my career highs in those days of covering the rock scene came from the personal relationships I developed with the stars I met. Though none of these evolved into lifelong friendships, these innocent, innocuous encounters helped me realize that even mighty rock 'n' roll icons are just people.

I interviewed the late Frank Zappa several times during my tenure with *The New Music*. A poet and a true intellectual, he managed to find a unique groove in the pop/rock scene, not by merely shocking with his scatological lyrics, but by making us think. As a teenager I'd lapped up what Zappa and his group, The Mothers of Invention, had to say. Their satirical commentaries on the rock world and pop culture provided irreverent political insights that jolted kids who'd been raised on a steady diet of commercial rock 'n' roll.

When I was assigned to interview him in 1981, I was awed by Zappa's reputation for brilliance and feared that his dark, nasty wit would make him a tough subject.

Zappa's intense, Rasputin-like looks were intimidating, but within minutes of our meeting in his Toronto hotel room, at the Windsor Arms, I realized he was a true gentleman: kind, respectful, gracious, and charming. He blew every stereotype I'd anticipated out of the water. I was especially surprised by his vehement anti-drug stance. Chain-smoking cigarettes and downing lots of caffeine were his biggest vices.

Frank Zappa was one of the kindest guys I'd ever met in rock. I was surprised to learn that, despite his irreverent music, he was so sensitive and caring. (Courtesy Citytv)

After an interview he invited me out to dinner at Three Small Rooms, the restaurant at the Windsor Arms. Three Small Rooms was the ultimate restaurant back then, famous for its fine wine cellar. I don't remember much about the meal except that Zappa ordered a very rare, very expensive bottle of Chateau Margaux. I recall thinking how classy that was — such a relief from all those beer- and whiskey-swilling musicians I was used to.

Afterwards he invited me up to his room. He just wanted to talk! Really. And I trusted him, wonderfully flattered that an icon like Frank Zappa actually wanted to spend time with me. He spoke about his wife, Gail, how much he loved her, and about how lonely he got on the road.

He asked me about my dreams and aspirations, and told me never to take bullshit from anybody.

When he came to town again a year later, I couldn't wait to interview him. We met in his trailer at Toronto's Exhibition Stadium. He greeted me warmly, like an old friend. I told him I was thinking about moving to L.A. to further my career. "Just make sure you take a pair of knee-pads and a jar of Vaseline," he advised. He tried to talk me out of going: I had a great gig already. Why would I want to subject myself to L.A. bullshit?

I took his warning to heart and treasured the time he spent with me. I was deeply saddened when he died of cancer in 1993 at the age of fifty-two.

Paul McCartney

When I was twelve, I slept with a poster of Paul McCartney over my bed. The first album I bought was the Beatles' *Twist and Shout*, during a Friday night outing with my parents to Sayvette, a bargain department store. I'd first heard "She Loves You" at a sleep-over at a friend's house. A few days later there was a shot of the Fab Four on the "People Are Talking About" page in my mother's new *Vogue*. They were so cute! Their suits and haircuts looked bizarre, but they oozed style.

The next week, I bought myself a fake Beatles sweatshirt at Sayvette. The real shirts with the licenced logos were too expensive, so the knock-off had to do.

When the Beatles played on the *Ed Sullivan Show*, I fell head over heels in love with Paul. I pinned my hair up, my long straight bangs taking on the semblance of a Beatles haircut, and wore my new hairdo and knock-off sweatshirt to school the next day, to the consternation of my grade six Hebrew teacher, Mr. Taube.

I cried my eyes out when the Beatles performed Toronto in 1964 when I was twelve. Unlike the mothers I read about in the newspapers, mine wouldn't even consider lining up in front of Maple Leaf Gardens for hours to buy tickets. I went on a mini hunger strike to express my outrage, vowing I'd see them the next time they came back, even if I had to sleep out on the sidewalk to get a ticket. Luckily, I didn't have to. Erica Kalmar's sweet Hungarian grandmother got us tickets. I can't believe she lined up for them, but I can't imagine how else she'd have had access to these coveted seats, even though they turned out to be way up in the rafters.

I was thirteen by the time the Beatles played that second Toronto concert, in 1965. Naturally, Erica's grandmother had to accompany us,

Meeting my favorite Beatle was the ultimate fantasy. It's wonderful when your heroes live up to your expectations.

and I remember thinking how embarrassing it was to have an old shopping bag–carrying Hungarian woman with us on the coolest outing of our lives.

From where we were sitting up in the grays at Maple Leaf Gardens, the Beatles looked like raisins on the stage, but before long, Erica and I were screaming and shouting along with everyone else. Throughout the insanity, Erica's grandmother clutched her shopping bag a little closer to her chest, probably contemplating how many cabbage rolls she'd have to make when she got home.

Flash forward to 1984. Paul McCartney came out that year with a lackluster movie called *Give My Regards to Broad Street*. The movie needed all the hype it could get, which explains why I was lucky enough to be invited on the press junket to New York. The interviews were to be held at the famed Plaza Hotel, where the Beatles had stayed on their first visit to New York on February 7, 1964.

Either fashion or I must have been having an unsexy moment, because I wore a pair of cream, twill parachute pants from a groovy Yorkville boutique with a black-and-white plaid flannel shirt from Roots. These were cozy, comfy clothes that just said "me." Maybe that's why I wore the outfit: he was my childhood hero, and I somehow felt I wouldn't have to impress him in that way. Still, I was a nervous wreck as I waited at the gilt elevator that would take me to his floor. And all the way up, as the butterflies danced in my belly, I prayed he wouldn't let me down.

As I walked through the door of his room, Paul rose to greet me, exuding a warmth I'd never encountered in a junket situation, let alone from such a major star. He looked boyishly adorable, and I felt like throwing my arms around him and thanking him for every song he'd ever written, every note he'd ever played, and every fantasy he'd ever given me.

"Oh hi, I'm Jeanne," I practically squealed.

"Oh hey, it's you," he said, pointing right at me. "I remember you — Maple Leaf Gardens, Toronto — you were up there in the stands!"

Even though he was just winding me up, he won my heart completely. Evidently, he'd been told the "next reporter up" was from Toronto, and when he saw me, he realized I'd be of the vintage to have been a Beatles fan all those years ago. No question, the man knew how to work the media. But delusional me just wanted to believe he really did like me after all. For days afterwards, I felt thirteen all over again.

Help, Police!

I had only heard rumblings about the three-man band called The Police, but reggae was hot, and the thought of an all-white band taking a stab at it was intriguing. The group had released two albums in 1979, *Outlandos d'Amour* and *Reggatta de Blanc*, but when they played Toronto's

Horseshoe Tavern that year, only a handful of fans showed up. Their record company, A&M, decided a media blitz was needed and Sting, the band's charismatic lead singer, appeared in town for interviews. My producer, John Martin, and I, along with a cameraman, went downtown to a low-end hotel to meet with him. I donned a pink-and-black striped T-shirt, hot-pink corduroy pants, black leather jacket, and red fox muffler. I also wore a pair of two-tone cowboy boots. Looking back, the outfit was a typical early '80s fashion disaster. But hey, this was rock 'n' roll.

Sting was in a black suit jacket, jeans, and a blue Mickey Mouse T-shirt. The boys had just returned from Disneyland, and evidently Sting was in love with at least some aspects of American culture.

I had rarely spoken to a rock musician as smart, polite, and witty as Sting. I was charmed as hell and actually asked him to autograph the magazine cover. Of all the hundreds of musicians I've interviewed in my life, Paul McCartney and Sting were the only ones I ever asked for an autograph. Okay, Paul is a bona fide legend. But I felt Sting was special, too — I knew that from the moment I first met him, and I had the feeling The Police were going to be huge. Sting and I got along famously and I left the hotel on a real high.

A few months later, I got a call from A&M asking me if I'd like to go to Regina to visit The Police on tour. I packed a bag filled with tight jeans and sexy tops and headed for the airport.

I arrived just in time for the sound-check. The boys were playing cuts from their new album, *Zenyatta Mondatta*, and were having fun with "Don't Stand So Close to Me" when we got there. Sting was playing the huge double bass. Afterwards, we rode back to the hotel in their private tour bus. But as nice as Sting was to me, he seemed a little distant, not anywhere near as chatty as Stewart Copeland and Andy Summers. I think he was feeling under the weather, with a bit of a cold.

That night the guys were pumped, excited about the gig. They camped it up for my camera, obviously knowing what made for great TV. They showed off their clothes, which were pretty understated, really, pretending to model them for the camera. They rolled me down the corridor on a dolly while I did my intro to the camera. And Sting stuck an apple in his mouth and "grabbed" me in the dressing room.

Later, back at the hotel, Sting excused himself and went back to his room early. I stayed with the band for a few more drinks and Stewart Copeland invited me back to his room to smoke some hash. There he talked about how lonely life on the road was, how he missed his wife. Suddenly, having a one-night stand with a rock star who was in love with his wife lost its luster. It was better to just be pals with these guys. How would I have reacted if I'd found myself in a similar situation with Sting? Man, he would have been hard to resist!

The next time The Police came to Toronto, I wound up interviewing Andy Summers in his suite. Wanting to do something outrageous, he took off his pants and got into the bath. I sat on the edge of the tub and attempted to keep a straight face as Andy scrambled to hide his privates with the rapidly dissipating bath bubbles. Just another classic moment in rock journalism.

Toller Cranston

While working at CBC Radio in St. John's, I'd become a huge fan of skating legend Toller Cranston, whose exquisite artistry and sense of drama enchanted me. About a year after I moved back to Toronto, I rented a groovy little apartment on Carlton Street, on the third floor of a big old Victorian house. The second floor of the house was an art gallery where Toller displayed his paintings. The house belonged to Ellen Burka, Toller's longtime coach and mentor.

The first time I met Toller, he commented, "Oh, you're the one I see on that music show. I just can't understand how you can talk to those spaced-out rock stars. It's fascinating." The two of us hit it off, and for a while he was my closest confidant. He took a strong interest in every aspect of my life, including my disintegrating first marriage and the affair I was having with my new lover. He was constantly giving me style advice and instructing me how to dress. "Put every penny you make on your back," he'd tell me. He asked me to be his date for the Genie Awards and bought me a dazzling Wayne Clark evening dress for the occasion: a white, strapless gown with a satin bodice and large organza "petals" cascading over the short, tulle skirt. It was a fantasy creation, and Toller always referred to it as The Dress. He presented it to me in a big box with a huge red ribbon. "I saw this hanging in a window," he said, "and knew it was you." It was my first real designer dress, and almost twenty years later it's still hanging in my closet.

Toller threw some amazing parties in the house he owned across the street from mine. One of the most memorable was an elegant dinner party at which a poet, whose name I can't remember, and modern dancer Robert Desrosiers gave salon-style performances. As always, Toller invited an interesting, eclectic bunch of people, and for this occasion he encouraged them to dress up as their fantasies. Few heeded him, but I was eager to comply and decided to play the naughty vamp.

I'd just done a news report on a Queen Street West gallery that featured paraphernalia from an infamous brothel. Inspired, I went out and got myself a black merry widow. Fishnet stockings, tarty, spike-heeled boots, and a riding crop completed the ensemble.

Toller sat me next to one of his CBC producers, Ivan Fecan, the former Citytv news director who now runs CTV. Ivan already knew I could be a little wild in the wardrobe department, and although he may have appreciated my originality he never did offer me a job at the CBC.

Toller was style personified. He went out into the night wearing cloaks and dramatic hats. Fine leather shoes and beautifully tailored, loose-fitting slacks were teamed with the finest cashmere turtleneck sweaters in shades of crimson or banana. When it was especially cold and he was taking his two English setters, Minkus and Lapus, out for a walk, he would wrap a long woollen scarf artfully around his neck.

When he wasn't practicing at the rink, I'd often drop by his garden or his big, sunny kitchen for a cup of coffee. There he'd be in some paint-splattered T-shirt and an old pair of chinos. But as soon as he got going, questioning me about my world and expounding on how he saw his, his physical gestures were so studied and deliberate that he could have been wearing a skating costume.

Toller was an avid collector of Canadian art. Hundreds of paintings lined his walls, and more were stashed in his basement. I knew little about fine art, and he was determined to educate me. On one of our first outings, we took a limo to a small art gallery where a friend of his, Marion Perlet, was showing. Marion and Toller had once shared a studio in

Montreal, and her work — colorful, whimsical, romantic — had influenced him strongly.

At the gallery, he introduced me to Marion immediately. He then took me around the show, explaining why certain pieces were better than others and pointing out the ones he liked best. "It's always important to show support to struggling artists," he told me. "We must buy one of these pieces. Since you don't own any art at all, I'll buy your first piece for you." He chose a pen-and-ink portrait of an Arab in earthy shades of sienna and russet and green. Together he and Marion took it off the wall right then and there, wrapped it in brown paper, and presented it to me.

My first original piece of art! I clutched it to my chest on the limo ride home as Toller talked about why this simple piece was the perfect one to launch my collection. It wasn't until a few years later that I could afford to buy more art, and the first pieces I bought were, of course, by the same artist.

Meanwhile, Toller loaned me an enormous oil he had stashed away in his basement, featuring giant buttocks in the throes of passion. He sagely suggested I hang it over the bed, and I must admit it served me well as a source of inspiration.

Years later, another artist friend of Toller's told me that a bird's-eye view of my uncurtained bedroom window was to be had from a spot on Toller's third floor. Perhaps I provided Toller with some equally inspiring pictures.

Fashion Forward

Fashion Television

In the spring of 1985, Denis Fitzgerald, the station manager of Citytv, an avuncular yet debonair gray-haired gentleman with whom I had a warm relationship, invited me into his office at the old Citytv building. Although he was in management, he always displayed a genuine interest in me and my work. I spoke first.

"What's this I hear about a new fashion program starting up?" I said, settling into the seat in front of his desk.

"Jay Levine in the on-air promotions department has pitched an idea for a fashion video show. We might try it. But it's just a pilot, you understand. We're not sure we'll even want the show."

"Who's gonna host it?" I asked, preparing to launch into a pitch of my own. I felt more than ready. Since 1983 I'd been Toronto correspondent for *Entertainment Tonight* along with being City's entertainment reporter.

Swedish beauty Helena Christensen's ice-blue eyes melted countless fashion hearts when super-models ruled the runways. (Courtesy Citytv)

"Well, Jay was thinking of a model. We really just need someone to introduce fashion videos."

"But the show could be so much more than that," I told him, the possibilities already popping.

Jay Levine had been on the assignment desk for a while when I was reporting entertainment news. He'd accompanied me on a junket to Quebec's Mont Tremblant one freezing winter, diligently schlepping camera gear in exchange for a free ski trip. He was intelligent and mild-mannered: definitely the kind of guy I could work with.

"Denis, you've got to give me a crack at hosting that show. I'd be perfect. I may not be a model, but I could bring so much more to it. *Please*. Besides, I need a change of pace."

Denis smiled, obviously amused at my eagerness. I had a reputation at the station as a glutton for work. If there was some action going down, I wanted to be part of it. Denis saw the fire in my eyes. "But you're doing so much already," he cautioned.

"Denis," I assured him, "this is something I'd really, really like to do. *Really*."

"Okay," he laughed. "I'll tell Marcie and Jay you're interested." Marcie was Marcia Martin, director of production at the station at the time. She was, and still is, the supervising producer of *Fashion Television* and countless other shows.

It was decided the show would be called *Fashion Television*. The station gave us the precious go-ahead to shoot a half-hour pilot, but a budget was another thing. John Martin had always joked that Citytv would better be known as "$1.98 Productions." But in a way, the lack of cash worked in our favor: we had to be especially creative, and a spirited team effort was mandatory. Jay pulled together a makeshift crew with a number of his buddies: Peter Whittington and Michael Proudfoot, also producers from the on-air department, helped with editing. Tim Powis, a writer, and John Gunn, a director, also lent their talents, as did cameramen Al Macpherson and Pat Pidgeon. The mother of Jay's pal Miles Dales had a friend who was a stylist, a real fashion maven named Jeanne Grierson. Determined to turn me into a diva, she borrowed designer duds from the city's swankiest boutiques for me to wear on camera. It was the '80s, and accessories were huge, so she brought shopping bags filled with them. And shoes, too. The piles of clothes available for me to choose from were dizzying. I felt like Barbie on Ecstasy!

For our first episode, we ran videos from Ralph Lauren and San Francisco designer Eletra Casadei, a clip from the new stage musical *Cats*, our own video montage of "street fashion," and a few sound bites from an interview I did with celebrity fashion photographer Francesco Scavullo, who had come to town recently for a gallery exhibit of his pictures. I was frustrated by my lack of participation in the pilot, but this initial offering was to be merely a "fashion video" show. My role was to look glamorous in a variety of over-the-top outfits I wouldn't normally dream of wearing.

We shot a couple of my intros for that first show on the street, and the others at the old Much Music/Entertainment department at 99 Queen Street East. Because the place was bustling with activity all day long, we ended up shooting in the middle of the night. We were wired, buzzed, intoxicated with the excitement of making something from nothing, carving out new territory. *Fashion Television*: it was obviously such a hot idea. Why hadn't anyone thought of it till now?

The pilot aired to some media fanfare, and the verdict was close to unanimous: the show had potential, and we should try now to put a little meat on its bones. We were told to do a series of one-hour specials. I jumped at the chance to produce profile pieces like the ones I'd churned out for *The New Music* and *Entertainment Tonight*. Now that we had a small budget, Jay booked a trip to New York, and I was off to interview the legendary designers Bob Mackie and the inimitable Betsey Johnson.

Meeting Bob Mackie was my first big fashion fantasy — as Cher's designer on *The Sonny and Cher Comedy Hour*, Mackie was responsible for providing me with my only hits of glamor while I was living in Newfoundland. He was terribly charming and very down to earth, and we clicked immediately. I got to try on one of his ostentatious ballgowns — an orange number that made me look like a pumpkin. At one point, on camera, he actually took the liberty of adjusting my shoulder pads while he was giving me a tour of his studio! We were being irreverent and having fun. Then it was off to Betsey Johnson's.

I fell in love with Betsey, too. She was kooky and inspiring, with her out-rageous way of dressing and neon tresses. She was big on Madonna at the time, and told me the Material Girl was her idea of a "true-blue woman." I appreciated Betsey's classic take on girly femininity, and oohed and ahhed over all her cheerful, funky creations. At the end of the shoot, she told me to pick out whatever I wanted. I was honored to think she deemed me worthy of her mad, colorful designs. I picked out a black jumpsuit with capri-length pants that had big, fuschia cherries printed all over it. And I also chose a wonderful black cotton dress with a lilac print. It had a very flared skirt and the bodice of the dress laced up, corset style. The matching gloves — with no fingers in them — were the perfect kinky complement.

Early Days

I'll forever be grateful to producers Marcia Martin and Jay Levine, who allowed a larger-than-life, big-mouthed broad like me in on their vision of fashion on the tube. Of course, I had my own ideas. Fashion itself made for pretty pictures, but I was determined to explore a different kind of color, exposing the personalities behind the labels. We never saw our-selves as fashion journalists, but rather as entertainment reporters. That mindset probably accounts for much of the program's success.

My makeup artist, Genya Hulak, experimented with a variety of eclectic looks, too: smokey eyes and dark lips one minute, fresh-faced pastels with pale lips the next. The attitude was forever changing.

My first few episodes of *FT* were, for me, a study in schizophre-nia. My hairdresser, Gregory Parvatan, was instructed to give me a dif-ferent do for every segment, and there were several within each show. I was cut, curled, crimped, and permed. One minute I'd be wearing my hair in an upsweep; the next, ironed below my shoulders. Behind the right ear, behind the left. For Oscar, a French twist; for Calvin, straight and simple; for Betsey Johnson, pigtails. The costume was equally contrived. Usually Canadian — something I'm still adamant about — these clothes were all over the map. As long as the fit was good, I was game to experiment.

For years before *FT* was in wide international syndication, we had to explain to designers what we were up to. Till that time, their only exposure to fashion on TV had been Elsa Klensch on CNN: a no-nonsense approach that considered hemlines serious news. We wanted to have more fun with our subject matter, and it wasn't long before designers saw our point. Bob Mackie and Bill Blass jumped at the chance to dress up their models and send them out on Seventh Avenue's crowded sidewalks for our camera. The late Patrick Kelly, a black designer from the South who

Patrick Kelly dressed up his models like paper dolls, as our camera captured the fantasy. Issey Miyake graciously gave us an inside peek at the creative process by inviting us into his studio in December 1986. (Courtesy Citytv)

based himself in Paris, was in heaven getting his gals dolled up against the backdrop of the Marais district. Japanese designer Issey Miyake had never allowed a TV crew into his Tokyo studio before, but in December 1986 he was convinced we'd capture him at his best.

We weren't in the business of stealing secrets or critiquing cuts — we simply wanted to celebrate the scene at a time when advertising and image were becoming everything in fashion.

Today, our fans run the gamut from little old ladies to little kids. Teenagers, cops, cabbies, housewives, professionals — they all have their own reasons for watching. It is intensely rewarding to be associated with a show that has that kind of mass appeal. It's also a phenomenal feeling to be recognized everywhere: whether it's in Red Square in Moscow, on a street in Dublin, in a New York department store, at a Hong Kong market, or in a Paris restaurant.

The first year *FT* was on the air, a PR woman from Montreal called to invite four of us — a cameraman, Al Macpherson; my producer, Jay; my supervising producer, Marcia; and me — to Paris to do a story on Christian Dior. In exchange for first-class tickets on Air France (where the Beluga caviar flows generously) and accommodation at the Bristol Hotel (one of the most luxurious in Paris), we would do a meaty feature on the house. Besides the obvious women's wear angle, we'd also look at their furs and men's wear line and make mention of their new fragrance, Poison.

The people at Christian Dior loaned me a voluminous burgundy cashmere cape to wear for my visit to the house. Inside the avenue Montagne front door, everything was perfumed, bright, and buzzing: there was a sale going on. Beneath the opulent crystal chandeliers, dozens of well-heeled women, all dressed to the nines and dripping with Christian Dior accessories, were picking through tables laden with expensive, lacy lingerie. They were all in search of a bargain — though I'm sure each could have bought the entire store out many times over.

Suddenly, my brand-new "no name" black suede and leather pumps with matching handbag — bought especially for this trip — seemed old, dowdy, and inadequate. I yearned to look like these women, to be wearing something — anything — with a big CD emblazoned on it. I yearned to appear as if cash were no object, to scrutinize *chaque petite chose* the way they did; I wanted to shop like them and talk like them and smell like them.

I floated up the plush carpeted stairway to meet the men who were perpetrating these fantasies.

At the time, Marc Bohan was the head women's wear designer for the house. Domenique Marlotti was designing men's wear, and Frederic Castet was doing the leathers, suedes, and furs. Castet, a short, silver-haired man in a black leather jacket, oozed Gallic charm, and I was especially impressed to meet him since he'd been working at the house since the days of Christian Dior himself.

The mid-'80s were a time for over-the-top excess, and nowhere was it more evident than in the fur department of Christian Dior. I don't know who was buying some of these creations, but they must have been akin to art collectors, because that's how spectacular — and expensive — some of the pieces were. Try the $100,000 range for some of the furs. One fur coat Castet showed me with great pride was made of shorn beaver pelts, dyed in an array of rich jewel tones and inspired by a stained-glass window. It was definitely suitable for hanging — and I don't mean on a coat rack.

In the early days of our show, in a blatant display of "reporter involvement," I'd often try on the designer's clothes and have fun modeling them for the camera. I'd certainly never make it as a professional model, but we felt it would be fun for the viewers at home to see some of these outrageous clothes on a "real" woman.

My theatrical sense lent itself well to showing off Castet's clothes. The designer and I had a great time playing dress-up in the privacy of the upstairs fur and leather department, with only a TV camera there to capture my oohing and ahhing and silly sashaying about in some of the world's most expensive and flamboyant creations. The pièce de résistance was a *faux* jewel-encrusted, black leather-and-suede dress with a big plastic peek-a-boo hole at the hip. It was revealing, kinky, and original — an '80s dress of the highest order — and Castet said it was totally me. The price tag was about 40,000 francs, or $8,000 — way out of my league. When my interview with Castet was over, the dress came off and went back on its hanger.

I left the Dior store with an "oh well, maybe next lifetime" feeling, but not before I bought a black lace teddy and tap pants from the picked-over lingerie sale table. Barely affordable, but at least now I owned something with the coveted Dior label.

That afternoon, on the way back from avenue Montagne, Marcie and I were in a gay, devil-may-care mood, so we dropped by the large Galeries Lafayette store and made a beeline for the hat department. In front of the crowded mirrors, I tried on several swank *chapeaux* — fantasy fare yet again. The experience was putting me even deeper into a Paris state of mind, and it was fun dreaming about all the transformational possibilities. Suddenly I looked down at my purse. Oh, my God — it was open! I quickly pulled a purple fedora off my head. A look inside the bag confirmed my fears: I'd been pickpocketed! My entire wallet was missing! Images of all the credit cards and cold hard cash I had stashed in there flashed through my panicked mind.

I found Marcie at the glove counter.

"I've been robbed! Pickpocketed — my wallet's gone!"

"Are you sure?" asked Marcie, ever the optimist.

"Yes. I was in a crowd at the mirrors and people were bumping up against me. What an idiot I am! My purse was just dangling from my shoulder and look at how easy this clasp is to undo."

I showed Marcie the open bag, telling myself that if I'd had a Dior bag, with its secure trademark clasp, this never would have happened.

"How much did you have in there?" Marcie asked.

"Oh, about eight hundred bucks — and all my credit cards. I'm gonna go report it." And I was off to find the customer service counter, even though I knew I'd probably never see my wallet and its contents again.

The woman at Galeries Lafayette suggested we make a report to the police. Other than that, she really couldn't help. Pickpocketing was a common problem in crowded Paris department stores.

"*Dommage*" was all she offered. "*Je suis désolée.*"

"*Quel* hassle," I thought.

Suddenly, I hated the French. I went back to the Bristol a little deflated, thinking of all the calls I'd have to make to cancel my cards and wondering if I was insured for the $800.

That night, we dined with one of the Christian Dior PR women and I told her about the experience. She was sorry, and hoped I wasn't too distraught to come back to the Dior boutique the next day to interview the other designers.

My chi-chi Paris experience had been marred; I felt stupid for having been so lax about my bag. I must have appeared the perfect target: a naive North American with nothing better to do than try on hats all afternoon, little black shoulder-bag with easy-to-open snap mindlessly dangling by my side.

I dragged my feet back to avenue Montagne the next morning for the rest of my Dior interviews, eager to get them over with so I could get out of this crook-filled country. My interview with Marc Bohan went well. The Dior PR people all thanked us, and then, just as I was about to leave, one of the women came out of a back room carrying a big, shiny box tied up with ribbon.

"This is a *cadeau* for you," she said sweetly.

I excitedly opened the box and found a card resting on top of the tissue inside. On the envelope was scrawled "Mlle Beker." Inside, the card read: *"Tu es vraiment marveilleuse dans cette robe. Merci milles fois! Tu es charmante."* It was signed Frederic Castet.

I peeled away the pristine layers of tissue to find the $8,000 leather-and-suede dress I had tried on the day before. The French had redeemed themselves. Life was beautiful again.

Celebrity

My eyes cruise the crammed conveyor belt at the supermarket checkout: anchovies, Instant Breakfast, Meow Mix, mayonnaise . . .

It's Sunday morning and my tired brain is trying its best to confirm that I'd covered all the bases. I grab the current *Marie Claire* magazine and savor a shot of Demi Moore at home in her pajamas. Joey, my bored ten-year-old, swings from the emptied cart, anxious to get back home. Outside, our dog Beau barks impatiently.

The woman behind me speaks up. "I can't believe you're actually doing this."

I turn to her in the "you talkin' ta me?" mode and her face breaks into a big grin.

"Sorry, but I've been watching you on TV for twenty years and I'm amazed that you're actually at a supermarket on a Sunday morning doing all this yourself. I mean, don't you have people doing these kinds of things for you?"

"It's life's simple pleasures that keep you grounded," I quip.

Then she starts telling me how she never misses my show, and asks me what it's like to have the best job in the world and travel to all those exotic locations and talk to all those amazing designers.

And as I stand there at the checkout in schleppy sweats, with limp hair and no lipstick, my kid whining, my dog barking, and a hazy shopping list at the back of my mind, I suddenly get this heart-warming feeling about the illusion of celebrity and what it can do for people on a dreary Sunday morning.

"I guess it's a glue, no?" Francesco Clemente, the shy and admittedly self-obsessed Italian-born art world star, is in the back seat of a sedan theorizing about the value of celebrity in our culture.

It's evening in Manhattan, and *Interview*'s editor-in-chief, Ingrid Sischy, and I are giving Clemente a ride back to his studio from the Guggenheim Museum, where a retrospective of his work is garnering mixed reviews.

"Francesco lives in Bob Dylan's old house," Ingrid informs me.

I can't believe we're giving one of the world's most famous living painters a lift anywhere. I was equally wowed when I first saw Clemente earlier that afternoon, lying half-asleep on the floor of the curator's office as hordes of art aficionados streamed into the gallery downstairs to check out his monumental work.

"Society is always looking for a glue to keep everything together," the painter explains. "It's not as bad as war or dictatorship — I mean, celebrity as a glue. Celebrity worship is not as terrible as all the other glues available, like authority or hatred."

Ingrid looks at me over her black-framed glasses and nods. If anyone understands why we want and need celebrities in our society, it's Ingrid.

Another close friend of Ingrid's is Helmut Lang, the Austrian-born design visionary who revolutionized fashion with his cool take on no-nonsense urban wear. Lang, whose ads are as ubiquitous as zippered flies, is another reluctant mega-celeb. I was thrilled to run into him on a casual basis, courtesy of Ingrid.

It's nighttime in Soho and I'm at the *Interview* offices on West Broadway. Lang, whose studio is down the street, is in the last throes of getting his next collection together and hasn't slept in who knows how long. He's decided to swing by for a cup of tea with Ingrid. Dressed in jeans, a simple navy sweater, and a brown suede jacket, he exudes style with his gentle warmth and cool, relaxed manner.

"You get used to the idea of celebrity in a certain way," Lang tells us between sips of chamomile tea. "Then you just sort out what the right balance is of being a public person on one hand and on the other hand, not at all. You do have a personal choice as to which degree you deliver yourself to the audience out there. And luckily, in my business, you can actually separate the trademark from the person a little bit. You don't have to be there all the time."

Ingrid sees Lang's attitude to celebrity as very modern. As she tells me later, "What's really interesting is the fact that he really shows this kind of new relationship to fame — that one can also stay totally true to one's self, totally private and public, as the situation demands. Your ideas can become public but that doesn't mean you have to become a kind of parody of the visible. And it doesn't mean that you have to dilute yourself."

Mel C., better known as Sporty Spice, recently told me she finds the whole idea of fame — and the effect it can have on people — pretty bizarre.

"Sometimes, when people meet us, they cry and stuff. A lot of it has to do with the media. I can't actually think of one [celebrity] who's lived up to what's been written about them."

Fueled by encouragement from the media, we've let our fantasies run amuck. Often, when we see someone famous in the flesh, our hopes and dreams come crashing down because the illusion is always better than the reality. Of course, some of us actually breathe a sigh of relief when we see those celebrity warts: *ahhhh*, nothing like a dose of good old reality to bring me down to level-headed earth. That's why I loved seeing Clemente asleep on the floor of his curator's office; and a weary Lang sipping a late-night chamomile tea; and Demi Moore in *Marie Claire*, wearing creased, baggy pajama bottoms and no makeup.

Meanwhile, back at the supermarket checkout, my fan and I are in the thick of talking about the virtues of shopping for one's own groceries. She still doesn't believe that a globe-trotting gal like me could find time for life's little chores. I tell her I've made it my business to strike that balance. And as I dutifully swipe my Interac card, I wonder how many of the celebrities I meet do their own grocery shopping, too.

Gianni Versace

I met Gianni Versace in 1986. We were on our first *FT* trip to Milan, and the designer's label was just starting to become known in North America. We'd made arrangements to interview him at his new palazzo in the center of town. An appointment had been made for me to get my hair done on the morning of the shoot. I rarely had the luxury, in the field, of going on camera with freshly coiffed hair, but we had a particularly organized production coordinator at the time. I decided the look should be an up-do: I knew little about Versace except that he was a classy, sophisticated designer with a penchant for opulent elegance.

Our production coordinator had also arranged for me to borrow something to wear from the Versace boutique. This was something I did often in the early days of the show, for the sake of fitting in with the designer's aesthetic and getting a better interview. The crew and I swung by the boutique on the way to Gianni's palazzo, and I selected a silver and taupe silk suit with a long jacket and tight, sexy skirt. The clothes felt better than anything I'd ever tried on before: the fit and fabric were sublime.

It was mid-morning when we arrived at the palazzo. The iron gates opened and we parked our car in a small courtyard. I wasn't sure whether this was Versace's private home or his business headquarters. As it turned out, it was both. The old stone building was pristine, freshly sand-blasted. We were escorted up a marble staircase toward a reception desk and told to wait. The place had a stark, modern feel to it, yet ancient urns and sculptures lined the long corridors. And there was light, lots of it, and beautiful black-and-white marble floors.

Finally, Gianni came to greet us. He was a gentle, soft-spoken man with graying hair. He was wearing baggy black trousers and a white shirt, sleeves rolled up. He had a quiet, casual elegance about him, so unlike the bold flamboyance associated with his label today. His English was poor, but he made apologies for it. He told us he'd prefer to do the interview in Italian, but I explained that it would be much better if our viewers didn't have to deal with subtitles.

"Don't worry, you'll be great," I assured him, realizing this was one designer who'd have to be coddled and coaxed.

"Okay, I try," he shrugged. "We go down to my office."

The crew and I followed him downstairs and across a cobblestone courtyard to a small, one-storey building that was older, cozier, filled with precious antiques.

Gianni took a seat beside his desk, explaining that this was his private workspace, away from the activity of the main house. Again, there was a pristine feel to the room: everything was neat, orderly, and in its

Gianni Versace was very elegant and low-key when I met him at his Milanese palazzo in 1986. We didn't have any idea of how famous and important his empire would one day become. (Courtesy Citytv)

place. I got the feeling that Gianni was a very calm, intense, private person.

He complimented me on my outfit and told me it looked very good on me.

"You recognize it, I hope," I said playfully.

"Yes, of course. Where did you get it?"

"I borrowed it this morning from the boutique. I hoped you'd approve."

"It suits you," he said, smiling. "Did you meet my sister, Donatella, there? She does all the accessories, sunglasses, shows. She's really fantastic. You must meet her — you should interview her, too."

It was clear Gianni adored his younger sister and was eager to promote her. When he died and Donatella took over the house, I knew it was exactly what he would have wanted.

By 1986, Versace was intent on conquering America. He'd hired the premiere PR firm Keeble Cavaco & Duka and opened a retrospective exhibition of his work at New York's renowned Fashion Institute of Technology. We were promised a short, exclusive interview with him on the afternoon of the opening, but the PR people tried to renege at the last minute. When my cameraman and I arrived at FIT, we were told Gianni had changed his mind about doing any one-on-ones. I kicked and screamed and raised a fuss, and eventually Gianni agreed to let us have five minutes with him.

I was surprised to see how much he'd changed since our first visit. He'd become a bit of a media monster, savvy to the techniques of manipulation. Suddenly he seemed a bit egomaniacal to me: "Like my friend Elton John," he told me quietly yet brazenly, "I can be a rock star, too."

But I stopping rolling my eyes when I had a preview of his retrospective. The scope of his work was awesome. His costumes for the opera were particularly impressive — the luxurious detail in these garments was exquisite. I forgave him for his gentle arrogance because I realized the man was a genius.

The night of the opening was bizarre: the PR people were intent on creating as much media hype as possible, and they succeeded. There were searchlights and a long red carpet in front of FIT with barriers installed to keep back the throngs of fans and curious bystanders. The press and paparazzi were out in full force — dozens of cameras and crews behind the velvet ropes — all waiting for glimpses of the stars.

The PR company had circulated a list with some hot names just to keep the media hanging in there, but whether names like Madonna, Cher, and Bette Midler were actually on that list, I can't remember. Everyone was buzzing that they were all going to be arriving any minute. I don't remember any big celebrities making it out that night; Gianni's popularity with the A-list names had yet to hit.

I decided to go out and ask the crowd what they thought all the hoopla was about. Very few of them, except for a handful of FIT students, even knew who Versace was. "Some big, important Italian designer," they guessed. No one had a clue just how big and how important he'd become before the decade was over — a decade in which designers truly did earn the iconic status shared by rock stars.

I met Gianni Versace many times over the next few years, mostly in New York at his own shows. He was the first big European designer to show in New York, and he luxuriated in American hype. Versace's vision epitomized the era: big, bold, colorful, flashy, trashy — and above all, sexy. His approach to showing fashion, pulling out all the stops and presenting runway shows with rock concert aplomb, was precisely what the media lusted after. TV had at last discovered fashion, and Versace was proving to be the P. T. Barnum of the scene.

No designer's girls looked more fabulous on the runway than Versace's: Naomi Campbell and Linda Evangelista in particular exuded just the right sultry exoticism. Their larger-than-life Versace-clad images defined the moment — a time dedicated to celebrating opulence. We were becoming addicted to eye candy, and Versace was fashion's greatest candyman.

In the fall of '96, Versace opened a big Manhattan store, and the Versus show that kicked off the evening was the hottest ticket in town. I opted to wear a new suit by Canadian designer Sunny Choi: pumpkin, with shiny black-vinyl trim. It looked a little over the top hanging in my closet, but the occasion called for that kind of statement. In the big tent in Bryant Park, the glitterati were filing in: Elizabeth Hurley and Hugh Grant; Jon Bon Jovi; Ice-T; Kirstie Alley.

"Oh, too bad. You just missed Elton John when you were talking to Jon Lovitz," taunted a hawk-eyed bystander.

"Shit. I better try getting backstage to schmooze," I thought.

"Okay, two minutes," the powerful PR honcho barked. "But Gianni isn't doing any interviews."

Moments later, amid the backstage chaos, I spotted Versace rushing around, looking especially happy and cool in brown leather.

"Hey Jeanne. Nice to see you," he said, and came right over.

I asked if he had to work at not getting too carried away with the business of fashion.

"Not only in my life, in my work," he replied. "I never take myself too seriously. That is stupid to take yourself too seriously. It's pretentious."

Versace's murder at the hands of a delusional gunman in Miami the following summer marked a loss of innocence for everyone in the scene. Fashion and celebrity weren't all frivolity and hedonistic glamor. Sometimes hard, cold horror darkens the brightest fantasies. I was angry at Gianni for making himself an easy target for a madman until I remembered something Israeli designer Isaac Mizrahi told me at Versace's first New York show: "What's great about Gianni is that he has his heart on his sleeve. He's vulnerable. And that's what makes him fabulous."

Donatella

In the spring of '98, less than a year after Gianni was murdered, his younger sister Donatella was firmly entrenched in the head design seat of his illustrious house. A couple of seasons into the collections, the jury was still out on whether the shy Donatella really possessed the talent and flair to carry her late brother's torch. But her determination to transcend her grief was matched by her determination to produce successful collections and put her own mark on the house, while staying true to her brother's spirit.

Not surprisingly, she'd been keeping a relatively low profile, refusing most interview requests. But she knew and appreciated our show, and granted us an exclusive interview at her home.

I stood there on 64th Street in my tailored navy suit, a little nervous but also proud that Donatella had invited us to the Versaces' New York home for our interview. I looked up at the stone Medusa over the big front door and felt as if I was entering a temple. A gorgeous man in a dark suit answered the doorbell and invited us in. "Ms. Versace will be down

Though self-conscious before the camera, Donatella was warm during our 1998 interview, and brought up Gianni's name without any prompting. (Courtesy Citytv)

in a few minutes," he informed us as we stepped into the marble foyer lined with Picassos.

A buff young man in a tight black T-shirt came down the winding staircase with an armload of Louis Vuitton luggage, which he took outside to a waiting car. Apparently, Donatella was leaving for the airport right after our interview. As my crew set up in the elegant living room, the PR man requested, "Please, no questions about Gianni. Only talk about the collections." I assured him I'd comply, knowing full well we'd eventually talk about Gianni.

Then in she walked, a diminutive figure in tight black jeans, a

T-shirt, and shiny black stilettos. Donatella was trim, tanned, and perfectly made up. Though nervous, she was also gracious. She took a deep breath as the camera began to roll.

"What's the biggest challenge in your mind before each collection?" I asked.

"To get it over with," she answered.

"So you get nervous?"

"Yes. This is very funny because when Gianni was alive, he was nervous before the collection. I was sitting next to him telling him that it's just a fashion show, relax. Now I'm alone there and I wish somebody would talk that way to me. It's a lot of pressure, expectations. And the audience out there, they're there to support you, but also see the mistakes."

Though I'd been warned not to ask about Gianni, it was Donatella who had brought up her late brother, with obvious sadness. She realized she'd been left with a legacy and understood completely the public's desire to know more about their close, collaborative relationship. I told her I had first met Gianni in Milan in 1986 and that he'd praised her to me. "What an incredible bond the two of you must have had," I said.

"We were very, very close, me and Gianni," she answered, tears welling up in her eyes.

"Do you ever sense that he's directing you?"

"No, but when I have some doubts during the show or I look at some outfit I'm not sure about, I just close my eyes and think, 'What would Gianni say?'"

I asked Donatella if she felt the concept of sensuality had changed at the house now that a woman was in charge. She pointed out that now that a woman was designing for women, there was more subtlety to the sexiness of the creations.

"I know better how an outfit makes you look sexy — it doesn't have to be a big split up your legs or anything. Maybe it's fabric, maybe it's cut. Maybe it's makeup that makes your eyes look sexy."

"What gives a person great style?" I asked.

"Intelligence," she said. "You can wear the best clothes but if you don't have a good attitude, it doesn't work."

"How do you find that confidence? Is it something you grew up with?"

"Yes, I did. Gianni always told me to be confident."

And then she left me with some sage advice: "We shouldn't be copying what we see. We should try to find our own sense of style, to believe in ourselves. We don't have to look perfect to look good — actually, some imperfections are sexier. You have to put an accent on those. That's what's good about a woman — don't be afraid to be not perfect."

Cottage Life

In April 1987, I gave a long and extremely laborious birth to our precious first daughter. Wanting to keep the "Beker" name alive, Denny and I named her "Rebecca Leigh" — "Becky" for short.

I remember the first instant I saw Becky's face — a howling, square-mouthed, vibrant little pink face, enraged at being forced to come out into this big, cold world and determined to make her tiny voice heard. She had a shock of pitch-black hair and I remember thinking she looked like me. I held her warm, tiny body, wrapped tenderly in snuggly pink flannel, close to my chest and suddenly felt completely, overwhelmingly fulfilled.

Two years later, in October '89, our dear little Sarah Jo was born. Named after my dad, who'd died the previous year, "Joey" was a quiet darling. Denny pointed out that she was "snarling like Elvis" when we first held her up in the delivery room. She had a distinctive, sweetly defiant personality all her own, and we were instantly charmed.

In 1990, when Becky was three and Joey was one, we purchased a wonderful old cottage on Peninsula Lake just east of Huntsville, Ontario. Built in the late '20s, the cottage, which we named "Bargaroop" for the Yiddish word meaning "downhill" (in honor of Mom's exclamation when she turned into the driveway for the first time), was the materialization of our sense of family. Here was a tiny spot in the world reserved for us alone where we could be cozy and alone and blissfully together. This was our little piece of heaven on earth, forty-eight weekends a year. It became an escape valve, my salvation.

When I was a little girl, I slept under a big eiderdown quilt Mom had brought with her from Austria. I would get under that big cover with my teddy bear, Pumpkinhead, and pull it right over our heads. By the

glow of my flashlight, I'd pretend we were on a ship, lost at sea — just me, Pumpkinhead, and my imaginary husband, all alone in the world, cozy and safe from the perils raging beyond our bed. So many years later, I got that same safe and cozy feeling when Denny, the kids, the cats, and I piled into our van and headed up to Bargaroop. Our weekly trips to Muskoka provided me with just the pause I needed to remember what was really important. No matter what crap went down during the week, I always took comfort knowing that on Friday afternoon we'd be on the road to paradise. With each mile we drove, the stress of my crazy life gradually dissipated and my heart swelled with happiness.

Each time we opened the cottage door, the woodsy aroma and the golden glow of all that pine made me melt with joy, because it felt as if I'd finally come home again. It was the best and only place I ever wanted to be. All I wanted to do here was to bake cookies, snuggle with the kids, make love with Denny, watch old movies, play silly songs on the piano, paint simple pictures, cook pots of chili, and listen to Nat King Cole and dance in the kitchen.

Every single thing in that cottage — the royalty plates lining the walls, the handmade willow furniture, the old souvenir pennants, the faded, braided rugs, and the flea-market paraphernalia: the funky old calendars and Indian curios and woven blankets and ancient biscuit tins and postcards and oil lamps and picture books — reminded me of the charmed life I thought I was living.

Dad's Prayer Shawl

The saddest thing I ever experienced was watching my dad work so hard and scrimp and save all his life, only to become ill around the time he reached retirement age. In and out of hospitals for several years with a worsening heart condition, he was eventually forced to give up his little business. Then he spent a good chunk of his savings trying to get help at a prestigious Boston hospital, after doctors in Toronto had given up on him. We had to hand over $10,000 U.S. in cash before they'd admit him.

I thought of all the vacations he'd missed sweating to earn that money. Watching how it was finally being spent was painful. I swore I would always try to live for the here and now and not ever put off enjoying my life.

My father died in 1988, nine months after seeing his first granddaughter born. I was glad that he lived to at least see a grandchild.

The morning of his death, my husband and I had the grim task of going to pick out his casket. The rabbi urged us to choose a humble pine box, in keeping with orthodox Jewish tradition. But my mother wanted us to choose something more special. "He worked so hard — at least he deserves that," she said.

Denny and I wandered around the casket showroom in disbelief. We were being sold a casket as if it were a car. We finally chose a maple model with brass handles — impressive, but not ostentatious.

Jewish men are traditionally buried in their prayer shawls. I planted a kiss on my father's blue velvet, gold-embroidered prayer-shawl bag and handed it over to the man, feeling like a stoic little girl. I had always loved and admired my dad's "tallis" bag and was always fascinated to see grown men walking to the synagogue on Saturday mornings carrying these precious velvet bags under one arm. I flashed on my father praying in shul, robed in his prayer shawl. And even though I said goodbye to him at that moment, relieved that all his suffering was finally over, I knew full well he'd never really be leaving me at all.

Ultimately, my dad taught me the true meaning of courage and the necessity of forging ahead no matter what. He was always my protector, and even though he's left me, physically, spiritually I feel his guidance and protection always. Whenever I start to doubt myself, or lose faith, I'm reminded of his presence in wonderful little ways: coincidences happen, magical synchronicities take place, and I am reminded of all the miracles that surround me every day. My father never let me down before his death — and never lets me down now.

Eyes Sore

"Your mother wouldn't tell you, your husband wouldn't tell you, and your best friend wouldn't tell you, but I'm telling you — you definitely need one."

I was in Marcie's office, and she was being frank: after a dozen years on TV, on the verge of turning forty, I was starting to look a little tired. She felt an eye job would be the perfect solution. The thought of someone taking a knife to my face was obscene. But hey, this was about survival — at least as far as my TV career was concerned. And what was the big deal, anyway? A plethora of L.A. types had already made a religion out of doctoring God's work.

"It's a reality of the business," Marcie insisted. "Everybody's doing it."

I went back to the screening room for another look at my puffy bags and decided it was probably time to do something. I called Dr. Bill the next day.

"You got this far with the nose you have, so it's good enough." That was always Mom's response when I entertained the possibility of getting a nose job. In my high school and university years, a large handful of my friends had had nose jobs, some with astounding results. But my nose, while far from the fashionably turned-up variety we all coveted in the '60s, went with my persona. It wasn't until I got into television that I realized my schnozz was not a thing of beauty from most angles. But I always took strength from my first producer's words — "Don't worry, they learned to love Streisand" — and had learned to live with it.

But the years were starting to gang up on my face, and I had to try and rectify the abuse. Marcie was elated that I was going to follow her advice. "You won't regret it," she promised.

The night before my initial consultation regarding my eyes, I had a bizarre nightmare: I dreamed I was meeting Dr. Bill for the first time and he came at me with a pair of gardening shears. "It's your nose that really needs work," he said. "Let me at it." I ran screaming from his office and woke up feeling troubled. But there was no turning back now. Besides, the more I looked at myself in the mirror those days, the more I hated those bags.

The first time I sat across from Dr. Bill, he mentally redesigned my far-from-perfect face, quickly homing in on my nose.

"It's fine that you want some work done on your eyes, but what about your nose?"

"No thanks. Just the eyes — for now anyway." Upstairs, on a mini-tour of his luxe clinic, he continued to razz me about my nose.

Grabbing a large piece of surgical equipment which eerily resembled a pair of gardening shears, he made a quip about having his work cut out for him.

Mildly freaked, I somehow decided I liked this guy — but then again, there was something a little crazy about what I was about to do. He evidently didn't think this kind of surgery was that big a deal, and I found that strangely comforting.

My friend Penny volunteered to escort me to the clinic on the big day. We pulled into the private parking lot and saw a blood-red Jeep with the licence plate "2 WILD." I had a sick feeling this was probably Dr. Bill's car.

There was fresh coffee brewing in the clinic's kitchen when we arrived. The place was plush and beautifully decorated with antiques and Persian rugs. A nurse assured Penny that I'd be fine and told her she could pick me up later that afternoon.

I donned a pair of paper slippers and was escorted upstairs to the operating room. The lights were bright, and country music blared as I settled down on the table. By this point, I was relaxed and excited about my impending transformation. Dr. Bill explained what he was going to do, and after the local anesthetic took effect, he proceeded. I couldn't feel a thing. As Garth Brooks wailed, Dr. Bill settled in to the "delicate" job at hand, chatting all the while. Every so often he'd report on exactly what he was doing. Several times he actually held up small blobs of fatty tissue he'd scraped from under my eyes. I promised myself I'd never eat bacon again.

There were mirrors strategically placed throughout the clinic. The one in the recovery room had a grand, gilded frame, and I couldn't wait to see myself in it. I'd been dozing for a couple of hours after my operation and knew it was time to get up. The vision in the mirror freaked me right out — there was a face I barely recognized as my own, looking like something out of a horror movie. Black stitching circled my swollen, red eyes. I looked like I'd run into a truck.

"Oh sure, it looks bad now," the nurse agreed. "But just wait a couple of weeks until the swelling goes down, the stitches dissolve, and the bruising disappears. You'll look gorgeous."

I put on my dark glasses and left the clinic feeling like I'd committed a sin. *Is there anything in the Bible about self-mutilation?* I wondered. This had to be against my religion; it all seemed grotesquely unnatural.

In the days that followed, my kids devotedly brought me countless bags of frozen peas and corn to act as compresses for my battered eyes. I was surprised they weren't terrified of me in this monstrous condition.

I can't say it was physically painful, but psychologically I still had trouble coming to terms with what I'd done. I refused to see any friends until my face recovered, and of course there was the anxiety that maybe it wouldn't heal right.

Finally, after three or four weeks, the last traces of bruising faded and I was ready to face the world again. The shape of my eyes had changed a bit — they seemed a little rounder, a little wider. The bags had gone, and almost all the puffiness under my eyes had disappeared. But these minute changes were almost imperceptible to everyone — except, of course, Marcie.

"Now, aren't you glad you had it done?" she demanded.

When I finally saw myself on camera, I started feeling that I'd possibly added a little longevity to my career.

It's been eight years since my eye job, and I've started noticing that other bits are beginning to sag. I often ask myself if I'd go through the ordeal of plastic surgery again.

My daughter Becky put things into perspective for me a few years back. I was driving the kids to school and caught a glimpse of my haggard reflection in the rear-view mirror.

"Becky, do you think I should get a face-lift?" I asked.

"No, Mom. Your face is high enough already."

Twiggy

By the time I reached junior high, I knew that clothes had the power to get you noticed. My family went on regular shopping sprees to Buffalo, where everything was new and shiny and cheap. We also visited relatives in Clifton, New Jersey, and Brooklyn, New York, and for the Christmas holidays, we started driving down to Miami Beach.

Because of all this exposure to America, I was the first kid at my school to have a "mod" watch, fishnet stockings, a miniskirt, a poorboy sweater, and go-go boots. In 1965, that was a big deal.

The following year, my sister graduated from university and took a trip to Europe by herself. She went to Carnaby Street in London and brought me some fabulous pieces: an emerald-green corduroy mod hat; a fitted, polished cotton shirt with a big collar in a wild orange-and-black print; and a minidress in a hot-pink, purple, and yellow psychedelic print. I was the envy of all my friends.

Twiggy is the kind of woman that makes me look forward to turning fifty: She's beautiful, down-to-earth, and exudes inner confidence. (Courtesy Citytv)

Back in the fearless '60s, when England was first starting to swing, a stick-thin girl with blue saucer eyes and a heart-melting pout made me believe in the magic of fashion: clearly, it possessed the magic to transform us. And as a young teenager, I craved nothing more than change.

Twiggy, a seventeen-year-old from Manchester whose real name was Leslie Hornby, turned the world on its ear by proving that you didn't need the height of Veruschka or the body of Jean Shrimpton to ooze glamor. Skinny girls who were only five feet six and one-half inches tall could be style icons, too.

Twiggy fueled our fashion fantasies: we got our hair cut like hers, painted on our "Twiggy" lashes, and started getting familiar with designers like Mary Quant and photographers like David Bailey. Twiggy's waifish, wistful image somehow empowered us. She was an emblem of our first real love affair with fashion and, for many of us, the harbinger of what would become a life-long obsession.

Since *Fashion Television* first started in 1985, we'd been trying to pin Twiggy down, but she'd long abandoned the world of fashion. Just four years into her stint as the most familiar face on the planet, Ken Russell cast her in his movie musical, *The Boyfriend*, opposite Tommy Tune. Having caught the performing bug, she'd chosen to pursue singing and dancing over primping and posing. She felt she had to turn her back on modeling completely in order to be taken seriously as an actor. Those were the days when nobody believed you could do it all. So in Twiggy's pursuit of credibility, fashion lost a precious muse; London lost a bit of its pop appeal; and we all grew up.

Still, years later we at *FT* would often say, "Wouldn't it be great to get Twiggy?" And we'd hear about her doing a show somewhere, and we'd hear about her writing her autobiography, and we'd hear she was living in L.A. We'd get the name of her agent, and we'd write little love letters to her pleading for a brief interview. But the response was always the same: "Sorry, she'd love to, but she's too busy." Or "Can't make her schedule jibe."

Sometimes her people would lead us on and tell us, "Maybe . . . she's considering . . . okay, all right." But always at the last minute, plans changed and we'd strike out. I was beginning to think she was either painfully shy, or a diva, or both. But we never gave up.

In the summer of '99, fifty-year-old Twiggy opened in a sweet little off-Broadway musical revue called *If Love Were All*, celebrating the songs of Noel Coward and his relationship with Gertrude Lawrence. Twiggy's husband, Leigh Lawson, directed the show. This, we felt, was certainly something she'd want to push.

This time she said yes. I was thrilled to think I'd finally be sitting down with a former icon, and I couldn't wait to see how much she had (or hadn't) changed over the years.

After a million phone calls and many changes of plans, a date and time were set for our rendezvous. I saw her show the night before because that's what she really wanted to talk about in the interview. I was determined to talk about her fashion days, too, and especially wanted to hear her take on the fashion scene today.

My friend Carol Leggett and I took a cab down to the theater on Christopher Street, where *If Love Were All* was playing. The audience had just started to file in. This was not a groovy crowd. As a matter of fact, most of the people were most unfashionable, and the average age was at least fifty. Noel Coward fans, perhaps. Or maybe these were people who were big Twiggy fans over thirty years ago but had somehow given up on fashion because their uncolorful lives got in the way.

Carole and I, looking out of place in our de rigueur black garb and designer handbags, spent the first part of the performance thinking we'd rather be at Fressen, a nouveau Belgian restaurant, or some other of-the-moment spot, far from the conservative corniness of Noel Coward, as brilliant as the man may have been. But partway through the show, I started appreciating how cute and earnest Twiggy was and realized that she really did have talent as an eager and energetic performer.

By the end of the show, I realized Twiggy was glowing because she loved being in this show. How super-smart and gutsy of her to have given up something as fleeting and frivolous as fashion; she certainly couldn't have still been modeling all these years later. Wisely, she'd carved out a little niche for herself, and though she might not be making any ground-breaking contributions to art and culture, she had followed her heart — something we rarely have the guts to do.

The next morning, before the interview, I dropped by a movie set down at the fashion-shoot mecca, Industria. New York fashion enthusiasts had been buzzing about *The Intern* for weeks — a send-up of the fashion scene written by two twenty-something former junior magazine editors. There were scores of young fashionable types on the set: actors, models, makeup artists, stylists, publicists. They asked who I was shooting with later that afternoon. When I told them "Twiggy," most had never even heard of her!

"But she was a '60s icon," I explained, "a legend!"

"Oh yeah . . . think I've heard of her," they said.

By the time Twiggy arrived at our meeting place, a Greenwich

Street tearoom called Tea & Sympathy, we'd changed our lighting and position half a dozen times. We were nervous, having been told by her PR guy that Twiggy insisted on things being just so. This was a woman who had spent a lot of time around lights and cameras, and she knew all her good and bad angles.

Finally, in a corner of the shop that sold old-fashioned English sweets and an eclectic assortment of British *tchotchkes*, we settled on our final set-up. Twiggy arrived promptly in a big gold Mercedes, and I held my breath as she walked through the door.

She was wearing a tuxedo suit, with a pastel pink T-shirt underneath and sneakers. And her hair was in teeny little pigtails. With a disarming smile, she introduced herself.

"Hi, I'm Twigs," she stated brightly and stuck out her hand.

My heart melted. She hadn't let me down. She was upbeat and generous, and seemed genuinely pleased that I had a handle on who she was. She recalled how she'd given up modeling to pursue a stage career and how she'd just fallen into it in the first place — she said her look was never really contrived at all.

She recounted how she'd met Noel Coward three times and talked about how great her relationship with her current husband was, and what a blessing it was to be working with him on something they were both so passionate about. She told me about her twenty-year-old daughter with great pride and maintained that she felt no qualms about being fifty — that it was a terrific time to be a woman, even an aging woman. And she filled me in on her plans to launch a beauty line and eventually a collection of clothes and accessories.

The whole time, I was drinking in her adorable beauty and genuine happy spirit, heartened to think that maybe, sometimes, there really *is* life after fashion.

Naomi

The first time I saw supermodel Naomi Campbell in the flesh, off a runway, was at a crowded party at Bergdorf Goodman's, where spacey-cool renegade designer Stephen Sprouse was launching his new men's line. It was an atypically hip fashion crowd, the sort that doesn't usually venture beyond the downtown scene. But the shy, disheveled Sprouse was their pal, and his friends had come out in full force to applaud his incarnation as a groovy, high-end men's wear designer.

There, huddling on the floor beside an elevator, were Naomi and her mini-entourage. I didn't recognize any of them except for the photographer who helped launch her stellar career, Steven Meisel. Naomi was wearing a big, floppy, patchwork velvet hat and a pair of wire-rimmed sunglasses. The effect was totally '70s, and this was way before the '70s look made a comeback in mainstream fashion.

I tried approaching her, and even though talking was probably the last thing she wanted to do — especially in front of my looming lens — she courteously gave me a quick, reverential sound bite about Sprouse.

Naomi on the runway — sleek and stellar. Up close and personal, she almost had a shy air about her. (Courtesy Citytv)

In addition to her stunning physical presence, she was surrounded by a force field of raw energy, and ready at an instant to get her back up or just run away if she sensed danger. She exuded vulnerability, but her magnetism was so powerful that you didn't know whether to comfort her or stay back in case she pounced.

The next time I ran into her was at Anna Sui's boutique in Soho. *FT* were there for a profile piece on the painfully shy designer. Suddenly, in walked Naomi, wearing a long black coat and hair extensions down to her elbows. She looked disheveled — almost spaced out, really — and her eyes looked glassy. I told myself she must have had a late night.

She needed something to wear that night and started going through the rack for anything in size 2. I approached, asking if she'd mind going on camera to say a few words about her friend Anna. She got a little giggly, but was most accommodating and even agreed to stand there while I did my intro to the story. Of course, it was all to support Anna. That's one thing I know about Naomi — she's extremely supportive of her friends.

Over the years, Naomi's heart-stopping beauty and magnificent runway presence were the stuff fashion dreams are made of. She is the original diva supermodel, a wild and exotic bird born to help redefine fashion. But intrigue never comes without controversy. No model in fashion had tongues wagging more than Naomi. They called her a "spoiled brat," a "prima donna," and an "evil bitch." According to some designers, she brought new meaning to the word "difficult."

For some reason, Naomi and I have always had a good relationship. In scrum situations backstage, she gives some reporters the cold shoulder, but she almost always agrees to talk to me. I guess she feels I've always been fair and supportive of her. We bonded when I did a profile piece on her gorgeous mother, Valerie Campbell. A former model and dancer, Campbell *mère* is a gracious person who, besides spectacular genes, imparted to her daughter a few lessons about tenacity and dreaming big. Naomi felt destined for a career in the public eye from the time she was a little girl — but it was as an actress and singer that she wanted to shine. The fashion gods had other plans.

A few years ago, Naomi allowed me to interview her over lunch at the Royalton Hotel. It was a special treat for me to sit across from one of the world's most glamorous creatures and watch her launch into a juicy hamburger. But more important, it was good to see her outside the context of a sizzling runway or a hot backstage scene and have her explain just what she goes through each time she has to get up for it all.

NC: Backstage, I just like to be chilled out and I can't get into the stew when there are tons of cameras — like at Chanel. It's hysterical backstage, you've seen it. I have to tuck myself away in a corner just to get my sanity before I go on the runway, otherwise, I get into this hysterical mode.

JB: But you always manage to turn it on for the camera, for the crowds.

NC: I'm nervous every single time I step out onto the runway. I think nerves help you not to be too sure of yourself and that helps you think about what you're doing. I've never actually walked out on the runway and said, "I know what I'm going to do and I know how I'm going to do it. And I'm here to show me." It's not about showing you — it's about showing what you're wearing in the right way.

JB: I don't mean to sound pretentious saying this, but I think it's probably because you have an artistic soul and that kind of sensitivity comes from you viewing what you do as a performance and you understand you must play the part.

NC: I do. And maybe that's because I studied performing arts since I was a kid and I think you have to realize that, sometimes, less is more. I really believe in that strategy.

JB: The fashion world has been entrenched in an incredible hysteria for the past few years now and you were there right at the start of it.

When that whole super-model craze started, you were one of the originals. It's a lot more relaxed now, isn't it?

NC: I don't think supermodels — even though I detest the word — are ever going to happen again. That's it. [The media] won't let it happen again because it got out of control. They wrote about us so much; it's not our fault. The media thought they could give us all this publicity and power and then just

take it away. But it wasn't so easy. And I think we've done really well! [Laughs.] Thank you very much! I don't think it's going to happen again but I'm very happy to have been part of it.

JB: I don't think people realize the drive you have to have to go to the top of your field the way you have. I mean, they just think you happen to be this gorgeous woman who happened to find herself in this position. They don't realize the work and ambition that you have to have to not only get to the top, but stay at the top.

NC: Also, you know, as you go along, you get thicker skin. There

I ran into Naomi unexpectedly at Anna Sui's Soho boutique one day, and she was eager to sing the designer's praises. (Courtesy Citytv)

are a lot of things you shouldn't take personally and that's something you should know from the beginning. But it's very hard to learn that and you have to go through mistakes to learn that.

JB: What's hurt you the most over the years?

NC: People are always going to be insensitive; I just don't care about what they write anymore. I know who I am and the people I know and care about know who I am and that's what really matters. I'm happy with who I am. You can't worry about what every person is going to say and write about you. Everybody has the right to have an opinion. So as long as I keep doing what I'm doing and giving it my best, I'm not complaining.

JB: Does it surprise you that you still look as great as you do on the runway? People are always in awe.

NC: I am surprised in myself. I did a picture with Mario Testino and all the models were told to wear what we love best. So I had on a jean miniskirt and a blue T-shirt and Vivienne Westwood shoes. And there I was with Amy Wesson, Guinevere, Shalom, Amber, Esther, Stella Tennant . . . and I'm sitting there in this bathroom, taking this picture and I said, "I don't fit here!"

But in fact, I do fit, otherwise they wouldn't have put me in the shot. So it's surprising and I find it funny. But I like all those [younger] girls and it's fun to still be around, watching all the changes. I mean, I'm not old! [Laughs again.]

Like all black models, Naomi has been victimized by the very real discrimination that exists in the fashion business. On one occasion, *Vogue* magazine, which features black models on its covers infrequently at best, did something that had us all a little miffed and very dismayed.

Vogue did a cover shot with blonde beauty Nikki Taylor and Naomi Campbell romping in bathing suits on the beach. But the cover was presented as a fold-out, with Naomi's "half" folded inside so that it was only Nikki we saw on the newsstand. You had to pull out the entire cover to see Naomi.

I told her I was devastated to see that being done. Naomi shot back, "Outraged!"

JB: What the heck was that all about?

NC: You should really ask *Vogue* because when I shot that, it was the actual cover. For political reasons — "having to have blondes on the cover" — I was bumped and put into the fold. But I have nothing bad to say about it. I hope that — I know that — I sell for who I am, and for being a girl of color. I hope that *Vogue* will take a chance and actually put me on the cover again.

JB: But is the situation getting any better?

NC: It pisses me off, to be honest. It pisses me off to hear these stories about why you can't be on the cover. I really hate the whole discrimination thing here. It really bugs me. I'm not used to it; coming from London, I never had it. I only became aware of it when I came here.

But for me, it's a big challenge and I try to fight it. Sometimes I conquer the obstacles and that's what I care about. You know, my mother always told me, "You're in a minority situation, so you don't try a hundred percent — try 120 percent!"

JB: It's almost like a karmic thing, like this was your path. It must be hard sometimes to maintain your sanity when there's so much craziness around you.

NC: I'm saner than people think. Sometimes I pretend to act crazier than I really am because I can get out of doing something I don't want to do. And people go, "We don't want her because she doesn't have it together."

I'm very together. I just sometimes appear not to be so, because it gets me out of things I don't want to do.

JB: [laughs] Oh, now the secret's out! You can't use craziness as an excuse anymore!

But as recently as the early fall of 1998, Naomi made headlines again when she allegedly hit one of her assistants with a cell phone. Naomi, who was subsequently arrested for assault, was in Toronto at the time starring in a low-budget movie called *Prisoner of Love*. It was ironic, because I'd just been granted an exclusive interview with her a couple of days before, on the movie set. Her co-star and producer were quick to sing her praises, claiming she was the consummate professional: hard-working and very cooperative.

What exactly transpired with Naomi and her "cell-phone fit," we'll probably never know. Eventually, she settled the case without having to appear in a Toronto courtroom. A substantial cash deal silenced the assistant. And Naomi's reputation as a wildcat diva was substantiated once more.

The Day of the Divas

By the early '90s, models had become the stars of the fashion and celebrity scene, and they seemed to wield all the power and influence of any designer — and more, in most cases. They were the glorified salesgirls, and their perfect images could launch a thousand cash registers. People wanted what they had: gorgeous faces, svelte bodies, glamorous lifestyles, and access to the best clothes on the planet. What got out of hand was their own perception of themselves and the role they were playing in the industry, and in our lives.

St. Catharines–born Linda Evangelista was the most striking of all, in terms of both physicality and attitude. Since she was from Canada, I rooted for her. While her classic supermodel quip, "I don't get out of bed for less than $10,000 a day," was appalling to many, I believe Linda was just trying to get a point across: "I'm ginormous now, so don't mess with me. And if you do, you'd better make it worth my while."

In 1990, shortly after she married powerful Paris modeling tycoon Gerald Marie of the Elite modeling agency, she dropped by Citytv for an interview. I didn't mind so much that Linda was well over an hour late for our meeting — what I couldn't understand was that she didn't apologize. She was defensive during the interview, especially when I asked her what she saw herself doing post-modeling.

"Why don't people always ask you what you'll do once your career as a broadcaster is over?" she snapped. "Why do I have to do anything?"

I suppose she was right: most of us just can't imagine a bright flame like Linda burning out and not begging to be rekindled. But Linda always seemed a bit prickly, anyway. For the longest time, she seemed to have it out for me. Once, backstage at a Valentino show in Paris, I went

The sublime Linda Evangelista encapsulated every fantastic notion we have about supermodels. (Courtesy Citytv)

112

up to her with the friendliest of intentions and she told me she was angry with me over something I'd said on the show.

"What do you mean?" I asked, nonplussed.

"Well, I'm not sure what was said," she explained, "but I heard it was something that wasn't fair."

I couldn't imagine what she was talking about, and told her I'd send a copy of any recent story we might have done that mentioned her so she could see for herself that we hadn't said anything offensive.

"Okay, do that," she said cynically.

A few seasons later, when she going with actor Kyle McLachlan and had begun to keep a somewhat lower profile, I caught up with her backstage at Isaac Mizrahi's show — the first New York show I'd seen her at that season. She was behind a clothes rack with Kyle, and he had just finished zipping her up.

"Hi Linda," I said, as they came into view. Under her breath, I

Backstage, Linda's responses sometimes ran hot and cold. (Photo by Taffi Rosen)

distinctly heard her say to Kyle, "Don't talk to her."

I had to pick up on it. "What? You're telling him not to talk to me?"

And then she piped up dramatically — and perhaps only half-jokingly — "Yeah, don't talk to her. She's a horrible person!"

Kyle smiled at me. Linda was obviously in a grumpy mood, but I still tried to win her over.

"Great to see you here, Linda. We haven't really seen you around too much this week."

She turned to me haughtily. "I did nineteen shows in Paris," she said, venom in her voice. "How many do you expect me to do?"

"It's just that we love seeing you on the runway," I said, switching over to stroke mode. "And I seemed to be missing your presence here in New York."

She turned away. "Well, it does get tiring," she muttered.

I slunk away, defeated at the microphone. Later, doing a piece about models and their attitude, we played that piece of tape. I'm sure Linda wouldn't have been too happy about it — she came across like a brat, making people suspect that there'd been some bad blood between us for years.

But honestly, I like Linda. I think the pressure of all the bullshit just got to her from time to time, and unfortunately she sometimes took it out on me. I have had some wonderful chats with her, and I wish her the best.

Kate and James Brown

One of the greatest advocates of cleavage power was Helen Gurley Brown, author of *Sex and the Single Girl* and the founding editor of *Cosmopolitan*. For years, *Cosmo* covers were famous for featuring girls who were "busting out all over." Brown said it was her way of celebrating the all-American female body — of glorifying youthful sexiness and free-wheeling femininity.

Even though most models have fairly small breasts, they were always made to look voluptuous for those *Cosmo* covers. I never realized the work that went into this illusion until we were allowed into a *Cosmo* cover shoot at Francesco Scavullo's New York studio in spring 1990.

Scavullo had been shooting *Cosmo* covers since the early days, and he and his stylist, Sean Byrnes, prided themselves on working with every hot model of the past twenty-five years. But nothing had prepared them for the challenge of making the new British waif sensation, Kate Moss, look the *Cosmo* part.

It was the spring of 1990, and rising young New York designer Victor Alfaro was creating some very sexy outfits. Scavullo and Byrnes had noticed them, so they were getting exposure on *Cosmo* covers. Victor arranged for me and my cameraman to drop by Scavullo's for the shoot for the October cover, which would feature Moss.

"But she's so skinny!" I told Victor. "I can't see her as a *Cosmo* girl."

"Well, she's going to be so huge, they felt they had to get her. I've designed an amazingly sexy little outfit for her. I know they'll make it work."

When we showed up at Scavullo's the next day, famous New York hairdresser Oribe was there, and François Nars was to do the makeup. He was excited because he'd just been up half the night with Madonna, working on her new video.

Kate had just arrived, looking like the furthest thing from a *Cosmo* cover girl. She was wearing a too-small, grungy, striped sweater, schleppy bell bottoms, and nerdy running shoes. Her hair was messily piled on top of her head, and she wore an old chiffon scarf around her neck. It was a thrift-store look, one that only a gorgeous young model like Kate can pull off.

As unstylish as I thought she looked, I knew that her anti-fashion statement would probably become the next big thing. Sure enough, a couple of seasons later, the anti-glamor "reality" trend hit.

Kate was talking on the phone and smoking up a storm as I grilled Sean and Victor about how they were going to make this waif fit the *Cosmo* image. Sean admitted it would be tough. They pulled out an outfit by Victor Alfaro, a purple two-piece suit consisting of hot pants and a bare-midriff halter top. The next ninety minutes were spent trying to pin the reserved Kate into the top, taping her boobs in an attempt to give her a bit of cleavage. Kate realized this was no easy feat, and seemed a little self-conscious as the stylist and designer struggled for the desired effect.

When presented with the results, Scavullo just shook his head in a "this will never do" kind of way. Then he asked me and my cameraman to leave and come back in a couple of hours. By the time we did, Kate was posing for Scavullo in a ruffly John Galliano dress, looking sweetly sexy but not quite as voluptuous as planned. Luckily, Sean had several outfits on hand to experiment with. Kate eventually appeared on the October *Cosmo* cover in a purple Betsey Johnson outfit. Just how much pinning and taping went into getting that one to look right, we'll never know.

In the early '70s, when I was studying acting in New York, I had a few dates with a bearded guy who claimed to be an artist but made his living as a bra designer. He lived in Westbeth, an artists' co-op in the West Village, just around the corner from my acting school. His work didn't impress me, because in those days I had abandoned wearing bras. I'd happily passed the "pencil test" (if a pencil stayed secure under your breast, you needed a bra) and preferred a liberating, bra-less look, as did most hip young women of the time. Of course, Mr. Bra Designer never failed to remind me that I'd end up looking like one of those women in *National Geographic* if I continued to shun bras. I thought it was sour grapes, because my sensibility was bad for his business.

But years later, I discovered the joys of fine lingerie. Besides providing necessary support and giving us the desired lines beneath our clothing, great underwear is good for the psyche and the soul — of both women and men. That probably explains why I ran into the legendary James Brown backstage at a Victoria's Secret show.

Undoubtedly, the Godfather of Soul was there because some savvy New York PR firm knew his presence would garner lots of attention. He'd also been hired to perform a set for a select crowd just after the show. I took advantage of this encounter with Brown to ask him how he liked his women to dress for bed.

"Oh, I like to see them in real pretty things," he gladly offered.

"Any special colors?" I asked.

"Oh, red. I love red," he replied.

"But exactly what types of things do you prefer?"

"Oh, that's a secret — between me and Victoria!" he joked, right on cue.

The Victoria's Secret models all admitted to wearing fabulous, sexy lingerie when trying to impress their boyfriends or husbands — but none claimed to wear it all the time. They did, however, concur on the importance of wearing quality underthings. They claimed good underwear can make you feel good about yourself, and what could be more important than that?

Claudia Schiffer told me her mother always warned her about the virtues of wearing nice underwear. You know the old line: "What if you get involved in a car accident and turn up at the hospital in crummy underwear? How embarrassing!" As if the state of one's panties would matter to anyone suffering from a concussion!

Still, I do agree that dressing well starts with what we wear under our clothes. And well-constructed undergarments that fit right, are comfortable to wear, and make us feel a little sexy are imperative.

Grammy-winning pop star Celine Dion once revealed her tour wardrobe to me: dozens and dozens of designer outfits and footwear that had been packed into about thirty Louis Vuitton trunks. But the piece of luggage she was most excited about was the LV case that contained her underwear: scores of matching bra-and-panty sets in every color imaginable, all neatly sorted.

"It all starts with the underwear," she told me. "And I'm obsessed about having it match what I'm wearing. I can't help it. I think it's important. I'm very proud of my underwear collection." And then she said, laughing, "Now, whenever you see me sing, you're always gonna be thinking 'I wonder which underwear she's wearing today?'"

Dark World

"Why do you suppose Naomi Campbell isn't speaking out against this?" The question was posed on the other end of my cell phone. All hell had broken loose in the fall of '99 with the sordid allegations that a couple of hot-shot execs from the powerful Elite modeling agency were sexually exploiting their models and corrupting underage teenagers with drugs and alcohol.

A BBC investigative team had caught Gerald Marie, former husband of Canadian supermodel Linda Evangelista, propositioning an undercover journalist posing as an aspiring model. His cohort, Xavier Moreau, was heard making racist comments. It was a dark, pathetic tale being exploited to the hilt by media vultures everywhere. In an effort to milk this sucker even more, a probing journalist from a major national newspaper had tracked me down, trying to get some inside poop on one of Elite's biggest stars — a black one at that — Naomi Campbell. The reporter seemed to think Naomi would have been outraged by the sleaziness and racial slurs and had fully expected her to speak out against her agency colleagues.

Naomi might have indeed been fuming, but she certainly hadn't spoken out. And I wasn't surprised. Naomi, like me and every other person who's been hanging around the world's fashion trenches for any length of time, knows only too well about the dark side of the scene. For all the pretty images, there are more ugly scenarios than you could ever imagine. The sleazy and criminal behavior these two men displayed came as no surprise to veterans of the fashion scene.

I won't name names or betray confidences; I'm still in the thick of things presenting an internationally syndicated TV program whose mandate is entertainment. But after fifteen years of following models around the globe and witnessing the rise and fall of a thousand pretty faces, there's little that shocks me anymore. There isn't a business on earth that features the elements of beauty, fame, sexuality, and big bucks that isn't at least a little shady and perverse. Gorgeous young girls are sought out and catapulted into so-called glamorous social and professional situations that they haven't the experience or intellectual skills to manage or even assess. You can easily imagine their vulnerability in light of their naivete and dreams of fame and fortune.

Of course, not all model agents are womanizing jerks. Many are earnest entrepreneurs who see themselves as Svengalis, there to give that adorable little gal the opportunity she so well deserves. They coddle and care for these babies, promising their mommies and daddies to answer all their precious girls' needs. Parents are assured that their darlings will be protected in the face of strong temptations and influences, like money, power, sex, and drugs — which are everywhere in the fashion world. You've got to be a pretty amazing sixteen-year-old to resist those things

when you're so far from home.

What never ceases to amaze me is how so many seemingly level-headed parents are intent on helping their daughters pursue modeling careers. Over the years I've received countless calls from starry-eyed parents asking my guidance on how to get their gorgeous offspring into the business. My first bit of advice is to send them to the most reputable agent possible.

There's something to be said for a successful reputation where modeling agencies are concerned. Outside a major market like New York, the biggest, higher-profile agencies are usually the best. Agencies that ask for money, or insist that modeling "classes" be taken before they sign a person on, should be avoided. Sometimes agencies will ask a potential client to pay a nominal fee for a photo shoot, taken to see how photogenic the aspiring model is. But for the most part, if they're interested in someone, they'll arrange for the photo session themselves. Good, reputable agents can usually tell right off the bat whether someone "has it" or not. However, rejection by one agency does not automatically mean rejection elsewhere.

I always urge kids and parents to keep their eyes open. Modeling agencies can be sordid organizations. They're dream factories, spinning fantasies about the jet-set life, always on the lookout for the next big face: one that's untouched, innocent, ripe for the picking. One that can be groomed and groped and exposed and exploited. I don't know of any agencies that have psychologists or social workers on staff to help young clients get a handle on the pitfalls of the new reality that they'll be confronting. Then again, is it ever really possible to prepare a girl for the rude awakenings she will inevitably face?

A while back, I did a story on a male chaperone from one of the world's largest agencies, a personable gay man in his early twenties. It was his job to "babysit" a number of girls who'd left home — many for the first time — to model at the European collections. I caught up with him and one of his young charges in Paris and followed them around town, as he made sure she got to all her bookings on time and that things were going smoothly. The young model was no more than seventeen, from the American Midwest, just out of high school, and obviously lacking in sophistication. Socially, she seemed to be having the time of her life,

The joyful, carefree, and sometimes whimsical attitude displayed on the runway is often in stark contrast with the dark realities of the fashion world. (Courtesy Citytv)

121

meeting an exciting new international set of friends and relishing life away from her parents.

The young chaperone admitted that this girl and some of the other new ones his agency was promoting were essentially babies and needed to be coddled and comforted and encouraged and reassured constantly. The pressure was on him to see that they didn't get into trouble, and to make sure they didn't upset clients by being late or unprofessional. I had a lot of respect for this guy — he was the caring big brother, and the girls adored him.

Toward the end of our day shadowing him, our good man had to get this young model to see an important photographer for a potential cover shoot. The girl was acting giddy on our way over to the studio, and when we got to the building, she pleaded with the chaperone to let her go up to this "audition" by herself. She said she felt "too shy and nervous" to have us accompany her to the meeting. We agreed to wait in the lobby.

She kept us waiting for an inordinate amount of time. Finally, she came downstairs, with the important photographer in tow. "I'm going to get a ride back with him," she explained breathlessly as the photographer slunk out the door. The chaperone tried to protest, but she quickly gave him a peck on the cheek and was off.

The chaperone looked at me and just shrugged, with a "that's life" kind of resignation. I got the feeling this kind of thing happened a lot. I wondered how the girl's parents would feel about their baby "making it" in this way.

In Yer Face

One of the most enigmatic photographers on the New York scene has got to be Steven Meisel. He's a phenomenal talent, responsible for igniting the careers of the holy triumvirate of original supermodels: Linda Evangelista, Naomi Campbell, and Christy Turlington.

Meisel grew up with a burning obsession to be a top fashion photographer. Twiggy once told me that when she first went to New York, she met a twelve-year-old boy who'd skipped school and come in to the city from Brooklyn just to meet her. He told her he was going to be a famous photographer and would shoot her one day. The kid turned out to be Steven Meisel. And in 1993, twenty-five years later, true to his word, he did shoot her for Italian *Vogue*.

Meisel is always dressed in a black nylon overcoat, dark glasses, and a hat, his long black hair hanging down. Many people have speculated that he's really bald under that hat and that the hair is a wig.

Though Meisel never grants interviews, we decided we still had to do a story on him. So we asked all kinds of people he'd worked with over the years about him: editors, designers, and models. And we certainly had enough tape of him out and about at parties and fashion shows to put something together and explain to viewers who he is and why he is important.

Howard Brull, my endearing but irreverent associate producer, wrote the piece, and he and my producer, Jay, decided that to illustrate Meisel's eccentricity, we should mention that he allegedly wears a wig. I felt a little uncomfortable with this, but I was assured it was accepted gossip. Besides, if Meisel wanted to set the record straight, he should have granted us an interview in the first place.

A few weeks after the story aired, I was at a Marc Jacobs fashion show, milling around before everyone took their seats. Suddenly I spotted Meisel — and he spotted me. He hopped out of the group he was standing with, pulled at his ultra-long hair, and started screaming at the top of his lungs, "See, it's real. It's real!"

Everybody stared as I forced a smile, mortified, cursing Howard and Jay for making me say what I had about Meisel. Afterwards, at a post-show reception, I spotted him again and felt I just had to say something. I was terrified he'd just tell me to "Fuck off!" in front of everybody.

"Steven," I said, timidly trying to get his attention. He turned toward me and glared.

"I'm so sorry, we have the utmost respect for you," I said. "It was a foolish comment that we made in the story and I really regret it. Please accept our deep apologies."

He closed his eyes for a moment and quietly said, "Okay. Fine."

I breathed a sigh of relief and vowed to never again say anything I felt uncomfortable with in a story. At the end of the day, I'm the one who has to answer for any hurtful comments we make in a piece.

Because of the often irreverent nature of the television we do, we feel comfortable running with the whole gamut of responses, snubs and all. My producers and I have never really worried about saving face — it's reality we're after. If people don't have time for us, either because they're rushed or just too snobby to talk, and if we're rolling tape on that moment of rejection, chances are we'll go with it. Maybe that's why designers have always been so nice to us — they realize they may be exposed if they tell me and my camera to take a hike.

This whole business of sucking up to people, coddling, coaxing, and stroking them, is sometimes distasteful to me, especially after twenty-five years in the business. But at the end of the day, it's product we're after, and if we don't get these celebrated people on camera saying something — anything — intelligible, we don't have a show.

As in-yer-face as my style has become, there's a fine line between pursuing people and actually bothering them. I hope I'm sensitive enough not to be a pain. I am always amazed at the power a TV camera can give you, and because of my ability to put people on the tube, it seems I have the *right* to shove my microphone into some of the world's most famous faces. Because I'm on a professional mission, it's my duty to get as many newsworthy people as possible — even if it's just for a few fleeting seconds.

Sometimes, during my more neurotic moments, I entertain thoughts of retiring the paparazzi approach. After all, I'm forty-eight years old, and I've spent over half my life in the pursuit of sound bites. Do I really want to continue to be at the mercy of abusive stars? Why can't I be more like Barbara Walters or Oprah Winfrey? Those two must have underlings to do the dirty work involved in approaching potential subjects off camera. And they must have days, weeks, maybe even months to prepare for encounters. And then, when they finally do get stars to agree, they sit down with them for hours.

But for better or worse, I've perfected the smash-and-grab approach. Sometimes it drives me crazy; sometimes I hate it. However, I have to admit that nothing compares with the thrill of landing yet another famous face, even if only for a heartbeat.

Prada

For all the falseness and pretension in fashion, it still amazes me to see the PR arm of a dignified house treat people poorly — sometimes with blatant disrespect. But such has been my experience with Prada — and in the past fifteen years of covering the scene, only Prada. I'm not suggesting we're owed any genuine displays of sincerity: those are hard to come by at the best of times in this fickle world. I'm just constantly dumbfounded by Prada's outright arrogance and apparent indifference toward *FT* despite the positive coverage our program has given the label over the years.

The last time I attempted to cover a Prada show, I wasn't even given a seat — until I said I was leaving. Suddenly one of the PR girls who'd been telling me a seat was completely out of the question did manage to find me one in the back row. But she acted as if I were pulling her teeth out. She also passed the blame on to "Mrs. Prada herself. She goes over the list personally."

I don't know whether that's true, but it was amusing to see all the empty seats in the house once the lights went down — seats that were being held for friends of the house who didn't have the courtesy to call and cancel. It never fails to amaze me that we keep coming back for this kind of abuse; I suppose that when a house is as important as Prada, one must stoop to conquer it.

Sour grapes aside, Prada is to be commended for pushing the fashion envelope, and Miuccia Prada, the granddaughter of the company's founder, must be admired for her ingenuity in taking over the helm of the label when it was known only for its bags and parlaying it into one of the most forceful, influential, and controlling names in fashion. I first became aware of her in 1991 at the CFDA (Council of Fashion Designers of America) awards, where her label won an international award for best accessories design. I couldn't believe my eyes when I saw this very unglamorous woman in clunky sandals and an unflattering skirt and sweater get up on stage to collect the award.

Prada was the first Western label to give us plain, unadulterated minimalism — a stark new uniform to help us get on with economic recovery after the recession of the early '90s. These were no-nonsense clothes and accessories in modern new fabrics that were tough, durable, and easy to wear. They were also featured largely in black — noncommittal, wear-everywhere, never-can-have-too-much-of-it black. There was an asexual quality to this manner of dressing: basic cuts and simple lines that never screamed feminine or masculine. With our bodies fitted this way, sensuality became headier and more intellectual.

Suddenly, there was this bag that you had to have and wear like a badge of honor. Suddenly, there was this sensibility you had to subscribe to if you really wanted to be in fashion. By the fall of 1996, Prada was the last word with editors. Miuccia, who had started the frenzy in the first place, finally granted me an interview at her Milan headquarters. Her time was precious. She had to take her boys shoe-shopping, she told me. I warmed to her a little, thinking of this successful powerhouse designer as just another working mom.

She was wearing huge platform sandals and a beautiful leather coat, her loose hair falling around her shoulders. She looked natural, not the kind of woman who really wore makeup. And despite her label's minimalism she sported large dangling earrings. She was responsible for setting huge global trends, yet she had the imagination and sense of independence to go against the grain.

Despite her intellectual self-assuredness, she seemed insecure about being on camera. We sat on a big couch in the stark Prada showroom. I started by asking her how her company had conquered the American market and what it was about her widely copied label that people loved so much. She found it difficult to explain, but tried to offer a few reasons.

"Prada is really a kind of transversal, in terms of age, and in terms of social class. It's not that Prada's right for young, or right for medium, or older people, or only for the bourgeois or intellectuals. It's really something that's flexible. My personality is complex, controversial, and I think that a lot of people like this. So the clothes need a lot of flexibility. You can wear them with a different spirit, in a different way. It's not a look. It also has something to do with me being a woman and liking clothes and fashion a lot, but still wanting to live a real life.

"The other thing is the quality, because our quality is really good and the prices are not crazy at all. Also, our pieces stand by themselves: It's not a look, it's a piece, an object, and that object is right in itself. It's good like this, it's good in another way. It has a force, it stands by itself."

JB: Are you flattered that you're knocked off to such a degree? That so many people are copying you?

MP: Yes, of course! The only thing is that I like to be different so I always have to move on. That is the pressure.

JB: But when you think of some of the major trends in fashion these past few seasons — uniform dressing, militaristic style, the '70s look being brought into the '90s — you started doing all these things in your own way before everyone else.

MP: Yes. What's good about a designer is that he is in relation with what's happening. So you have to be having a certain dialogue with people, so there's a kind of instinct for what is right for that moment. It's instinctive, not merely invention. Another reason why Prada is successful is because it's not the invention of a look, fashion for the sake of fashion.

JB: It's a reaction to what's going on in the world.

MP: Yes. It's fashion, but it relates to what's happening.

JB: One of the first things people say about you is, "She's such an intelligent designer." That's not saying you're merely smart as a person, but that your approach to fashion is intelligent.

MP: Yes, because it's real. For instance, I like the fact that everything in the show is in the store. I hate the idea that something is false, only for a fashion show. I like a lot of eccentricity, strange things, but things that are wearable. It's the little eccentricities that are interesting in life, like, for instance, a bare leg in winter. That's something that I always liked in my life and something that when people see you, it's strange, no? But you can do it.

JB: People have to take risks.

MP: Yes, but real ones. And the ones that make you feel better or you enjoy a little. So in the end, what's fashion is just to have a little better life.

JB: It seems now that image is almost as important to a designer as the product. Do you enjoy that?

MP: No, no! I hate that. I think that the product and the way you live with that product is what's important.

JB: Do you think that fashion can, in some way, help us get closer to who we are?

MP: Fashion is like a little pleasure in your life. When I'm depressed, I go buy something and I get a little better. It's also important the way you present yourself, just as important as your home or the place you choose to vacation. It's part of your aesthetic. So what you wear is important because it's part of yourself.

It's good when clothes help express your personality. They should be something that relates to your feeling; to your vision of yourself; to what you want to express that moment. They should be used in clever ways. You dress different for a business appointment, different if you're going different places. I like the idea that this helps make you more in harmony with the place. For example, I hate it when you go to Egypt and the tourists are dressed so badly, they destroy the panorama. It's all part of your aesthetic vision.

To Russia with Love

My first true taste of exotica growing up came from my dad's brother, Srul Hersh, who lived in Russia. Uncle, as he was simply called, only seemed real to me about twice a year when he sent us fabulous packages filled with lacquered boxes and beautiful Chinese paper cut-outs and records with songs like "Midnight in Moscow." Sometimes, he'd enclose aromatic Russian cigarettes that were quite stale by the time they made it over here and interesting Russian fairy-tale books that were written in English. I remember one about a farmer called *They Got the Better of Mr. Fetter.*

He also sent us the most beautiful book I'd ever seen about the paintings at the Hermitage Museum. I studied that book religiously and it offered me a great education in art. But the most impressive gifts "that Uncle from Russia," as we called him, ever sent were a very grand silver samovar, and a babushka doll that was actually a tea-cozy.

These gift packages were always crudely opened before we got them. My parents explained that the Communists were nosy and mistrusting and who knows what other precious treasures Uncle might have tried to send us that were stolen by the Russian government. Having an

Katya Philipova's avant-garde creations were a big hit as our camera captured them in Red Square.

128

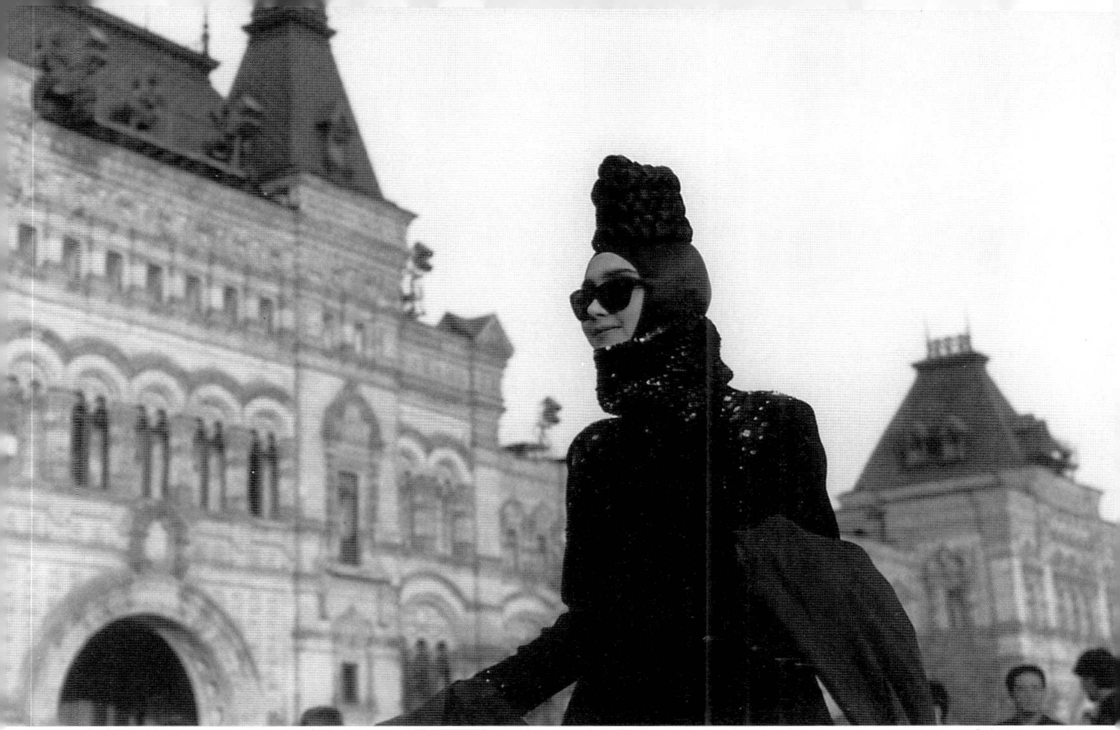
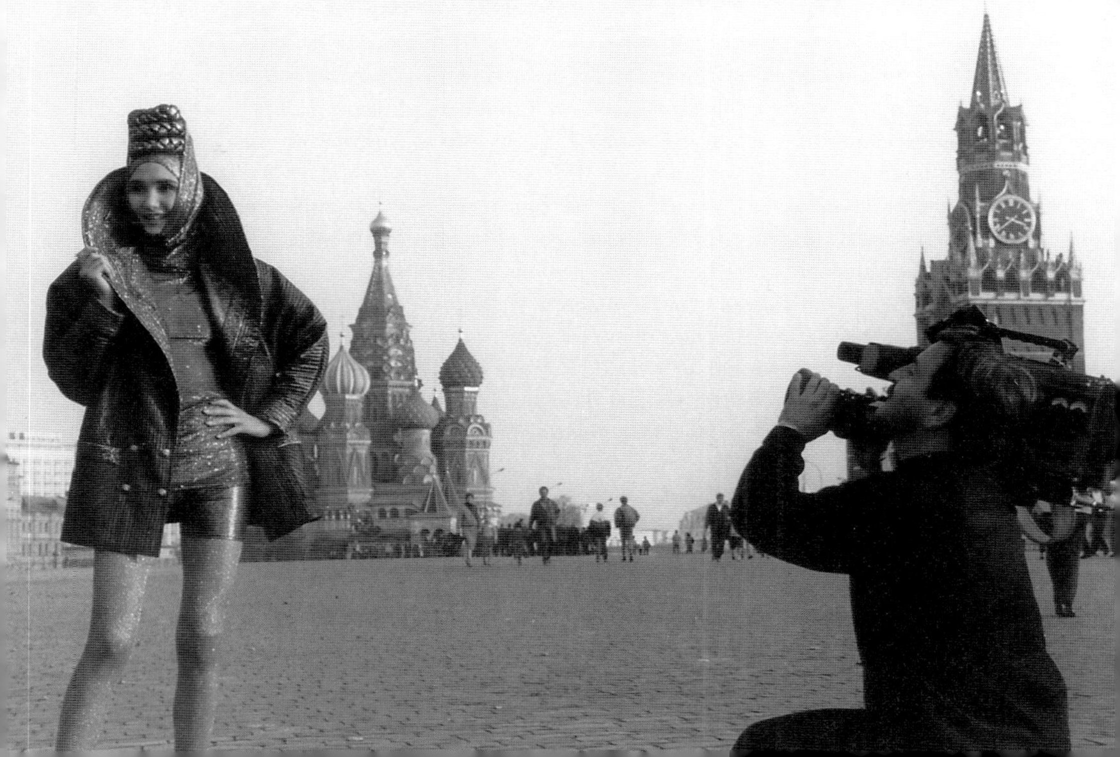

obviously affluent — or at least well-connected — uncle in a dark, mysterious place like Moscow who sent such exotic gifts seemed exciting and dangerous and it always made me feel very special to be so privileged.

Then I got a chance to see the country for myself.

Russia Journal (1991)

Friday. We're in the VIP lounge of Moscow airport when I get the bad news: My suitcase and half our camera gear have been lost. Hosting an entire *FT* special in the one outfit I'm wearing — a black-and-white houndstooth suit — will not be fun, not to mention that our batteries and microphone are missing. But whoever said life in Russia was easy?

The VIP lounge is a modern, smoke-filled setting where guys in black leather trench coats are knocking back cognac and caviar canapés. Our hired guide, Luba Shaks, is the head of PR for *Moscow News* and obviously has connections. In the next few days we'd learn that connections are all-important in this country.

My producer, Jay, my cameraman, Hernan Morris, and I are told not to ask how or why we're here, just to accept the fact that we're not forced to stand in the long line-ups with the others. Luba asks if I have a gift for the official-looking woman who's helped us thus far. I hand over one of the many eye-shadow compacts I've brought with me. Evidently, eye shadow can make wonderful things happen in this country. We pray our lost baggage will arrive tomorrow.

Saturday. There is a God. Our lost bags arrive and we take a trip to Red Square. Throngs of people have come here on a kind of weekend outing. I'm conscious of the lack of style — a collage of '50s, '60s, '70s, and '80s dress. A few wedding parties are here for photos, a tradition here in Moscow. These folks are wearing their best: mismatched pieces, but worn with such pride that you realize attitude in dress is all that really matters.

The sixteenth-century basilica here is visually stunning, a myriad of colorful onion-shaped domes. The crowds of people gathered here seem all the more colorless in the basilica's commanding presence. Photographers have set up stands in an effort to capitalize on those who haven't brought cameras. To the right, Lenin's Tomb, a hard-lined, solid brown structure guarded by a pair of khaki-clad soldiers. At the other end of the square, a Russian Orthodox prayer service is in progress. And just over from that, GUM, the legendary department store — a sprawling, antiquated atrium featuring rows of stalls, barely stocked with boring goods. There are dull woolen scarves for 30 rubles; a few cheap embroidered blouses; a counter with soap; another with souvenirs. There isn't a lot of anything, but people are in line-ups, waiting.

Sunday. We take an early trip to the outdoor market Ysmylovo, located in the northeast end of town, to do a bit of shopping and shooting. This craft fair started a few years back and was originally meant as an opportunity for artists to exhibit their work, but since perestroika three years ago, the artists and craftspeople have become more sales-oriented.

Now, hundreds of vendors set up shop in this muddy open field. Countless, freshly painted Matryoshka dolls form a sea of color. Balalaikas, bowls, and lacquered boxes are displayed on tiny tables scattered everywhere. Other things up for grabs include "Gorby" (Gorbachev) novelties, old Red Army uniforms, traditional flowered scarves and strings of amber beads. Open fires and roasting *shashliks* — shish kebabs — fill the air with a smoky, spicy scent.

Everything is incomprehensibly cheap. Several sacs of souvenirs later, I've spent only 3,000 rubles. I clutch my bulging bags, gleefully thinking Christmas as we dash back to our hotel for a quick change.

I must seem so materialistic to my new friend, Luba. She has never seen rubles fly this fast. While I'm dressing, I hand Luba an extra couple of pairs of pantyhose I've brought. She can't thank me enough. Pantyhose are almost impossible to come by in these parts, even if you are willing to pay the 50 rubles they cost — more than half a week's wages. I'll never take pantyhose for granted again.

Slava Zaitsev is Russia's most celebrated designer. He occupies a small fourth-floor apartment in a very "happening" street called Arbat, which is alive with street musicians and rows of vendors pushing old Communist party paraphernalia. He has a cheerful voice, rosy cheeks, and an alarming brush cut. He's wearing a black, raw silk suit, accented with a bright red tie, belt, and hanky puffing out of his breast pocket. This man has more flair than anyone I've seen here yet, and his forthright charm sweeps me off my feet. He's articulate, passionate, and strikes me as an artist.

Though his business is state-backed, he refuses to give Raisa

Gorbachev credit for helping him achieve his success, though many in the fashion industry credit the fashionable First Lady with making the world aware of Soviet style.

"I would never be artist of the court, a slave," he insists. "I am a free artist. I find it even difficult to speak with those involved in politics."

I ask Zaitsev if he sometimes thinks fashion a bit frivolous in a land where eating is becoming a growing concern. He responds that fashion is good for the soul, the outward affirmation of an individual's freedom of expression.

"What could be more important than that?" he asks.

He is optimistic about the future of Russian designers. Some of them have been forced to use drapery — even bed sheets — for their creations, since good fabric is so very scarce. Anyone that resourceful, says Zaitsev, is bound not only to survive, but thrive.

Monday. Russia's foremost avant-garde designer is Katya Philipova. Dubbed the Jean Paul Gaultier of Moscow, her lavish creations were shown in Paris last year and she manages to spend a fair bit of time in New York, garnering publicity and hanging out with her American MTV-producer boyfriend.

It's in New York that she hunts for interesting bits of fabric. She's incredibly inventive — she even made an outfit out of old Red Army flags a couple of years ago, before the Communist Party ever dreamed it could lose face.

Excited to see how this artist lived, I am disheartened when we pull up in front of a shabby old high-rise. Philipova greets us at the door of a dark, minuscule apartment. Her skin is alabaster, her hair jet-black. Her tiny bedroom studio manages to accommodate an old baby grand piano and a riot of lamé fabric swatches, strips of sequins and various sparkling stones are scattered everywhere. An easel displays a religious watercolor painting and posters from her Paris show line the walls.

Philipova has a great sense of humor. Her creations are more like wearable art than high fashion. She tells me she was at the barricades the night three young heroes lost their lives. When Boris Yeltsin and the people were victorious, she was fiercely proud. But now, a month later, she questions what it all means: the poverty, the diminishing supplies, the inevitable struggles that lie ahead. She says a dark depression fills her soul.

She's not alone. People everywhere are wondering how they'll survive. She's also not optimistic about the future of fashion designers in Russia. Only those who sell out can make it, she claims. Would she sell out, if given the chance?

"Of course," she jokes.

To show my support, I order a custom jacket from her. And she beams. She'll charge me $250 U.S. for this one-of-a-kind creation. I realize this is an outrageous price in this country, but I also realize that Philipova has spent time in Paris and New York. Why should she settle for rubles when she's dealing with a customer who's used to high-priced fashion?

Tuesday. My last night in Moscow, Luba and I take a drive to Katya Philipova's apartment to claim the jacket I had commissioned. Incredibly, in three short days, she's managed to craft a wonderful piece, culled from scraps of brown satin and black velvet and gold brocade I'd seen scrunched up in a shopping bag in her bedroom earlier in the week. It's hand-stitched — the workmanship is meticulous. Not only has she made good on her promise to have the jacket ready, but she's proved to be an extraordinary artisan, every bit as talented as Zaitsev, I'm sure.

Luba and I head back to the hotel, huddled in the back seat, sharing secrets, hopes, and dreams. Will she, like so many of the other young people we've met, leave for the West? She says it's hard to tell, because now, like always, the Russian people wait: Wait for things to get better; wait for change; wait to see what happens.

I think of all the waiting eyes I've seen in this dark country: waiting in lines, for fabric, for food, for life to begin. Together, we pray it won't be long now.

A Touch of Blass

It was well before noon, but Bill Blass and I were feeling extravagant and a little outré, so we ordered a bottle of champagne for breakfast. It was October 1999, just before the launch of his new fragrance, "Amazing." Okay, so the breakfast was at a mere dining hall in a Toronto department store (though the crystal chandeliers and friendly service were very nice).

And the "champagne" brought to us was some insipid local sparkling wine.

I love the way this country grounds me.

Still, it isn't everyday a girl gets to schmooze with one of the most influential forces in American fashion. The bottom line for me, though, is that, at seventy-eight, Blass is one of the classiest men I've ever shared a table with and one of the most down-to-earth people in fashion.

Back in 1986, when our show was in its first year, we requested an interview with him and were told we could have fifteen minutes. His office also asked to see a copy of our show. We sent one, and a few days later his office called back to say we could have three hours with him.

Up in his Seventh Avenue showroom, the affable Mr. Blass, a cigarette casually dangling from his mouth, picked through his glorious racks and pulled a variety of looks. Handsome and rugged, he seemed more like a football coach than a designer. I immediately understood why America's most important socialites wanted nothing more than to hang with the Indiana native and wear his fabulous clothes.

We suggested taking Blass's model outside so we could shoot the clothing in the context of the street. Blass conceded, and dressed his girl up in a floppy-brimmed hat to match her stunning black-and-white ensemble. She stopped traffic on Seventh Avenue. Horns honked and faces lit up. It was thrilling to bring a blast of Blass to the midtown Manhattan workday. When we rushed upstairs to tell the designer about the scene he'd helped create, he was delighted and promptly started dressing his model in another sensational outfit in which she could strut.

Blass's love affair with fashion started long ago.

"As a kid, for fifteen cents on a Saturday afternoon in the height of the Depression, I'd go to the movies and see Dietrich and Garbo and all of those legendary clothes horses. I realized then that's what I wanted to do — I wanted to be a dress designer."

So in 1939, at the age of eighteen, he moved from Fort Wayne to New York City and began studying fashion design at Parsons. He did a brief stint as a sketch artist before serving in the army as a sergeant and was thankful for his three years in the army: the experience exposed him to a group of men and a side of life he would never have known otherwise.

Once that grounding experience was over, it was back to design-

Bill Blass, class personified, has always been very special to me. I joined him for lunch on the day of his perfume launch in Toronto in the fall of 1999. Earlier that spring, I dropped by his apartment just hours before he presented his fall collection at Le Cirque.

(Bottom photo courtesy Citytv)

ing on Seventh Avenue. He bought his own company in 1970 and was one of the first Americans to put his name on a label. He quickly became one of the most recognizable designers around. Soon the licencing of his name became a major business. Bill Blass was associated with everything from swimwear to jeans, furs, shoes, perfume, and chocolates. He even did a car. Today, designers everywhere are scrambling to jump on the home-line bandwagon, but Blass had been hip to the concept for years, having made a small fortune with his huge collection of bed linens and towels.

But mostly, he loved to dress ladies. And he always knew what they wanted and needed. He socialized with his high-class customers, witnessing first-hand the lives they led. These gals were never fashion victims; they were fashion plates.

"I hate a woman who shops all the time and spends all of her hours in the fitting room and going from one boutique to another," he told me. "That woman's a bore. My customer is a woman — no age to her — who takes care of her figure, loves her house, serves great food, and is involved in her community. She's a woman who I admire."

There they were in the front row: dames like Nancy Kissinger, Blaine Trump, and Barbara Walters — at New York's Le Cirque last spring, lapping up that pizzazz only Blass could give them. It was his fall/winter show, the first he had given since recovering from a stroke the previous December. And he was his usual cool, charming self. He invited me and my camera up to his Sutton Place address first thing that morning.

We wanted to do a profile piece on him; there had been rumors that the "Senator of Seventh Avenue," the "Dean of Fashion" as he was known, might be retiring. He was eager to inform us he wasn't.

He greeted me at the door of his ultra-chic Sutton Place apartment, an elegant study in design perfection.

"I hope you're not here because you think I'm doing my last show," he said off the top. "It's not."

And as he poured coffee into my exquisite bone china cup, he told me he especially relished his time in the country these days. Back in '86, he also impressed on me how much he valued his privacy.

"You can only stand people so much. When you're constantly on, as you have to be in this business, you need desperately that other facet of life."

As I toured his apartment, I felt a definite sense of calm. This was a man who had an uncompromising sense of self and was likely preparing to trade in the craziness of fashion for a little sanity. I looked out at the magnificent view from his living-room window and imagined the satisfaction he must have felt knowing he'd conquered his childhood ambitions and become the quintessential New York designer, spinning dreams of luxury and glamor into modern, wearable realities.

Though Blass wasn't ready to pack in his sketchpad just yet, he would be by the fall. The spring 2000 show was a spectacular swan song. It was somewhat poignant that the rain poured down outside the Bryant Park tent where he presented his final collection. Inside, we were all cozy and enchanted by the razzmatazz he gave us: hot, dazzling, pretty clothes that made us realize how much he was going to be missed.

Backstage, Blass finally admitted to me that he'd decided "not to hang in anymore." He wanted to spend more time in the country.

"And what has a life in fashion given you, in the end?" I asked.

"A great deal of satisfaction," he answered.

"What did he tell you?" Blass's lovely assistant, Yvonne, asked when she saw me wrap my interview.

"He said this would be his final collection," I told her.

"Really? You mean he actually said that, on the record? You know, he hasn't really announced anything official just yet. You're the first one he's told."

"Yeah, well, I'm flattered I'd be the one he'd tell first," I told her. "God — he'll be missed so much."

Tears welled up in Yvonne's eyes. She took off to a corner and wept, sad, as we all were, that Bill Blass had decided to bow out before the new millennium got underway.

The Good, the Bad, and the Beautiful

Madonna

Initially, I couldn't understand what the hype around Madonna was about. I went to one of her concerts in the late '80s and saw little more than a girl with chubby legs dancing her heart out in front of a cheering crowd. But I dug the way she dressed. It was a mishmash of styles — romantic, vintage, sexy — thrown together in a way that was contrived but whimsical. It was precisely that talent of Madonna's that eventually made me appreciate her. She was a brilliant role model for girls everywhere; she knew how to market herself and proved you can be sexy, smart, and successful at the same time.

Betsey Johnson once told me that Madonna was her "ideal woman, a true-blue girl." A free-spirited original, she was a great inspiration for a plethora of designers in the late '80s and '90s, from Betsey, to Anna Sui, to Marc Jacobs, to Jean Paul Gaultier. Those in the fashion crowd with a sense of humor got Madonna, and by the time her star peaked, the fashion scene could not get enough of her. By constantly evolving her image, she was also setting an important example for those who found themselves stuck in style ruts, afraid to take fashion risks because they were so used to seeing themselves in a certain way.

New York's Anna Sui was one of Madonna's biggest fans. The pop star was the perfect muse for Sui, who caters to hip young girls and their older counterparts with clothes that are wildly romantic, sometimes nostalgic, and often larger than life.

Sui is fairly shy — early in her career, she was painfully so. When we interviewed her at her Soho shop (the time Naomi Campbell dropped by looking a little bleary-eyed), it struck me that her boutique was just like a big, dreamy closet. After our interview, I began picking through the racks, determined to find a little something to buy. My fellow shopper Naomi's enthusiasm for Anna's work was not surprising; every supermodel on the circuit in those days was singing Anna's praises. Hers was the only show they'd all come out for — in their eyes she was *the* designer, the one with a rock 'n' roll sensibility. Naomi always had a place of honor at Anna's shows, either opening or closing them.

Anna was helping Naomi and me simultaneously. I came across an outrageous pair of black-velvet bell-bottom trousers with humongous bells, that somehow felt right. Bell bottoms had just made a comeback on the runway and I thought it would be great to wear such a striking pair. I bought them, already plotting just where I might make an impact with this theatrical fashion statement.

I'd been dying to interview Madonna, but since I wasn't working the music beat, there wasn't much opportunity. But I was still contributing pieces about movies to Citytv's *Movie Television*, so when her starring vehicle *Body of Evidence* was being hyped, it was a great opportunity to get Madonna and air bits of the interview on both shows.

The studio was holding a junket in New York at the Regis Hotel, and I couldn't wait. What to wear became the big issue at hand — I figured it had to be something slightly fabulous. I wanted her to know I subscribed to forward fashion and certainly appreciated her style and talent as a trendsetter. Then I flashed on the Anna Sui bell bottoms and knew God was talking to me. No question Madonna would have an appreciation for Anna Sui anything.

Movie junkets are demeaning by nature. Scores of entertainment reporters and lowbrow critics from across North America come out in droves for freebie weekends at upscale hotels, usually in New York or Los Angeles. Most of the media types who take advantage of these junkets take themselves and their work very seriously. The TV folks get a maximum of five minutes, if they're lucky, for their one-on-one interview with the stars of the film.

You wait way too long in a holding room at the hotel, where at least you can drink lots of coffee and hear about some of the inane questions these stars-in-their-local-market types are planning to ask. Then you go into a suite where there is a major crew set up with two cameras, tons of lighting, and countless production assistants scurrying about, making sure everything is running smoothly.

The head PA, who is holding an ominous stopwatch, comes over. You introduce yourself and are escorted over to where the star is sitting, usually in the process of getting his or her makeup retouched. Introductions take place at the speed of light because these people are involved in a major project, you're made to understand, and they're mega-stars of course, and who cares that you've hauled your ass across the continent to converse with this celebrity and ultimately push his or her product. They're doing you a favor — a big, giant favor — and you are at their mercy. And don't take advantage of their kindness or you'll be out on your ass, without any precious tape to bring home.

It was under these circumstances that I was to meet pop's biggest icon. I proudly sashayed through the hotel suite door in my over-the-top bell bottoms, feeling that I would probably fare better than most of the nervous interviewers she was obligated to meet that day. After all, I was wearing one of Madonna's favorite designers.

Madonna was sitting in a straight-back chair in the center of the room, looking much tinier than I expected. She was, understandably, not in a good mood. *Body of Evidence* had been screened the night before to actual catcalls — it was that bad. And Madonna's dramatic performance was a joke. No wonder she wasn't smiling, or exuding any positive energy at all, for that matter.

"Hi, I'm Jeanne Beker," I said, introducing myself to the PA at hand.

"Hey, cool pants!" one of the cameramen called out.

"Thanks."

Madonna turned her head around.

"Hi, great to see you," I said, settling into the chair in front of her.

And then my heart skipped a beat. She was wearing the exact same black-velvet bell bottoms! I looked up to see Madonna eyeing my pants.

"Oh how funny," I offered, "we're wearing exactly the same pants."

Madonna didn't look amused. "Oh, are we?" she said.

"Yeah. They're Anna Sui. I was just in her shop last week."

"Hmmm."

We were wasting precious time. I'd better launch into the interview. My first question: "How close are you to the image you project to us?"

"Not very," she retorted.

She was being honest, and perhaps resigned that with the speed fashion was moving, it was becoming harder and harder to keep a step ahead of everyone — including the earnest interviewer at hand. Or maybe she was thinking that next time she did a press junket, she'd have something custom-made.

Raquel

I met Raquel Welch for the first time about five years ago in New York at a Richard Avedon retrospective. The legendary fashion photographer had managed to attract a healthy handful of glittering guests, and none was more arresting than Raquel. She was dressed in diamonds and white, a symphony of generous curves.

Celebrity hog that I am, I thrust my microphone in front of her face just as she was getting onto an elevator. She looked me right in the eye and somehow I felt we connected. I can't remember what flippant question I posed to her, nor can I recall her answer, I just remember thinking how articulate and gracious she was, strong and definitive. Even at that ultra-close vantage point, her physical beauty was astounding.

Fast forward to the summer of '99. My cameraman is sweating buckets, rearranging the lighting for the umpteenth time as the diva snaps for her hairdresser across the room. Raquel and I are sitting on the tasseled couch in the elegant living room of her classic new Beverly Hills

Raquel invited my crew into her bedroom, and outfitted me with one of her name-brand wigs. I think I'll stick to my own hair! (Courtesy Citytv)

mansion, her love nest with pizza restaurateur Richie Palmer, whom she married on the day John Kennedy Jr. and Carolyn Bessette were reported missing.

Within view is the dining-room table, which is laden with a delicious mess of blue Tiffany boxes filled with wedding presents. Raquel's entourage nervously looks on as she checks the lighting in a small hand mirror one more time, fretting over whether her freshly altered, body-hugging mesh outfit looks all right. I assure her it does, pointing out that mesh is the hottest thing. "Look," I say, "I'm wearing mesh myself!" I wonder how I'm going to get this legend to lighten up.

"Of course we can talk about the wedding," she reminds me, clutching a sheet of points she wants to make about her new line of synthetic wigs. "We got married right here at the house," she informs me, producing a current copy of *Hello!* magazine with a hefty photo spread to prove it. "I'll give you a magazine to take back with you so you can include some of those shots in your piece," she says, playing the role of producer. "But we have to talk about the wigs, too, of course. That's why we're here."

And then, not missing a beat, she demands to check the shot in our monitor one more time.

"What's this?" she says, alarmed as she notices a shadow she doesn't like. My cameraman apologizes and sweats some more.

"When I came to Hollywood, it was really not a glamorous era at all, and everybody was saying, 'You're a sex object, you're a sell-out, you're not a good role model for women.'"

Raquel is starting to get cozy, finally relinquishing the reins to the TV gods and hoping for the best. She's fifty-eight now and a little full in the tush. But you know what they say: after forty, it's either your butt or your face — and if you're too thin, your face will look haggard. Raquel's face is radiant, emanating the kind of healthy beauty you can't get from plastic surgery alone. She's entirely deserving of her *Playboy* magazine honor, having been named the #3 "Sex Star of the Century."

She's also damn smart.

"It's almost a cliché," she tells me, "that one way you can equalize everything if somebody seems to have a lot of luck in the looks department is to say that they're not really very smart. We do that with the supermodels, and actually there are a lot of these beautiful young girls who are anything but dumb, and they really have to work like dogs in the life they've chosen. But it sort of makes us feel better if we can think that's all they have to offer."

Raquel's ride to the glamor throne only looked easy; I well know it was anything but. Looking fab all the time takes a lot of work.

"I think glamor is one of the hardest things in the world," she says. "It's very time-consuming and very high-maintenance, and women are much busier than they've ever been, so they really don't have time."

I marvel at Raquel's ability to have kept it together all these years. Okay, so this is her fourth marriage — but she tells me it's the first time she's ever married for love, so it's bound to work out. At least she's managed to maintain her own mythology. But I soon learn that maybe her inward journey has to do with more than cosmetics or the gym. She's been practicing yoga since she was thirty-five.

"I think it's that connection with the inner me that was really responsible for all my success," she says. "I know somebody's going to laugh their head off over the fact I'd say this, but I think that basically there was a kind of fierceness and independence in the way I was, even as a starlet, that came through. There was a very independent and forceful character there; I was an antidote to the overvulnerability of a Marilyn Monroe, who was so hypnotically fascinating in her helplessness. I just think I didn't represent helplessness."

Raquel takes me upstairs to see her bedroom. We decide that I should try on some of her wigs. Hey, maybe a synthetic, tousled do is just the quick fix I've been looking for in my hectic life. Raquel and her hairdresser sit me down in front of the vanity and proceed to transform me. In no time, they have me looking like "Gina Lola Beker." Resigned to the fact that wigs just aren't my trip, I give it up.

"Okay, just before we wrap, can I shoot an intro to the story from here?" I ask.

Raquel obliges and positions herself beside me in the mirror. The camera starts rolling and I deliver my off-the-cuff lines: "Well, it's not every day you get invited into a sex symbol's bedroom. But Raquel Welch . . ."

Suddenly, Raquel steps back, getting testy.

"No, forget it. Stop right now. Don't even go there," she fumes.

I start dancing around my apparent faux pas, pleading forgiveness. I certainly didn't want to piss off my new best friend. "Oh, you're right. Sorry, I was only joking. Don't worry, I wouldn't dare say that," I fumble. "I don't know what I was thinking, just trying to be funny, I guess."

Raquel composes herself and stands by for another take.

"Was that okay?" I ask when it's over.

"Yes. And you know what? Try not to use the part where you were trying on the wigs. They really weren't the right color for you."

"Yeah, but I don't mind looking a little silly on camera sometimes. It really doesn't bother me."

"Never do that to yourself," she cautions. "It really doesn't do you any good to look anything but great all the time; don't do yourself a disservice."

Behind the smoke and mirrors, it's all about control.

People Tell Me

People tell me I have one of the most glamorous jobs on the planet. Sometimes I believe them. But not on those nights before each big trip, when I'm trying to convince my kids that I'll be back before they know it. Like most working mothers, I have a love/hate relationship with the travel aspect of my job. I'd be lying if I didn't tell you how great it feels to get away sometimes: the limbo of a plane ride, the other-worldliness of a hotel room, the exoticism of a foreign city, and the chance to meet interesting people are all things I crave. What *is* hard is the guilt and sadness I feel when I look into my children's eyes the night before.

Just an example of one of my "assignment sheets" — my associate producer, Mary Benadiba, usually makes sure I never have a dull moment.

Sometimes magic happens and the whole thing actually works. And it's those episodes I live for.

Joey had her tenth birthday on October 4, 1999, the same day I was scheduled to start covering yet another set of collections in Paris. There was no way I was going to miss Joey's big day, so thanks to a couple of understanding producers, I was given a day of grace — if, of course, I would immediately get to work as soon as my plane landed.

"No problem," I said. I might look a little dragged out for my first

NEW YORK TRIP

ITINERARY   FEB. 1 - 5th

LIMO PICKUPS: EMILIO @ CITY @ 9:15AM
JEANNE AT HOME @ 9:45

MON. FEB. 1   JEANNE DEPARTURE FROM NY
AC FLT # 706 @ 10:50   WED. FEB. 4th
ARRIVE 12:12   AC: FLT # 709 @ 12:53 ARRIVE T.O @ 2:19

HOTEL RENAISSANCE
2 TIMES SQUARE

JEFF KLUMPP

ue VHS) drop off For Jeff.   JEANNE CALL FRAN LEIBOWITZ TO CONFIRM
                                     TUES. INTV AT THE HOTEL RESTAURANT

MON. FEB 1/93   INTV MARCUS SHENKENBERG AT PHOTO SHOOT
2:00PM   LOCATION: Leight ST. (DOWNTOWN)
                           CONTACT: JASON   By wall street

                           photographer; PATRICK ANDERSSON
                             INTV MARCUS @ 2:00pm

5:45-5:00PM   B-ROLL OF KEVIN AND ANDIE MCDOWELL
                       LOCATION: THE RITZ CARLTON HOTEL
                                 ANDIE'S SUITE

6:30PM   CFDA'S
                       THE NEW YORK STATE THEATRE
                       LINCOLN CENTRE   (Jeanne THROW)
                       BROADWAY +63RD
9:00PM   POOL FEED OF SHOW

                       THERE'S DESSERT AFTER SHOW
                       CONTACT: LAURIE FLATER

JES. FEB. 2/93   11- Helen Gurley Brown - COSMO
                       224 W. 57th - 8th. (near Broadway)
2:00PM   FRAN LEIBOWITZ
                       LOCATION: RESTAURANT AT THE RENAISSANCE (THROW)

                       TONY FROM THE HOTEL HAS CLEARED THIS USE HIS NAME IF ANY PROBLEM

:30   INTV: KEVIN AUCOIN
                       LOCATION: SPRING ST
ve FED Express   BETWEEN LAYFETTE AND MULBERRRY
+ TAPES   BOTTOM BUZZER
FED #
104951007   1 2 Mark Kostabi   Melis 20 7th. (10k   SUSAN

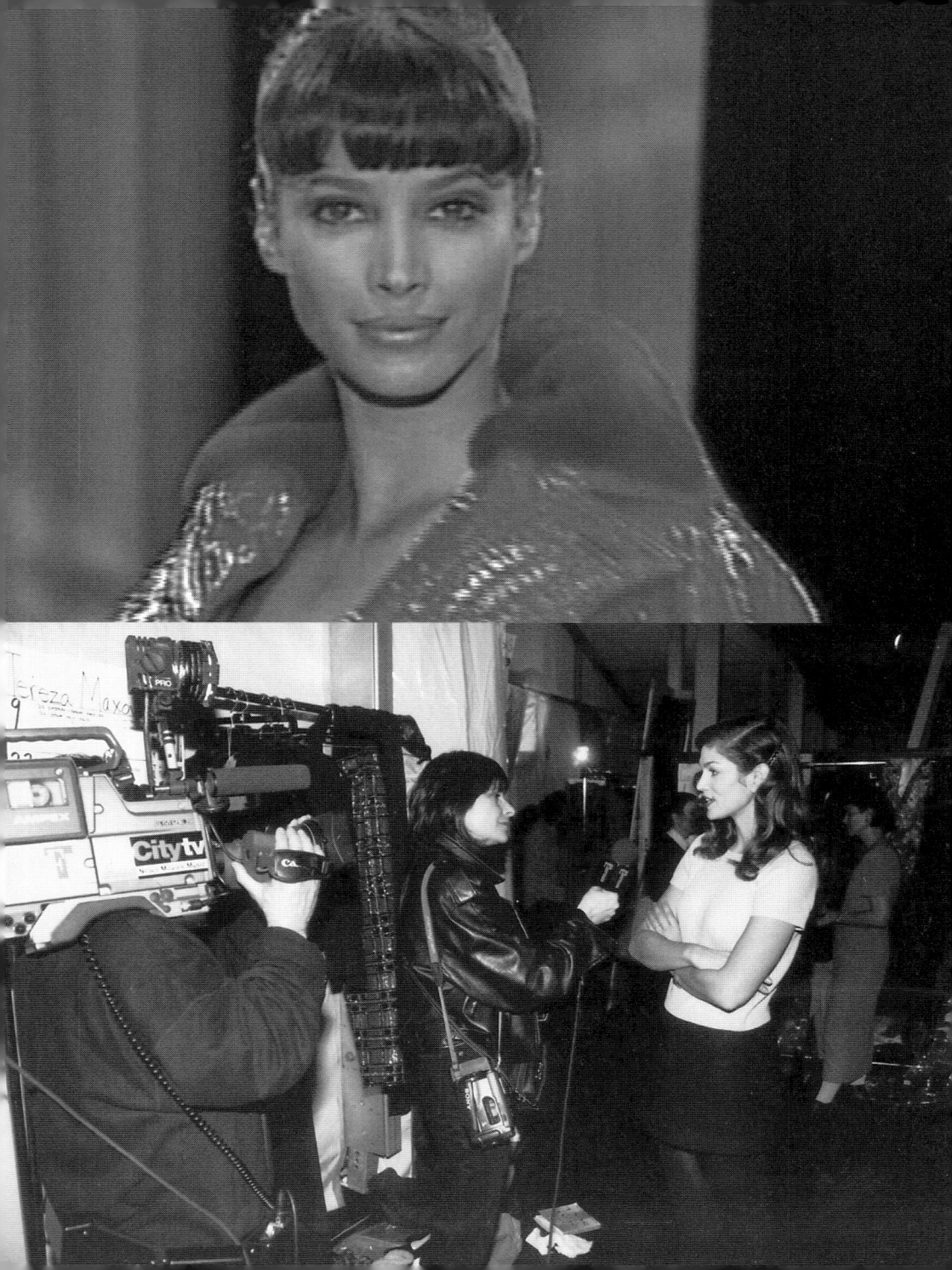

show of the week; at the same time, it was a relief that Joey wouldn't remember her tenth birthday as the one mom missed.

Right from the plane, my driver drops me off at Le Petit Palais with minutes to go before Stella McCartney's runway show for Chloé. Sir Paul's daughter has been designing for the French house for the past few seasons, and she's quite the media darling. There are rumors flying that the talented young Stella is thinking of leaving Chloé for some other prestigious French label.

I find my crew inside the crowded ballroom, and we try to get backstage.

"After the show," says the New York PR type. "It's about to start."

Minutes later, all signs of weariness disappear as I bop to Stella's music and delight in all the skin and glitz she's dishing out for next spring. There goes hot Brazilian model Giselle in a gold lamé bikini. The photographers go wild. This is a dangerously sexy collection, complete with super-cheeky short shorts and ultra-low-rise skin-tight jeans: an ode to perfect young female bodies.

Backstage, after the show, there's a scrum around Stella. She remembers me from a couple of years back, when she was first starting, before Chloé snatched her.

"You've come a long way from that small studio in Notting Hill," I point out. "Ever imagine it would get this crazy?"

"Not a chance," she says. "Never even dreamed it'd turn out like this."

She's coy when I ask her how long she'll continue at Chloé.

Over in the next room at a makeshift champagne bar, Paul is schmoozing some attractive woman. And he's singing in her ear!

Security guards ask us to hold off shooting until Paul says it's okay. The former Beatle is boyishly charming in a rumpled linen suit and blue Nikes. Finally, he looks up at me. Again, a flash of recognition and a big, warm "Hi!"

Ever the supportive dad, he's eager to talk about his precious girl. "She's cool, isn't she?" he says.

"What do you think she learned from you in terms of handling all the hype?" I ask.

"Well, she just grew up with that sort of thing, so knowing what

Christy Turlington, one of the original supermodels, is among the most grounded and intelligent of them all. Cindy Crawford has become an icon in her own right, and has always been a very savvy businesswoman. (Top photo courtesy Citytv)

to do comes naturally to her, I guess. You should hear her sing. She's got a great voice, always singing around the house."

"Hey, maybe you'll do a duet with her someday," I suggest.

"You never know."

"Then maybe you can design a line of clothes with her, too."

"Hmmm, yeah. A whole McCartney family show!"

And I'm off to the hotel for a quick shower before show number two.

Up next: Alexander McQueen for Givenchy. This one is at the big salons under the Louvre, venues designed especially for the collections. McQueen, the young British upstart who was snagged by Givenchy a couple of years back, always puts on lively, unusual shows. This time around, the runway is a gymnasium floor.

Ivana Trump arrives well before show time, looking groomed and gorgeous in a drop-dead white suit. A huge tarantula brooch rests above her heart.

"Veee all vant close zat verk for us. Modern vomen lead actif lives."

Ivana's working it beautifully for my camera. After all, she has a self-titled lifestyle magazine of her own she wants to push these days.

The Givenchy collection is an upbeat take on disco gym wear, complete with sparkly mesh pieces and leather gym shorts. It's geared to make you feel rich when you sweat.

Backstage, mini-interviews with McQueen are being conducted behind a white curtain. It's finally our turn, and the Boy Wonder lets out a hearty laugh when he sees me. The last time we met, a few weeks earlier for his own signature collection in New York, Hurricane Floyd was raging.

"So you survived the storm," he notes.

"Yeah, and I followed you right to the gym!"

"Sports are sexy," McQueen tells me.

"So, do you work out these days?"

"Oh yeah, got myself a trainer. Can't ya tell?" he demands, showing off his formerly chubby midriff. "All I know is that if I were a bird [English-speak for woman], this is what I'd want to wear."

We say our goodbyes and beat it over to the house of Balmain for a photo shoot with Claudia Schiffer. She is the muse for the label's new designer, Gilles Dufour, former creative director for Karl Lagerfeld at Chanel. Gilles was at Chanel for sixteen years and remembers when a very young, very shy Claudia first came to Paris to model for that house.

"I just knew she had something special when I first laid eyes on her," he says.

Claudia looks especially babe-acious in flowing mint-green chiffon, and camps it up for the camera. She doesn't do much modeling anymore and is appearing in Balmain's runway show as a personal favor to Dufour. He's quick to tell me she's seriously studying acting now.

"She gets offered lots of big parts but she's only doing small ones for now. She wants to get really good before she takes on anything too big."

Claudia smiles demurely, acknowledging that she's got too much respect for the art and craft of acting to plunge in headfirst. "But I still love fashion, of course," she assures me.

Then it's over to rue de Rivoli and the Musée des arts décoratifs for a meeting with Gucci's Tom Ford. The Texas-born whiz kid, who singlehandedly revived Gucci's tired old image and made it into a must-have label once again, is behind an impressive new exhibition by the late, great French interior designer Jean Royère.

The furniture on display, designed from the '30s to the '60s, is whimsical, organic, forward. The thirty-eight-year-old mild-mannered Ford, dressed in a black T-shirt, black jeans, and black leather jacket, guides me through the gallery like some pop culture guru. At one time, Ford studied architecture and interior design.

"Our sense of aesthetics has become increasingly sophisticated. Our environments reflect our personal style as much as our clothing," Ford waxes on.

He's extremely focused, but what's really going on in his busy mind is anybody's guess. A couple of days later, it will be announced that Gucci is buying Yves St. Laurent. Ford will undoubtedly take the helm, if not creatively then at least in a business sense. This dude is one sharp cookie.

"I'm incredibly obsessive," he admits. "For me, every detail always has to be perfect."

I grab my Gucci bag and run back to the hotel for another quick change. Tom is hosting a party for the exhibit that evening. His new best friend, Stella McCartney, shows up at the bash, which leads to all kinds of speculation about where Stella might end up next.

Back in my tiny St. Germain room that night after a late dinner at Livingston's, the new rue St. Honoré eatery, I digest my remarkable day. Already missing my kids like crazy, I ring them across the waves.

"Hi Mom," answers my twelve-year-old, Becky. "Whatcha doing?"

"Well, I've had an amazing day. Saw Claudia Schiffer — you know, that gorgeous blonde who used to go out with David Copperfield. And I got to do a little interview with Paul McCartney. You know, that cute old Beatle."

"Yeah, right. Okay, Mom. I really miss you, Mom."

"Yeah, me too, Beck. But I'll be home in a couple of days. Love you, Sweetie. Good night."

Suddenly, the night feels lonely. Exhausted, I snuggle in for a much needed rest and a bit of middle-of-the-night reflection. Will this roller coaster ever stop? Yes, this may well be the most glamorous job in the world, and I love being away. I also hate being away. Another typical workday in Paris comes to an end.

Bad Attitude

It has always bothered me how designers and PR types expect the media to act as publicists. They want and expect coverage — lots of it — but if they provide you with the access you need, they expect all the coverage to be positive. Even if something goes wrong with the interview they've granted you, or the event they've invited you to, they want you to make like nothing negative happened. So we in the media — especially those of us in television who are not critics and need access in order to get our stories — are really up against a wall. Our mission is to relay the color of the encounter or the event. If access is denied, we can't get the pictures we need to tell our story. As a result, we inevitably have to suck up to people, greasing them enough to let us in — and enough to let us come back. Season after season, year after year. It isn't fun.

Sometimes, if you're with a popular publication or show, it's almost a badge of honor to be denied access to a designer's collection. It

Backstage passes have always been my tickets to those fantasy worlds where beauty and imagination reign supreme.
(Photo: Bill Douglas)

means there was some bad blood between you and the designer — that you had the nerve not to portray them in the best light; that you spoke your mind, dissed them perhaps, or for once just didn't treat them like gods. For example, the great Geoffrey Beene had a long-standing feud with the all-powerful *Women's Wear Daily*; for a long time, their people were not invited to his shows. Ditto with Yves St. Laurent and *Vogue*. The higher-up folks at these publications may know why they're being denied access, but the average reporter doesn't. It just becomes a known fact.

For fifteen years, our good manners and positive style of reporting and dealing with designers pretty much ensured us a spot at each and every collection. We aimed to please because in the medium of TV —

especially when it comes to covering fashion — access is everything. Then in March '99, at the fall/winter collection of France's most flamboyant and enigmatic designer, Jean Paul Gaultier, a controversy erupted. And that was the beginning of the end for us and Gaultier.

It certainly isn't news that most press photographers get treated like shit at the shows. More often than not, space at the venues where shows are presented is extremely limited. Most of the time, the press photographers are positioned at the end of the runway on a riser and by the time the show starts that riser is an overcrowded mess, with countless tripods and tired shooters packed onto the platform. It's survival of the fittest, and those with the brashest manners and sharpest elbows get the prime spots. The pushing, shoving, and fighting that take place just before show time are legendary. Once the banks of cameras are finally assembled, it's an awesome sea of lenses.

Jean Paul Gaultier was obviously upset when press photographers boycotted his fall '99 presentation, and surprised to see me and my camera backstage after the show.
(Courtesy Citytv)

It was early evening when we arrived at the Musée des arts décoratifs on Paris's rue de Rivoli. A crowd was gathered outside, and as my crew and I approached, something wasn't right. People were yelling at each other, and it was apparent that the photographers were not filing into the venue. We quickly learned that the photographers had decided to boycott the show because the area set aside for them was minuscule: there was room for only twenty or thirty, not the sixty or so expected at the show.

It was near the end of collections week in Paris, and these people were justifiably tired and angry. They'd had enough abuse and had decided en masse not to shoot Gaultier's show. I sympathized with the photographers and decided to stay out with them. Other TV crews that showed up made the same decision and split immediately to go for dinner.

But to me, this was a great story — even better than simply covering another collection. The newsgirl in me came out, and I decided to capture the anger and passion outside the venue, and to try to get backstage after the show to get Gaultier's reaction. Since all the other TV crews were leaving, it would be like having an exclusive.

Gaultier's American PR lady, Lisa Lawrence, was only too happy to help me secure a post-show interview with Gaultier, promising that if I'd hang on and wait outside until after the show, she'd get us backstage. About an hour later, people started filing out. My cameraman started rolling as I proceeded to get the mandatory post-show reactions. "What a shame the photographers weren't there to capture it" was the consensus. "It may have been the best collection of his career."

Finally, Lisa came out to get us and showed us backstage. Gaultier was surrounded by print journalists and ranting on to Constance White of *The New York Times* about how he was sorry and that he was not responsible for organizational problems: his only concern was for the collection itself. Suddenly, he turned and saw my camera.

"Oh *mon dieu! Un camera!*" he said, feigning shock in his comically theatrical fashion. I congratulated him and expressed my apologies that we couldn't see the show. He was obviously riled up, and kept going on about how the situation was not his fault and how he hoped it wouldn't happen again next season. "But for me, the important thing are the clothes. That is what I do."

"Well, then, tell us about the clothes."

"I have done my job," he snapped. "Now go do yours. Look at the tape if you want to see the clothes."

Our story aired, complete with all the inherent drama. It wasn't really a negative piece — if anything, it made one sympathize with Gaultier while realizing how tough a job photographers face during collections. It also gave us the opportunity to show Gaultier's house tape of the collection itself — and it looked great.

A few months later it was time for the couture collections, and we made our usual calls to all the designers, confirming our attendance. But when we called Gaultier's people they said there was a problem. *Fashion Television* was not being invited to the show. The edict had come down from Gaultier himself. Apparently he was unhappy about our last back-stage encounter and felt I shouldn't have broached the subject of the boycott at all and should have talked more about the collection.

"But that's not what really happened," I argued in our defense. "He went on about the boycott, unsolicited, and I have the raw tape to prove it!"

But Gaultier's mind was made up. Lisa Lawrence in New York understood the value of our coverage, and was dismayed and urged me to write a personal letter to Gaultier, begging his forgiveness for any misunderstanding. So even though I felt he was being unreasonable, I wrote a letter of appeasement. After some opening pleasantries, I wrote:

> I plead with you to view our raw tape so that you can recall exactly what transpired between us backstage. Your memories now might simply be colored by the heat of the moment.
>
> Jean Paul: We are among your biggest fans. Our show has millions of viewers the world over who are also your fans. We were compelled to cover the presentation of your collection in the best way we could and we felt that included addressing the issue of the boycott. We are not a program that talks merely about hemlines, cuts, and colors. For over fourteen years, we've been concerned with the spirit, energy, and attitude of the international fashion scene. Since you are one of its most vibrant and instrumental players, any hoopla surrounding what you do on

the runway is of interest.

I believe we were fair in our reporting because we let you have your say. And finally, and most importantly, we let your beautiful creations speak for themselves, as always.

I hope you get to see the piece we ran on you and understand we were only trying to tell a story.

Sincerely . . .

Unfortunately, my plea fell on deaf ears. I don't know if Gaultier ever even saw my letter or the story we aired. But he wouldn't change his mind.

"Maybe he'll come around next season," Lisa said hopefully.

It looks as if Jean Paul and I have reconciled. I ran into him early in the summer of 2000 at the American Fashion Awards in New York, where he was being honored as Best International Designer. He was very charming and friendly when I approached him for some sound bites. At the end of my session with him, with the camera still rolling, I asked him if I could come to his next show.

"Of course!" he said. "You must! Are you coming for the couture?"

I said probably not, that I'd see him next probably at the next ready-to-wear collection.

Later that night I caught his eye and he winked at me. So maybe he's come around already.

Bad Boy

It was the 1999 annual Costume Institute Ball at New York's Metropolitan Museum and the grand foyer was bubbling with hundreds of beautiful people making trite conversation over sparkling champagne glasses. I brushed by the dutifully smiling familiar faces, but I was not into it. This was New York high society *fashionista* time, and I felt like an outsider. I scoured the crowd, hoping to detect a kindred spirit.

Suddenly, I spotted Alexander McQueen, unusually dapper in

Givenchy shades and tailored pinstripes, puffing on a cigarette and chatting up an unassuming, gray-haired lady. She certainly wasn't a *fashionista*.

McQueen looked up and waved me over.

"This scene is unreal," I whispered in his ear as we hugged hello. "I really don't feel like I belong here."

"That makes two of us," he laughed. "Jeanne, have you met my mother?" he asked, turning to the gray-haired lady.

That the world's so-called *enfant terrible* designer would come to this chi-chi bash with dear old mum was a refreshing revelation.

I first met Alexander McQueen in Capetown in the fall of '95. We were on a judging panel for the Smirnoff International Fashion Awards, and he was being a pain in the ass. Contrary in deliberations, he kept insisting that his personal favorite, a poorly sewn rollerblade costume made of baby-blue parachute nylon, finish in the top three. The rest of us felt the entry was a dud. But McQueen, the brat, refused to give in. At about 2 a.m., we finally relented and indulged the shit-disturbing renegade in his power-tripping mockery.

We — the entire Smirnoff entourage of judges and their guests — were scheduled to go on safari that weekend, and he promised to do a major interview with me while we were out on the safari. But one of my kids got sick and I had to fly home. Still, I knew McQueen would keep his promise, even though past TV efforts had always been thwarted. The designer had become infamous for allowing only the back of his head to be shot.

Alexander McQueen and I have always gotten along famously. I appreciate his sensitivity; he appreciates my enthusiasm. (Courtesy Citytv)

By spring, McQueen was playing with fire. He'd shown his latest collection at an old church in London, in an attempt to turn fashion into a religious experience. He then tried to grab New York media attention by taking that same show to an abandoned old synagogue in Brooklyn. The scene outside the synagogue was bedlam as hundreds of invited guests pushed and shoved their way into the small venue. The doors were locked before many of the important editors got in: it was interpreted as poor organization, or brilliant strategy, depending on who you talked to. The only thing for certain was that everybody was talking about Alexander McQueen.

"It's all about manipulating the media," McQueen told me a few days later. "People are bored, they want excitement, so I'm giving it to 'em."

He was acting smug, and rightly so: he'd done what he set out to do, and an offer to design for Givenchy was brewing.

McQueen's first collection for the French house was a disaster, and the press reviews were ruthless. Finally I was granted my long-awaited interview with the wounded young talent, in his London studio days before his own show. Animal hides were being used for that particular collection, and he pointed out one from a bull that had a gash in it.

"See this? I'm making a coat out of it. It represents the pain I went through in Paris. That's what it was like for me, this twenty-six-year-old kid, thrown into the ring and they killed me." Tears welled up in his eyes as he remembered his recent ordeal.

By show time, he was back to his rebellious, mischievous self. Though the evening was sponsored by Smirnoff, he wasn't about to kowtow to corporate protocol: he brazenly served tequila to his invited guests, mocking the Smirnoff PR people and telegraphing the message that he hadn't sold out.

The following season, I interviewed McQueen in Paris just after his second ready-to-wear collection for Givenchy. He was decidedly down, and miffed that the crowd hadn't appreciated his fun, in-yer-face take on Cowgirls Go Vegas.

"What's the matter with these people? Don't they realize how much work I put into this?"

"But this business has nothing to do with fairness," I reminded him. "You know, it's mostly based on bullshit. How can you expect to maintain your artistic sensitivity in this *faux*, dishonest world?"

"Well, I'm not sure that I can. Maybe I'll get out after all."

Still, a few weeks later it was announced that McQueen had renewed his Givenchy contract for another three years. Bravo. It was high time he accepted the reality of business and commerce.

In November '97 I found myself judging for the Smirnoff Awards once again with McQueen. It was a business deal: the vodka company was still sponsoring his shows, despite the tequila caper.

A Croatian student had submitted a design that was covered in raw meat, and organizers were refusing to let the girl put her creation on the runway. McQueen stood up and threatened to walk if the meat dress was censored. Again, he got his way. The night of the competition, I caught McQueen's eye as the gown cruised down the catwalk. We gave each other a knowing smile and the thumbs-up sign.

Bad Fashion

March 2000. Curaçao: A large lizard darts out from under my lounge chair and scrambles silently into a lush flowerbed. I marvel at the natural beauty and exoticism of the here and now. Warm and weary, I'm trying to calm my cluttered brain after weeks of covering the collections — seeing too much fashion and trying to digest it all. I look beyond my frosty piña colada and am reminded of the frivolity that lies in store for dedicated followers of fashion.

There's a bleached blonde in a glitzy pink bikini a few lounges over, nose buried deep in *Valley of the Dolls*, the '70s novel by Jacqueline Susann that documents the world of pills and beauty, dishing up a dated brand of dangerous glamor we'd already learned to live without. The book has been a cult classic with the gay community for years now. But this new hardcover edition, in the hands of some babe from Middle America, is a sure sign that that scary sensibility has crept back into the hearts and minds of the general public. And judging from most of the collections we've been shown for fall, the world's style mavens and trendsetters are determined to carry us away with all the gauche possibilities. So dust off the gold chain belts and tease up the hair: fashion has embarked on a *Dynasty* trip, the result of too much money and not enough taste.

I suck up the rest of my piña colada and try to find a waiter. Maybe I'll order a tequila sunrise next.

Paris: Backstage at the Dior show, and everybody's jubilant.

"Faaaaaa-BEW-lous!" is the overused word on everybody's lips, but this time they may even mean it. Head designer extraordinaire John Galliano has expanded on his hobo-inspired couture collection from January — which featured a mishmash of ripped dresses and unraveling sweaters — and given us a raunchy kind of street chic complete with newspaper-print frocks and shredded chiffon. And there are oodles of big fur coats, too, in fox and chinchilla, and even fur-lined jean jackets. And dangerous lace-up boots with towering heels. And reams of gold chains. And enough leopard print to put you off zebra forever.

"It's Ghetto Fabulous!" gushes *Vogue*'s André Leon Talley. Talley's been around since Diana Vreeland's day, and if he says something is cool, it's cool. "The boy's a genius, no question," he gushes.

I want to concur. You just have to applaud Galliano's wild extravagance and his ability to get everybody so excited about mere *shmattes* in the first place.

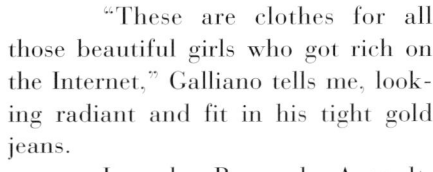

"These are clothes for all those beautiful girls who got rich on the Internet," Galliano tells me, looking radiant and fit in his tight gold jeans.

I nab Bernard Arnault, Galliano's boss and the magnate who heads LVMH, the company that owns Dior, Givenchy, Louis Vuitton, and Celine, to name a few.

"You must love what Galliano's done for the house," I say.

"What's really great about Galliano," the mild-mannered barracuda retorts, "is that these things sell. He's making clothes that people want to buy."

I wonder how true this is, just how many of these shredded tulle, newsprint fantasies will actually get out there into the world. Then again, it's image that Dior and all the fashion houses are selling these days. Even if you don't buy the actual extravagant outfits, the designer's vision has usually seduced you enough that you'll at least buy the bag or the scent. And we all know that bags and perfumes are big business these days.

Backstage over at Givenchy's, Isabella Blow, the eccentric British stylist and one-time muse to some of the U.K.'s most cutting-edge designers, is sipping champagne, shaking her Philip Treacy hat, and swirling about in her Givenchy cocktail skirt, showing off just a couple of the

John Galliano was glowing backstage after his fall 2000 presentation for Dior. The collection was "Ghetto Fabulous": decadent, opulent, and reminiscent of the '80s. (Courtesy Citytv)

extreme pieces she so adores to strut. I compliment her on her look, but she rolls her eyes.

"Yes, well, the vultures are killing fashion, you know. Commercialism is totally sucking the romance out of design; all they care about at the end of the day is selling. And you can't create great clothing with that mindset. I think I'm going to give it all up and open an art gallery in New York. Things have just gotten too commercial."

Toronto: The Grammy Awards have been over for well over a week, but that green silk–print demi-dress that Jennifer Lopez half-wore is still making headlines. Over my morning coffee, I study the look in the paper, charmed that Jennifer's crafty stylist had the good sense to use toupée tape to help the thing stay up. The story says the dress is actually being carried in Versace stores, for about $10,000. While the costly get-up may have been garish and overly risqué, all the gawking and tongue-wagging have paid off in spades for both Jennifer and Donatella Versace, who had the chutzpah to design the frock in the first place.

Simply by wearing it so provocatively, so casually, Jennifer Lopez has become a bona fide icon in modern fashion history: the sensibility of that frock is bound to make waves on our own style psyches for seasons to come. It encouraged us at least to think about daring. It'll be interesting to see who, if anyone, has the guts to try and outdo her at the upcoming Oscars. Just where all this flash, opulence, and garishness in fashion will take us is anybody's guess. But as long as the economy continues to boom, stay tuned for more of the same.

I suppose I'm secretly delighted that "bad fashion" is in. The curious love/hate relationship I have with the fashion world has become more pronounced and passionate as a result — besides, it all makes for great television. And while the celebrity quotient at the shows may be dwindling, the theatrical frenzy still occasionally attracts the most unexpected enthusiasts. I'm not sure what enticed Jerry Seinfeld to drop in on Stella McCartney's show for Chloé at the Opera House in Paris this season. Maybe he just wanted to hang backstage with her father, Paul. But when I asked the comedian if he was indeed a big fan of fashion, he quipped, "Oh yes. I always wear clothes."

Perhaps it's the high-tech lifestyle we're living that's making us hungry for the playfulness and innocence of days gone by. But there's a definite new exuberance to dressing up these days and a determination to have some decadent fun when we look in the mirror. Best forget about natural beauty and exoticism for now — just pass the toupée tape.

I'm on to my next tequila sunrise.

Clean-Cut Calvin

I'd been wearing his name on my butt for years but it wasn't until '86 that I first met the man behind the label.

Calvin Klein, America's most influential designer, was coming to a Toronto department store to launch his new fragrance, Obsession. The provocative ads for the scent were proving to be some of the decade's most memorable: harbingers of the cutting-edge, sometimes shocking campaigns Calvin would become even more famous for in the decade to come.

On the appointed day, Calvin walked into one of the corporate offices of Toronto's downtown Simpsons store looking conservative in a nondescript sports jacket. His boyish good looks were still pretty much intact, and he was suave, thoughtful, interesting, and generous in his answers.

We talked mostly about his new perfume and why he had chosen to call it Obsession in the first place. Naturally, Calvin revealed that he himself was obsessed by his work, by his desire to get it right. And he pointed out that all of us are obsessed by something and that is ultimately what drives us. He also talked about the power of effective advertising and the importance of having a clear image.

I once asked him what his idea of design perfection was. He thought for a long moment and then said, "A flower. I'm seeing a Georgia O'Keeffe painting: the petals, the pistil, the stem. You can only get that kind of design perfection in nature."

Fast forward to the fall 2000 collections in New York. To our surprise, Calvin Klein has agreed to our bold request to drop by his design studio on the eve of his runway presentation. He'd been up till 4:30 that morning, wired to his work, pursuing elusive perfection. Those were the final hours of editing for Klein and his design staff: what to show, what to omit. They were refining the overall message of yet another season.

Calvin allowed us to pay a rare visit to a fitting just a couple of days before his fall/winter 2000 show. He'd been up all night, working obsessively.
(Courtesy Citytv)

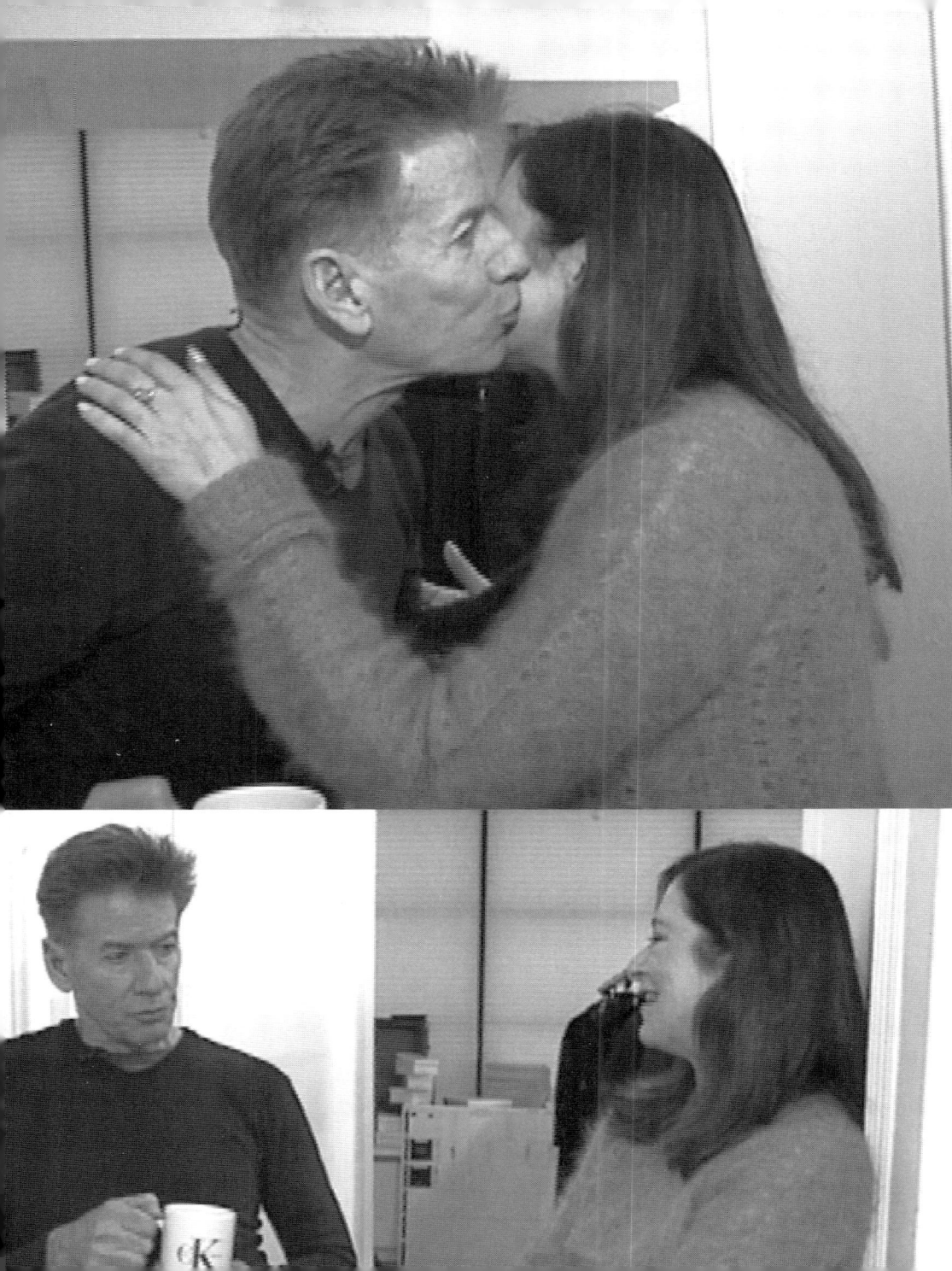

My crew and I wait in a rack-filled showroom. Lunch is just wrapping up, and Calvin will be with us shortly. According to his PR woman, he's cancelled just about everything for the day, but surprisingly to her, not our interview. Not yet, anyway. I try to be optimistic but always expect the worst.

A good half-hour later, we're told that Calvin will indeed be with us momentarily. I down my second cup of coffee just as he bursts through the door. It's obvious that he's been up all night: he looks tired, haggard really, in a sweater and ill-fitting blue jeans. He's drawn, understandably exhausted. But somehow he maintains his edge: always in control and sharply alert. He runs a hand through his close-cropped gray hair, psychologically taxed to be facing this TV camera in the first place.

"Okay, sorry, I've been up all night. How do you want to do this? I should get started with fittings."

I agree, absolutely. We want to watch the master at work. We'll put a mike on him for any salient sound bites we can pick up.

"Please, just carry on, Calvin. We'd love to see you do your thing."

Polish beauty Malgosia emerges from behind a curtain wearing a demure, claret-colored skirt-and-sweater ensemble. Calvin turns to her abruptly and begins scrutinizing, fussing, assessing, critiquing.

She does, and he examines the line with hawk-eyed intensity. Our camera is capturing it all. I decide to casually fire a question at him.

"So, what do you think? Satisfied?"

"Oh." His concentration is broken. "You mean you want to do this interview now?" he snaps. "No, no! I can't deal with this now."

"Sorry, sorry," I apologize. "Of course, just go ahead with the fitting, we'll talk when you finish." I hope I haven't blown the interview opportunity completely.

Calvin finishes up seconds later, dismissing Malgosia with a request to see another look. He heads over to me directly.

"Okay, now. Sorry, Jeanne, but I can't talk and work at the same time. It's too demanding."

I ask him how he's able to give people a taste of the times while remaining true to his vision.

"Well, that's what we're supposed to do. You have to be on top of it, in touch with what's happening, because it's always changing. And you have to be true to yourself, to your sensibility. That doesn't change. The feeling for refinement, for shape, or for sensuality, those things are always there. What changes are the fabrics, the silhouettes, the mood. It should be fun, but my idea of fun is someone who looks hot and sexy and young and great and never silly. Never silly. I'm always thinking about the woman I enjoy dressing, who's into this sensibility. And she's young, regardless of her age. She has a very young, cool attitude. I want it to be easy, relaxed — I mean, it's American."

And then in a flash, he's gone. Giselle, the fashion world's hottest model-of-the-moment, has just breezed in. The Brazilian beauty's time is at a premium, and there's no time to waste. Calvin hustles her away to try something on, and I'm left in the dust. Moments later, Giselle emerges in another look: a simple, black sleeveless leather dress, cut as if it were on the bias. The dress is basic, but Giselle exudes a breathtaking confidence and beauty.

The designer looks pleased: this is what great dressing has always been about for him. Giselle retreats to try another look, and Calvin pops back into our interview.

"How has your idea of beauty changed as you've grown older?" I ask.

He tells me about the Hollywood sirens he looked up to in his youth, stars like Carole Lombard, "that kind of blonde certain type. Or Katharine Hepburn, women that had a certain kind of masculine thing about them and yet at the same time there was a sexy, tailored quality to them as well. Like Grace Kelly."

He also mentions his admiration for Gwyneth Paltrow, whom he's been dressing for the past few years. "She's that kind of woman today because she's easy. She doesn't come with press agents, there's no pretense. She's young, she's cool, she's very fine, and she has wonderful taste. She's the modern Grace Kelly."

Then it's back to Giselle, in yet another stunning, streamlined look. "Now it's really about healthy, big bodies," Calvin explains, still pondering the notion of what's beautiful today. "These girls look like they've just come off the track running, or out of the gymnasium. They're tanned, healthy, gorgeous. It's Brazilian, you know. I mean I always think American, but usually, what's American is never born here anyway. It comes from Sweden or it comes from Brazil. It's really what I feel is right for the moment, and I think, 'Now *that's* American!' And she happens to be from Brazil."

I thank Calvin for allowing us behind the scenes.

"I hope that was all right," he says.

I'll Be in Scotland Before You

In the spring of 1990, the Scottish Wool Bureau hosted an international fashion event in the south of Scotland, and my cameraman and I were invited on an all-expenses-paid trip to cover it. The trip afforded me the luxury of being a houseguest in an Edwardian mansion. I would dine with dukes; shoot clay pigeons with young American designers Marc Jacobs and Michael Kors; and ride down deserted country roads with Britain's grande dame of fashion, Vivienne Westwood.

It was a three-day fantasy, and I kept a diary.

Day One. The setting is sensational. Pat (Patrick Pidgeon, my cameraman) and I are driven from Glasgow to the Scottish Borders, where Fashion '90 is to take place. The scenery is stunning: green, rolling hills, paint-blue skies, manicured hedges, country inns, old stone cottages, and marshmallow sheep drift by. Everything is tidy and charming.

Near Duns, a town in Berwickshire, our car enters an imposing driveway and stops in front of a huge mansion. Manderston was begun in the 1790s, and successive generations added to it until the final version was completed in 1905.

A fortyish couple emerges from the majestic doorway, smiling. Adrian Palmer, heir to the Huntley & Palmer biscuit fortune, inherited the estate from a great-great-uncle, and in order not to pay inheritance taxes he and his wife Cornelia must open their home to the public two days a week.

It was Fashion '90's idea to put up a handful of media people at this magnificent house, and we are certainly not about to complain.

Inside it is breathtaking: a silver-plated staircase; 24 karat gold–encrusted drapes in the ballroom; and 109 rooms full of rare antiques. My room has a mahogany vanity, chintz curtains, a fireplace, and a view of endless green lawns and flowerbeds.

The house is surrounded by 22 hectares of gardens. The grounds include a marble dairy, a wood-paneled teahouse, and what are reputed to be the finest stables in the world.

After Pat and I explore them all, we drive over to Sunlaws House, a country hotel where the designers are staying. We come across some of them shooting clay pigeons in a clearing in the woods.

There they are: Britain's Bruce Oldfield, who designs a lot for Princess Diana; Jasper Conran, Mary Quant's godson and son of U.K. entrepreneur Terence Conran; and Marc Jacobs and Michael Kors, who are so "Manhattan" that it's weird to see them in this context. They're wondering if they've dressed appropriately: Jacobs is in his trademark stretched-out cotton turtleneck, and Kors is in his standard white crewneck jersey. A butler stands by with a silver tray of glasses filled with sloe gin.

Sunlaws House is owned by the Duke of Roxburgh, one of the wealthiest men in the region. He also owns Floors Castle, where the closing night party will take place. Recently divorced, he is, at thirty-six, one of the world's most eligible bachelors.

That night, there's a small reception for the designers at Sunlaws House. The group now includes France's Chantal Thomas, Spain's Roser Marce, and England's Arabella Pollen.

Michael Kors asks if any of them remembers the first celebrity customer they wanted to die for. He admits his was Faye Dunaway. Marc Jacobs won't say, but recalls his terror when, as an up-and-coming young designer, he had to take the measurements of all-powerful *Vogue* editor Anna Wintour, who can make or break any designer.

Day Two. We follow the designers to a couple of mills, then go to the Scottish College of Textiles for a luncheon with the Duke and Duchess of Kent, who are late.

By then, more designers have turned up: Britain's Jean Muir, Ireland's Paul Costelloe, and England's Vivienne Westwood, who invented punk fashion. And three more New York designers have appeared: Rebecca Moses, Carmelo Pomodoro, and Joseph Abboud.

The Royals arrive, she in a peach-and-beige print suit, he looking like an older version of Prince Charles. Michael Kors pulls me aside and squeals that he met Her Royal Highness earlier on and *oh my god*, she's bare-legged! I squint at her ankles but can't tell.

British designer Jasper Conran and I have a glass of champagne in the garden at Manderston, while a butler stands by — opulent glamor at its best!

The luncheon starts, with the royal party sitting at a table feasting on poached salmon. The designers, college students, and press plebes stand and eat from a buffet of hard-boiled quail eggs and cold fried mushroom caps. Apparently, segregation is the usual style at royal events. I find it grossly impolite, but none of the Brits I question about it are surprised.

Jasper Conran comes back with us to Manderston for an interview.

We head out to the garden, butler and champagne in tow. There, among the azaleas, Conran laments that British women don't spend enough money on clothes.

In the evening, there is a party and barbecue at Bowhill, the stately home of the Duke and Duchess of Buccleuch. The duke is reputed to be the second-wealthiest man in Britain, owning some 197,200 hectares of land and one of the most impressive art collections in Europe. But even

Michael Kors and Marc Jacobs had no idea during our trip to Scotland that one day they'd be designing collections for powerful European fashion houses (Kors for Celine, Jacobs for Louis Vuitton).

with all this wealth and a beautiful wife, his life has been tragic. Fifteen years ago, a horse he was riding rolled on him, leaving him with a spinal injury. He now views the world from a wheelchair.

These dukes and duchesses are taking an interest in Fashion '90 because it is sponsored in part by the South of Scotland Chamber of Commerce. Bringing over top designers is a means to promote local textiles, which are facing hot competition from Italy, and to give mill owners a chance to learn what today's fashion market wants.

No one is quite sure what to wear to the barbecue, but once there, we realize that anything goes. Vivienne Westwood is wearing a long

Lurex-knit dress, tweed blazer, and platform shoes.

We dine on a mixed grill, followed by strawberries and meringue, while sitting at tables under a huge marquee. The Duke and Duchess of Roxburgh are not there (they've recently been divorced), and neither is Bruce Oldfield, whom we learn later is not in the mood for socializing.

That dynamic duo, Jacobs and Kors, pose for photos à la Marilyn Monroe singing "Happy Birthday, Mr. President," jackets slung over their shoulders. By now, the Kents and the Buccleuchs have split the scene.

Day Three. A TV feature on Manderston itself is a must. We spend the morning toting our camera through masses of rhododendrons, sculpted hedges, and sparkling fountains.

Off to meet Vivienne Westwood at a mill, I become concerned that we haven't shot enough sheep.

"Pat, shoot some sheep!" I plead with my cameraman, who gets out of the car and heads for the nearest flock. The sheep scoot away from our looming lens.

"Rats!" I scream. "We'll just have to stop again!"

At the textile mill, Westwood is going through old fabric swatches with a magnifying glass. She must be working on a new collection that combines the traditional with the modern; the only thing we can be sure of is that the results will be outlandish.

We nab Vivienne for a backseat interview en route to Peebles High School, where she and Marc Jacobs are scheduled to address school kids. She tells me she finds American culture vulgar and will have nothing to

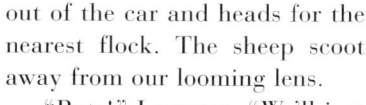

Vivienne Westwood has always had very definite opinions about the lack of personal style in the world. She, of course, is in a league of her own.

say to Marc Jacobs, who exults in American culture. At the school, she predicts she'll just have to keep quiet and let him do the talking. But when we get there, Westwood launches into a speech about what makes her tick; how she sees the world; and how the media are trying to brainwash us all. The kids look stunned. Jacobs looks perplexed, but when he does get to talk, he comes off as honest and unpretentious.

Back at Manderston for a quick change into party clothes, I chat with Adrian Palmer over a glass of champagne. I'm wearing a Debra Kuchmé gold, chemise-style mini made of English lace, with fringes galore. Adrian tells me the Duke of Roxburgh had rung him up that afternoon and told him I'd be sitting at his table at the dinner at Floors Castle.

Oh my, dinner with a duke — I don't know if I'm ready.

We drink more champagne at huge, crenellated Floors Castle, which was built for the first Duke of Roxburgh in 1721 and enlarged and embellished through the ages. The walls are hung with priceless tapestries, and the lavish furnishings are Louis XV and XVI. All the designers arrive, decked out in their own designs: an international fashion parade of the highest order.

A quick look at the seating plan tells me I am indeed to be at the duke's table. Be still my beating heart! What do I know from dukes? Will I look like a goof? Or as if I belong? Is my dress too risqué? Is it risqué enough?

My commoner complex is in full bloom; I just hope it's not showing.

The duke is a tall, lanky, relaxed man with thinning hair, sparkling eyes, and a fun-loving air. After dinner, I ask him for an interview and he agrees.

The duke is kind and cool, and our little chat goes well. He admits to knowing nothing about fashion, but he knows what he likes. No, he doesn't throw parties like this often, but he hopes we're having fun and that the party meets with our approval. I assure him we are and it does.

While we're talking, we hear bagpipes in the distance. We dash outside to see a glorious Highland band emerge from the darkness — and they're playing Gershwin! Suddenly, the castle grounds are illuminated by a dazzling display of fireworks.

A short while later, as I'm getting ready to leave, someone runs over and says, "You can't go yet! Bring your camera! Bruce Oldfield is wearing a kilt!" Sure enough, he's sitting modestly in a chair, a mass of photographers madly snapping away.

Back at Manderston, over a fireside brandy, we review the evening. When the other members of the press party arrive, they report that Marc Jacobs, Michael Kors, and Jasper Conran have all been doing Donna Karan imitations at a post-party party at Sunlaws House. They have her sprawled on a couch, eating doughnuts and talking about design inspiration: "Take a bath towel and wrap it around yourself . . ."

"You had to see it!" the *Sunday Times* reporter gushes.

Somehow, I'm glad I didn't. I go up to my room and crawl under my comforter, cozy, happy, exhausted. I've dined with a duke. And if kilts abound on fashion runways next season, I'll know why.

Fashion Cares

There's no question that AIDS had a profound effect on sex and what we considered sexy in the '90s. Pre-AIDS, we all dressed rather vulnerably, invitingly. In the '80s, as the fear of AIDS infiltrated society's mainstream, fashion took on a kind of "look but don't touch" sensibility. Now, it has evolved into a "look, touch, but don't you dare mess with me" approach. This attitude was also one of the driving influences behind the duality theme in fashion: strong enough on the outside to be wearing a man-style suit, soft enough on the inside to be wearing feminine lace. Mixing messages became the thing to do: hard/soft; masculine/feminine; uptown/downtown. It was all indicative of our search for true identity and a kind of sexual and sensual experimentation that had been going on for years but had only started to surface in a big way.

It was just since the mid-'90s that pop idols, mega-designers, and even movie and TV stars started coming out proudly, paving the way for average people to begin being honest with themselves and the rest of society. This new awareness made for some interesting fashion — a bit scary maybe, but interesting nonetheless.

"Fashion is the ultimate drag," New York–based screenwriter Tom Hedley told me over drinks in a Greenwich Village bar named Allison's. "That's because it's simply dressing up and acting out. You know, I wouldn't be surprised to see a kind of drag style incorporated by the major designers in the next little while."

Sure enough, a few months later, in January of '95, Jean Paul Gaultier was sending his men's wear models down the Paris catwalk in *faux* mink stoles and riding skirts.

Drag also works on another level that I ultimately subscribe to: fashion should never be taken too seriously. It's a concept even the indus-

Makeup artist Kevyn Aucoin and the inimitable RuPaul have always been outspoken about gay rights and issues. Backstage at Todd Oldham, amid the party atmosphere, they were in their element. (Courtesy Citytv)

try finally got hip to when super drag star RuPaul was named the face of MAC Cosmetics in the spring of '95, making him the first drag queen to become international spokesperson for a cosmetics company.

I was proud to have emceed Ru's official launch at Henri Bendel's in New York. The promotional ploy worked in a number of ways: naming a gay male as the official face of a respected makeup line helped democratize high-end glamor. As RuPaul told me, "If makeup can make a big old black man look like this, think of what it can do for you!" But it was also a vote of confidence for the gay population in general, an encouraging pat on the back for all those who had the courage to come out and be counted. And since the MAC AIDS Fund had already done so much in terms of supporting an already ravaged community, who better to help pump up the charity work that MAC was doing than one of the scene's best-loved icons?

RuPaul was stellar in his role for MAC and especially good whenever he appeared at "Fashion Cares," the annual MAC-sponsored fashion gala benefit that celebrates the unparalleled creative spirit of the Toronto fashion community.

I have been involved with Fashion Cares since its inception fifteen years ago. The most heartening thing about this benefit — besides the outlandish creativity exercised by the community in staging the event — is the fact that corporate sponsorship has grown so much, so steadily over the years. In its first few years, there was a strong stigma associated with the cause and no one wanted anything to do with it. AIDS was a scary thing, and most corporations wanted to steer clear. But eventually, as the disease began to touch all our lives in some way, other corporations joined MAC in supporting Fashion Cares. Now it seems that corporate sponsors are clamoring each year to hop on board.

I never fail to find the evening moving and bittersweet. No one loves an outrageous party and the opportunity to dress up and celebrate life more than the creative spirits I've met in the gay community.

One special friend, a makeup artist and jewelry designer named Terry Wood, became my hero in the light of Fashion Cares. Although Terry had never even been to Europe, his taste was wonderfully sophisticated. He adored the glamorous life, and though his own humble lifestyle didn't allow him to wallow in luxury he had a vivid imagination and fantasy life. He used to say that he sometimes lived vicariously through me.

Each year, Terry would take great delight in helping dress me for the event, fussing over me, making sure I had just the right accessories to wear, doing my makeup. He was such a sweetheart. But by 1988, Terry had developed full-blown AIDS. Though he rarely complained, his intense suffering broke my heart. Still, we never gave up hope that a cure would be found. Terry was confident there'd be a breakthrough any day.

Terry was a native of Calgary, Alberta, and had gravitated to the bright lights of Toronto as a young man, in search of a more worldly existence. One afternoon I found myself in Terry's hometown, on a movie set with Canadian actor Gordon Pinsent. I'd never been to Calgary before, and it was a glorious day. We were at a picture-perfect farm, standing in a huge, golden wheat field under a brilliantly blue sky. Suddenly, someone came running out of the farmhouse to tell me there was an urgent phone call for me.

I ran inside the house. Terry's companion was on the other end of the line, telling me that Terry was in hospital and slipping fast. He was asking to see me. I said I'd be there as soon as I could, and raced for the airport.

It was eerie: Terry couldn't come back to Calgary one last time, so it was as if I'd been there for him, to say goodbye.

I went directly to the hospital as soon as I landed. Terry was in the intensive care unit, in a great deal of pain and barely conscious. But he came to a bit when he heard my voice, and managed a smile when I told him I'd just jetted in from his "glamorous" hometown. I told him how beautiful it had been there: how bright the sun was, how blue the sky, how the wheat fields seemed to go on forever.

He told me he was scared. And I said that was all right. "Even if you think you're going somewhere, Terry, you're not really going anywhere at all, because I'm going to carry you around with me in my heart forever," I told him. As I said goodbye, I held back the tears and borrowed a line from *E.T.*, when the little boy is being torn away from E.T.: "I'll be right here."

I left the hospital and went home to hug my children and pray for Terry's suffering to end. Late that night, I returned to the hospital. Terry was in his own quiet room now, intensely sedated on morphine, drifting in and out of consciousness. His mother and his companion were there. His mother was going over all his final wishes. "And you want Jeanne to get your little gold ring, don't you?" she asked him.

Terry opened his eyes, saw me in the room, and nodded. And I couldn't believe that I had the honor of being there with him in that room, in the precious little time he had left in this life. As I held his hand, he drifted off again. I told his mother I'd be back in the morning.

Around 5 a.m., I got the call that Terry had passed away. I was relieved that he was finally out of his excruciating pain, but sad because I knew I'd miss him so much.

A couple of weeks later, a small box arrived from Terry's mother in Calgary. Inside was Terry's beautiful gold pinky ring, which he'd designed himself. I slipped it on the ring finger of my right hand, and it fit perfectly. It hasn't come off since — a constant reminder of Terry's courage, talent, and friendship. I especially enjoy seeing it on my hand when I'm at some exciting event like Fashion Cares; or in some exotic location; or interviewing one of the world's great designers or glamorous stars. It's as if Terry is along for the ride, and I know he's absolutely adoring it.

It Came as a Gift

It came as a gift from a young American designer in the winter of 2000. As I pondered the ominous black garment bag in my dark New York hotel room, I feared what it might be. Throwing caution to the gift horse, I unzipped the bag. There, within, lay the seductive piece: sweet, precious, luxurious, waiting to at least be stroked if not tried on. Banana yellow bunny fur never looked so tempting.

My first impulse was to zip the bag up immediately and send the thing back to wherever it came from. This was something for the runway or the back of a young Hollywood starlet — not a forty-something, hard-working fashion reporter with a sensitive public and a twelve-year-old vegetarian daughter to answer to.

I had succumbed to political correctness in the mid-'80s and stopped wearing fur altogether, but the decadent spirit of the current season called me. Maybe it wouldn't be so bad to just try it on, even if only for a minute — just to see if it fit and remember what fur felt like after all these years.

By the time I found myself backstage at Puff Daddy's show, I was feeling fabulous and funky. "They like it — they really like it," the happy little girl in me mused, as countless fashion folk oohed and ahhed and stroked my new bunny jacket. When I ran into Puff Daddy's mother I was amazed to see she was wearing lemon-yellow fox in the form of an outrageous hat and fur-trimmed cashmere cape. She immediately related to me in my banana yellow number.

A few minutes later, rap sensation Li'l Kim swooped by in a multi-colored rabbit coat that gave new meaning to hip-hop. She made a bee-line for Puffy, who was chatting me up about his new "Sean Jean" men's wear line.

"No doubt we're taking it to the next level tonight," Puffy boasted. "This is my lifestyle and I feed off everybody else around me. We like to dress; we like to look good; we like our jeans to fit just right. We take that very personally and so we just want to take it to the fashion world and create a label that everybody out there will like in every community."

I scanned the racks laden with high-end leather and fur — lots and lots of it: lynx, sheared mink, fox — you name it. My bunny suddenly felt a tad cheap. Still, it made me feel like I belonged.

In a small room reserved for hair and makeup, *Vogue* fashion icon André Leon Talley was holding court, looking like the Pope in a Fendi fur-lined robe. He immediately gave my jacket the nod, pooh-poohing the slight remorse I confessed feeling for wearing the thing in the first place.

"Sweetheart, let me just tell you one thing," he said, waving his giant hand through the air. "Wear it before it eats you. Because if you were out there, you would be the snack."

I was charmed by his way of thinking, even though I knew Thumper was harmless.

"But what is this indicative of, all this luxury?" I asked him.

"People are into luxury and glamor," he proclaimed, "and it's positive and optimistic. What do you do with fashion? You enhance your own inner world. And if you feel good in banana-yellow bunny fur, that's what makes you tick."

Puffy's runway was a constant stream of larger-than-life outfits for the urban jungle: guys in baggy leather jeans and oversized coveralls, draped in fabulous fur, accessorized with flashy diamond chains and rings. There was a sheared mink hooded cape and even mink pants. Man oh man, this was fashion at its hedonistic best. The crowd went wild.

The next day, the *National Post*'s Linda Frum flew to New York to follow me around for a profile. It was freezing outside and again I was tempted to wear my new jacket. I agonized for a bit, fearing she'd tell on me, expose my folly to my kids, and just think I was a bad human being in general for wearing fur in the first place. But my *fashionista* instinct told me to go for it, and rightly so: when Linda caught up with me, I was delighted to see that her coat was trimmed in bunny fur, too.

And that's the way it was all week long, running around at the New York shows seeing all kinds of friends, colleagues, and (of course) models decked out in a variety of furry garments. Many chose to go the vintage route, perhaps feeling less guilty because the critters had been killed so long ago. Director Tim Burton's girlfriend, Lisa Marie, wore jaguar from the '20s to Marc Jacobs's show.

But PETA, People for the Ethical Treatment of Animals, was not amused. Determined to make its voice heard, the organization sent a couple of reps out to storm the runway of the Oscar de la Renta show with a "Fur Shame" banner. The reps were hauled away quickly, but not before my heart started beating faster. I was paranoid that they might be coming after me — never mind *Vogue* editor Anna Wintour and Ivana Trump, both of whom dashed out the side door in their opulent fur jackets the second the show was over. I actually thought about dumping the darned jacket before I made my way out. But I took strength from the *National Post*'s Serena French, sitting next to me in a black fur hunting hat she had bought on the street a day earlier.

I wasn't alone in my paranoia. *People* magazine's West Coast fashion editor, Steven Cojocaru, was wearing a jacket identical to mine, but in ivory, a gift from the same designer.

"I just felt like sinking into my seat so they wouldn't notice me."

he said. "How neurotic — like it's all about me!"

PETA made a couple more feeble efforts: spraying red paint at the Randolph Duke show, and allegedly hitting CNN's Elsa Klensch and Hollywood stylist Phillip Bloch, who'd been wearing a vintage bear coat all week. And then there was the tofu cream-pie incident at the Michael Kors show. I heard André Leon Talley and Anna Wintour got a dollop of that. In the end, PETA's voice was muffled by the thunderous roar of what had become fashionable once again.

Where would it all end? Admittedly, it did start to feel a bit perverse and icky toward the end of the week, at the preview of a young designer's collection in his showroom.

"The trim on these cardigans feels divine," I said, admiring the ultra-soft brown and gray fur. "What is it?"

Covering his microphone, he confessed, "Well, it's something a lot of designers are using but no one wants to talk about. People might get a little creeped out. It's hamster."

Yeesh! Just what the world needs — another ratty sweater. I told Hilary Alexander from the *London Daily Telegraph* the sorry tale.

"That's nothing," she said. "I was admiring a young London designer's garments recently and commented on the wonderful silkiness of the fur he'd used. Then he told me it was rat's belly."

Now that I'm back home, far from the wilds of New York Fashion Week, I'm unsure how to proceed with my winter fashion statement. It's darn cold in Canada. Dare I wear my bunny? And if so, how often? Exactly where will I be safe from the scrutiny of those who feel that fur is offensive?

Meanwhile, the jacket has been relegated to the back of my closet. I'll probably pull it out for special occasions. I just hope my daughter Becky isn't watching — I'd hate for her to think I'm a mere fashion victim.

VH1 Awards

Of all the magical nights in my career, the first VH1 Fashion Awards, held in New York in December 1995, was the most moving. I don't think as many greats from the worlds of music and fashion had ever gathered

in one place before. And I don't think as many will ever come together again.

VH1, an adult-oriented music channel owned by MTV Networks, had been broadcasting our show in the United States since 1993. Almost from the start it was one of the most highly rated programs on the channel. Its programmers realized there was a vital connection between fashion and music — after all, style was an important aspect of the pop scene, and rock stars and designers were quickly forming powerful bonds, both personally and in the public eye. Among the couplings to emerge: Madonna and Gaultier; Tina Turner and Azzedine Alaïa; k.d. lang and Richard Tyler; and most obviously, Elton John and Versace. The time was right to stage a music/fashion extravaganza, and in order to get the big stars to show, awards would have to be presented. Egos can rarely resist accolades.

So the annual VH1 Fashion Awards were born.

Since *FT* was the key to VH1's credibility as a station that cared about fashion in the first place, and since I was the face of *FT*, it seemed appropriate to the organizers that I play a role in the evening. I certainly wasn't high-profile enough to host the event, but few could schmooze better backstage. And besides, all the designers already knew me and they had to feel as comfortable as possible in a live situation.

So I was to be co-host of the pre-show and the post-show and would be the official backstage color reporter during the awards program itself. I was proud that *FT* had had such an impact on American TV, and that fashion on TV was evolving to this next level.

With the help of Hollywood stylist Phillip Bloch, I felt like Cinderella at the bal for the first VH1 Fashion Awards.

John Sykes, the president of VH1, held a press conference at Bryant Park during New York Fashion Week to announce the station's plans for the special. He publicly credited me and *FT* for popularizing fashion to such a degree. Naturally, the New York press was true to cynical form, and many of its members — especially in the fashion press — were reserving their opinions about whether a big awards show like this was a good idea. Certainly everyone understood that VH1 was capitalizing on the fashion hype of the moment. And as good as all this was for the industry, the fashion snobs were miffed that these music programmers wanted to dabble in their arena.

Fortuitously, the VH1 event was scheduled the night before a huge

couture gala at the Metropolitan Museum. *Vogue* editor Anna Wintour
was honorary chair, which meant fashion's European heavyweights were
in New York at her behest and could attend our bash. Only too happy to
attend were Thierry Mugler, Karl Lagerfeld, Gianni Versace, Jean Paul
Gaultier, and Valentino. American designers included Tommy Hilfiger,
Isaac Mizrahi, and Richard Tyler. Calvin Klein was too cool to attend and
give the event credibility just yet, and Donna Karan, perhaps following
Calvin's cue, also bowed out. Ralph Lauren also didn't show.

The night of the awards arrived, and the confirmed guest list read
like a who's who of fashion and music: slated to perform were Tina
Turner, Elton John, the Artist Formerly Known as Prince, and k.d. lang.
Madonna was to be honored with a personal style award, which ensured
that she would show. There were also plenty of supermodels: Naomi
Campbell, Claudia Schiffer, Kate Moss, and Shalom Harlow, who actually
picked up an award herself that night as best model overall. Even the
male supermodels were out in full force: Marcus Schenkenberg, Mark
Vanderloo, Alex Lundqvist, Tyson Beckford, Michael Bergin, anxious to
ooze as much sex appeal as their female counterparts.

What to wear to such an image-driven event was a crucial consideration,
so the producers hired a hotshot Hollywood stylist to dress us. I'd been in
my hotel room less than fifteen minutes when Phillip Bloch and his two
assistants arrived, towing a rack laden with designer duds.

"Oh honey, is this work or what?" Bloch was happily chattering
away, telling me about all the running around he'd been doing, borrowing top-label designers for the program's presenters — who ran the gamut
from Mariel Hemingway to Chynna Phillips to RuPaul.

"Mariel wants to wear Calvin but she's not a sample size, so it's
not easy," he gushed in his Long Island accent. "And I was dying to put
RuPaul in Valentino, but nooooooo. She insists on wearing something Bob
Mackie made. Who knows what Madonna's gonna do? She's got Dolce &
Gabbana's entire collection over at her house, along with everything from
Gucci and Prada. It's totally insane. But don't ya just love it?"

Yes, I did. I'd been working in television for sixteen years at that
point, and I'd never had this particular kind of service. *This is something
I could get used to very, very quickly*, I thought, as I shuffled through the

hangers dripping with Ralph Lauren, Valentino, Giorgio Armani, and Richard Tyler — all in my size!

Bloch initially pushed for the Valentinos. I was slated to do an interview with the Rome-based designer backstage, and Bloch told me how happy it would make Valentino to see me in one of his creations. But the Valentino offerings, as gorgeous as they were, didn't feel funky enough for me. My new best friend/stylist soon saw it my way and turned to the Richard Tylers. He gave his approval the moment the Richard Tyler tuxedo jacket slipped over the lavender silk/satin Tyler shirt. "It's understated but very chic and rock 'n' roll," he observed. "Now try on the pants."

But the pants were too voluminous. "Lose the pants," he said. "You've got great legs — show 'em off. The jacket's long enough; it'll make a gutsy statement. I'll run around tomorrow and find some sexy shoes. It'll be perfect."

It's funny how one can bond so quickly with a hip stranger who comes into your room with tons of designer clothes. Within minutes of meeting Bloch, I was running around in my bra and panties, lamenting the fact that I hadn't had time to wax my nakedly exposed legs. But according to Bloch, even the biggest stars get insecure.

As for hair and makeup, we went for a '60s mod look, making me look tastefully raunchy. I felt like a rock 'n' roll Cinderella going to the big ball.

The backstage area at the Lexington Street Armory was the size of a small gymnasium. I was nervous as hell, running around with an entire production team, who were putting me through the paces and giving me thousands of instructions. Heavyweights started arriving, each with his or her own handlers. There went Elton, over that way, Tina. Suddenly, Valentino showed. Then came Gaultier. Versace was asking to see the questions I was planning to ask him on camera.

"But I don't ever really prepare my questions," I tried explaining to his assistant. No matter. He wanted to see them anyway. Now.

So I jotted down a few on a sheet of paper and had it delivered to his dressing room. Thierry Mugler was in charge of the runway presentation, so you can imagine how incredible the models looked, outfitted in costumes of the most theatrical order, sexy and larger than life. The male models were hanging around the food table, obviously in awe of the scene unfolding around them. The Artist Formerly Known as Prince whisked by us, decked out in a bright red suit, intent on checking out the stage set-up.

That night was probably the most satisfying of my career. All of us involved in the production felt we were breaking new ground. But more poignantly for me, it felt like the culmination of all those years of trailblazing — first putting rock stars on TV, then fashion designers, and helping mark a path so many around the world would soon follow. Finally, I was having the chance to simply do my thing — chat to the stars of the scene in the backstage milieu in which I was so totally at home. I was proud that except for my throws to commercial breaks, my segments hadn't been scripted. The rest of the awards show followed a ridiculously tight script. I was nervous as hell, but it was a positive kind of nervousness.

The only weird bit was a quickie interview I did with Mariel Hemingway. Because the producers wanted to keep my segments as off-the-cuff as possible, most of the chats I was expected to do weren't planned at all. We were all confident in my ability to wing it, so we figured we'd just grab celebs as we needed them.

At one point I was required to go out to the front of the house and collar an audience member for an impromptu little schtick. Well, minutes before airtime, the wranglers I had working with me couldn't decide who to get for my mini-chat. I suggested Kate Moss, who'd just picked up an award for Calvin (who couldn't make it to the show), but it was decided that she was too shy.

"What about Jean Paul Gaultier?" I offered.

"No. We want someone who can speak English," one of the exec producers said. "His accent is too thick for the folks at home."

We entertained a few other ideas, but dismissed them all. Then I spotted Mariel Hemingway in a gorgeous gown, right on the aisle.

"What about Mariel?" I asked. I'd interviewed her a couple of weeks earlier at the launch of her TV series *Central Park West*, in which she played a fashion magazine editor. She seemed pretty cool. Maybe she wouldn't mind giving us a minute live.

One of the wranglers went over to ask her about it, and she obliged. I started making my way up the aisle, moments before we were going to go live. I passed by Richard Tyler, who smiled at me and told me I looked great in his jacket.

"Hope you don't mind I wore it without the pants," I pointed out.

"Nah. Looks good."

I continued toward Mariel. I did my thing to camera, and introduced her. But instead of greeting me with enthusiasm, she looked bored and almost annoyed.

Her iciness threw me, and I compensated by being especially perky. When I asked her how she first developed a passion for fashion, she rolled her eyes and said she wasn't particularly passionate about fashion in the first place — that one day you just show up somewhere in a dress and everyone just assumes you're really into it.

Her response was honest enough — fine, really. But it was a little off-putting, and on TV it made her come across as bitchy. I made some inane comment just to wrap up the bit, and before I knew it, we were off the air. I thanked Mariel and disappeared backstage for more schmoozing.

There's Got to Be a Morning After

The next day, gossip columnist Liz Smith led her column off by relaying the brief encounter with Hemingway, using it as an example of how insipid the fashion world really is anyway, and aren't we all just sick to death of all the hype surrounding fashion these days? I felt a little bad, but just resigned myself to the fact that not everyone was out to applaud what we were doing. But the worst hit a few days later, when a friend called from New York with bad news.

"Jeanne, I don't want to hurt your feelings, but I thought I should be the one to tell you. *Women's Wear Daily* just really dissed the fashion awards, and the writer actually pointed you out and said some not-so-nice things about you!"

My heart sank as my mind raced: How bad was "not so nice"? Then my friend proceeded to read me the review, in which the writer trashed the presentation itself and inferred that I was out of my league — and why hadn't they got someone like Rosie O'Donnell, who was really funny and quick on her feet, to provide the color backstage reporting?

My friend tried to comfort me by telling me that the people at *WWD* were probably just jealous because they hadn't had anything to do with the awards. And that being an outsider was my biggest strength — real people could relate to me and my energy and to the fact that I was excited about being on the show. Those die-hard, insider fashion types were cold, pretentious bitches without a morsel of humanity. But I still felt like an incompetent loser who had no business trying to play in the fashion big leagues, especially on live American TV. I tried telling myself that I'd worked in the fashion trenches all those years, and had been the first to profile some of the biggest names in the business on TV, and had helped turn millions of people on to the whole groove of the fashion scene. So why shouldn't I have been part of this important event?

Sure, Karl Lagerfeld liked me, and Versace and Valentino had agreed to their live interviews because they knew me and knew I wouldn't throw them for a loop out there in Live TV Land. But it didn't change the fact that I still had a gazillion dues to pay before I'd ever really arrive in fashion. My years of hard work in the scene just didn't cut it. Everybody was probably expecting to see a real fashion star in that gig and that wasn't me.

My bubble had burst. I wasn't — and would never be — a member of that inside fashion club. It seemed so unfair.

Real Life

Two days later, my phone rang. It was a woman named Anna-Marie Kostura from L.A., who was head of daytime programming at NBC.

"I was working out on the treadmill the other evening and I caught you on the VH1 Fashion Awards. I thought you were great."

She went on to say she really liked my style and found it refreshing to see this "real" woman in such a star-studded scene.

"We're launching a new magazine show for women on the network called *Real Life*, and we need someone to cover style. Could you send me some tape?"

Wow. There really is a God after all, and He was making sure I wasn't going to give up yet. I sent some tape out by FedEx the next day, and Kostura phoned back a couple of days later.

"Great stuff. Now, have you ever done anything with a consumer edge — you know, stuff to do with trends?"

Earlier that spring, the telecommunications giant MCI had made me editorial director of a web site that was part of its Internet MCI division. To encourage more women to use the Internet, they wanted to develop a fashion site, and they gave me responsibility for all the content for @fashion, the web's first official site dedicated to style. Besides contributing interviews, reviewing collections, and writing designer and model profiles, I did a style advice column where I answered questions posed by visitors to the site. I sent printouts of this material to Kostura.

Shortly afterwards, *Real Life's* executive producer called and offered me the job of style correspondent for the show, which was based in Boston. *Real Life* was actually a replacement show — a daily strip that ran for only eight months. But it gave me major U.S. network exposure and, more important, the opportunity to cover fashion stories with a "real people" angle. It was refreshing to look at style through the eyes of Middle America.

"Our average viewer might live in a trailer park in Tennessee," the producers would often say. "The high-end, East Coast sophistication of New York means nothing to them."

Hallelujah! This was my chance to dismiss all the bullshit as just that, and talk to women where they really live. It was my idea to do an interactive fashion-help segment. For "Fashion Hang-Ups," we solicited women from across America to tell us their style dilemmas on video; then we enlisted experts to try and help them out. A few years later, E! Entertainment Television came out with a similar concept called *Fashion Emergency*, and the show proved to be a big hit for them. I'm happy to have gotten there first.

Galliano

Being on the judging panel of the Smirnoff International Fashion Awards for five years presented me with a host of opportunities, including the chance to travel to some wonderfully exotic locations like Rio and Capetown. But best of all was being able to sit next to some of the greatest young minds in fashion today, like Alexander McQueen and John

Galliano, and hear them intellectualize — sometimes even rant and rave — about the fashion vision of aspiring designers.

The annual competition is open to fashion students from around the world; in some schools the competition is actually integrated into the students' course work. They're given a theme — usually very broad-based and open to wide interpretation — and then encouraged to let their fantasies fly. Truthfully, the winning designs were much more interesting in the early years of the competition, when many art-to-wear pieces were celebrated. In recent years, students have been told to take practicality and wearability into account. It makes sense, since Smirnoff wants to award students who are likely to pursue successful careers in commercial design.

But the competition's early years was often characterized by some truly awesome, over-the-top fare. In 1994 the finals were held in Brazil, and the judging panel's star attraction was John Galliano, the British designer whose mad, elaborate visions helped keep the artistry and romance alive in fashion in the late '90s. At the time of the awards in Rio, Galliano's star had just begun to rise internationally. He hadn't yet been recruited by Dior to help revive that label's image. It was blazingly hot in Rio, so Galliano's fur hat, complete with ear-flaps, was more than noticeable. He wore that hat religiously throughout the three-day competition, obviously determined to make a statement: here was a man who couldn't care less about practicality — he was mainly concerned with image, and took great delight in shocking people with his irreverent approach.

You had to love him for his sense of fun, seeing him wear that monstrous hat with a little white T-shirt on the porch of the Copacabana Palace. The sand, surf, and palm trees provided the perfect dramatic backdrop for Galliano's fashion shenanigans. It was inspiring to see someone so revered be so in-your-face with his personal style. Suddenly, everybody else seemed too earnest.

For the entire trip, Galliano was joined at the hip to a very pleasant, down-to-earth fellow. This young man was evidently his personal assistant — a caretaker, actually. He was even allowed to sit in on the jury's private deliberations. In the final stages of the judging process, he began putting his two cents in — as if it weren't already difficult enough to deal with so many varied opinions.

Co-judging with John Galliano at the Smirnoff International Fashion Awards in Rio was a real education for me. The students, too, found him to be most inspiring. (Courtesy Citytv)

In recent years the judges have been allowed to inspect the garments up close well before the final runway presentation. But that particular year, the first time we really got to see the garments was up on the runway during dress rehearsals. Because the competition was Smirnoff's baby, let's just say the vodka flowed generously at all times.

As we sat down for our first serious look at the fit and general runway impact of the entries, we were served an assortment of exotic drinks and encouraged to indulge. Before long we were all having a very good time indeed. It makes me sad now to think of some of the poor students who'd worked their butts off preparing for the competition, finally revealing the fruits of their intense labor to a panel of judges who'd been plied with liquor.

We did all try to be fair, but coming to terms with the required criteria and making that jibe with our own personal mandates was tough. There's no accounting for taste in fashion, and without question there's little in fashion besides technical execution that one can be objective about.

It was interesting to see how adamant Galliano was to recognize the theatrical sensibility of the entries. I don't think it was the garments that impressed him, but the way they were modeled. One young model, in a pretty basic jacket and poorly cut pants, ran wildly down the runway carrying a suitcase; he looked rushed and a little maniacal. When he got to the end of the catwalk, the suitcase opened and all kinds of stuff came spilling out. The model looked distressed, and hurriedly packed up again, scrambling back up the runway. I'm not sure what Galliano read into this bizarre little performance, but he seemed to think it was genius. And while I couldn't really see much brilliance at all in this entry — especially because the garments weren't well executed — Galliano ranted and raved to have it included at least as a finalist.

Later, he told me it was indeed the theatrics of the presentation that he liked so much. He was eager to see young talent push the envelope of convention and concentrate on how the clothes were being worn, rather than the clothes themselves. I saw his point, but I didn't think that was what the competition was about. Galliano is famous now for the stories he tells with his collections. And while that's important to the creative side of fashion, it's not what makes a designer's bottom line. At the end of the day, people have to be able to relate to the clothing: seducing them with a fantasy only gets you so far. Maybe that's why Galliano's clothing is usually appreciated more in conceptual than in practical terms.

I didn't agree with his judging criteria, but I was certain I was in the presence of a mad genius. In public, Galliano behaved incredibly sweetly at all times, coming off as a very shy, reluctant celebrity. Behind closed doors it was another matter. One of my producers was staying in the room right next to his and came down each morning with tales of the designer's middle-of-the-night ravings and screaming fits.

I catch planes the way some people grab cabs, and it's a part of my job I love. And it's a part of my job I hate. But when the opportunity arose to fly to New York for the afternoon to interview Galliano, it wasn't a question of love or hate: it was simply do or die. Even though I'd just come off a plane from Hong Kong, I wouldn't have dreamed of saying no.

With his constant themes of glamor, extravagance, and fantasy, Galliano has contributed more to the spirit of turn-of-the-century fashion than any other designer. I've interviewed him several times over the years — only when he was in the mood, of course. This is one artist (and certainly not many designers are artists) who is subject to magnificent mood swings.

Now here were the Dior people calling our office and inviting me to New York for a one-on-one with him the night before the opening of the new Dior boutique. This was a good sign. Galliano was ready to talk again.

I get there an hour early, all dolled up in black Misura with my new orange Christina Perrin coat and ultra-high Pradas on my weary feet. I peer over my Chanel sunglasses at the construction guys, who are still readying the new digs on West 57th. No one's expecting a TV crew of any kind just yet, so I head for Bergdorf's to kill time.

I'm cruising the handbags when my cell phone rings. The Dior publicist apologizes; Galliano is running late. Would I mind waiting? Of course not. So I pretend to shop a little more, psyching myself up, praying that the Great One won't change his mind after all.

At the boutique, Mesh Chebers, Galliano's right-hand man, greets me at the door.

"I'm off to get John. He'll be right over," he assures me.

My crew and I head upstairs to set up. We wait a little longer. And longer still.

Apparently, Galliano has been feeling a little under the weather and is waiting for the doctor. I'm getting concerned that he'll be a no-show — this stuff happens all the time. But suddenly there are rumblings downstairs. Moments later, the designer appears: a swashbuckling figure in an ostrich overcoat, acid-wash jeans, Hermès silk print vest with denim trim, a crocheted skull cap, and an enormous diamante skull-and-cross-bones belt buckle. It's the ultimate, dangerously decadent statement.

"So sorry I'm late," he apologizes. "I felt as though I was getting a cold, so I had to get a pill."

Galliano looks fit and relaxed. He oozes vulnerability and boyish charm, an Old World gentility with a hint of roguishness. If you're a woman, you have to love him.

He took over design duties at Dior in the fall of '96, which made him the first young upstart designer to join Bernard Arnault's prestigious LVMH stable. Always a sensation with his own dramatic collections, he revamped Dior's image, spinning powerfully seductive fantasies the likes of which the house hadn't produced since the days of Dior himself. The young man from Gibraltar showed us the virtues of old-fashioned glamor and reinstated over-the-top romance. His storybook collections smacked of sensual indulgence — clothes worthy of movie stars.

The Galliano moment had arrived, complete with rumors of back-stage rantings and tales of turbulence befitting the most distinguished of divas. The style cognoscenti deemed him a genius, and we silently thanked the fashion gods for sending us this inspired new savior. But critics adore building you up and then tearing you down. The past couple of seasons had been rough for Galliano. His detractors were claiming that his opulent dresses weren't selling and that he'd lost his magic touch. Some were even proclaiming that his spring collection for Dior, inspired by Lauryn Hill, was downright vulgar.

Knowing how sensitive Galliano must be in order to tell the stories he does, I'm sure the heinous reviews have hurt him deeply. But when asked, he claims he doesn't even read his reviews right after a show.

"I think it's good to have some sort of recoil," he tells me, but admits that some reviews do actually affect the house.

"Then I have to explain," he tells me. "Hey, Mr. Dior would have loved this! We're on the cover of the *Herald Tribune*, we've been slagged off as unwearable. Mr. Dior would have loved this in 1947. Sometimes, it's the covers that count."

Galliano shares the happy news that he's just signed again with the house for another three years.

"I don't really see women returning to the 'bag lady,' no-look, shapeless gray moment," he says. "I mean, it's a great time to be an individual, to be able to express yourself through your clothing, to feel it. Clothing can make you feel a certain way: from morning till noon, dusk, dawn. And one should be able to express oneself through their clothing. That eclecticism is a forward move after the whole separates revolution. The feeling in the air now is like a mix of the soft with the hard — the savage with the very rare, and that you find in Dior. It's that rare and savage, a bit like me."

By the end of our chat, I want to take him home for tea. He's sweet and gentle and I forgive him for the countless times over the years that he's kept me waiting, or snubbed me, or just been too busy and stressed to deal with any of it. Mesh tells me my interview with John has been terrific, one of the best he's ever given.

"You obviously made him feel relaxed," he says.

I don't judge designers. That's not my role. Instead, I allow myself the luxury of picking the brains of some of the world's most flamboyant and creative visionaries. And while I sit there, lapping up their brilliance and discovering what drives them, I don't give a hoot about things like commercial viability and practical wearability: I just let myself get off on their larger-than-life personas and be energized by their originality and exuberance.

Yes, Giorgio

Throughout the '90s, the dark, design-conscious lobby of New York's Royalton Hotel was often illuminated by a wide variety of international fashion stars. So it wasn't really surprising to look up over my pot of tea one morning and see Giorgio Armani hovering near the elevators. It was

September of '96, and the Italian master of elegance had breezed into town to celebrate the opening of his flashy new Emporio boutique at 58th and Madison. It was part of a flurry of innovative marketing ploys by some of fashion's biggest names: each house vying for its moment in the spotlight by opening bigger, more luxurious retail headquarters in Manhattan.

But a mere reception at the store wouldn't be enough to make the desired splash. The town was buzzing about a rock concert/fashion show bash Armani would be hosting two nights later at the Lexington Avenue Armory for a thousand guests: Lauryn Hill and the Fugees, Jakob Dylan and the Wallflowers, Me'Shell Ndgiocello, D'Angelo, and Eric Clapton were all slated to play. No doubt the celebrities would be out in full force.

I got up from my tiny table and made a beeline for the tanned, fit, and charming designer, eager to tell him how much I was looking forward to his party and to our scheduled interview the following day. The timing for my one-on-one with Armani couldn't have been better. Besides the hype surrounding the upcoming party — the hottest ticket that had come along in a while — the sixty-two-year-old designer had just made the cover of *New York* magazine with his shocking proclamation that "fashion is finished." He was undoubtedly looking for attention, striving to ensure he would stay relevant now that other Italian labels like Prada, Gucci, and Dolce & Gabbana were making big waves in America.

After all his dealings on this side of the Atlantic, you'd think his English would be pretty decent, but he's one designer who almost always insists on answering questions in his native tongue. I can't blame him: he's a highly intelligent, articulate man, and he just feels more comfortable in Italian.

With a translator standing by, we took over a couple of big leather chairs in the second-floor privacy of his new flagship store. I commented on his aura of calm on this the eve of his big exciting party.

"I'm a great actor," he told me, "and great at interpreting different roles. At the moment, I'm playing the role of a very secure person, one whose life has always gone perfectly. But deep inside I'm very nervous."

I told him it was nice to know he was human after all.

(margin note) Armani told me he was "a great actor ... great at interpreting different roles." He was playing the part of a very cool designer during our interview, just before his big Manhattan splash in September 1996.

JB: You came out with a fairly shocking comment recently: "Fashion is finished." That's a scary concept for some people. Could you explain what you meant by that?

GA: The quote on the magazine cover was shocking and from a journalistic point of view, it was a great headline. But from a realistic point of view, it emphasizes something which isn't true. When I said "Fashion is finished" I meant "finished" as a "diktat," as "input" by one or more designer. For me, the time has ended in which everyone must follow these directions without adding their own personality to this choice, without looking in the mirror and judging themselves. That is finished, in my opinion.

It's not modern: we are all free to be ourselves, dress as we wish, to feel comfortable. There are so many options, so there is no longer *a* trend, but *many* trends that could make a person happy without following particular rules.

JB: Designers have been saying for the past decade that they don't want to dictate, yet women are still looking to designers for direction. It seems they don't feel confident or secure unless someone is putting their stamp of approval on it. Do you ever get uncomfortable with that level of responsibility?

GA: I didn't choose an easy job; I chose a job through which I speak to people, so it's clear that some risk and effort on my part are involved. However, it's also a wonderful job. Out of one hundred women, there might be ten who know how to dress, the others need to be guided. That is one of my duties.

JB: You understand the media so well — really understand how to play it. That's something that's become increasingly important for designers — to some, even more important than the clothes themselves. How much does it please you to dabble in this arena of publicity and celebrity — to be staging a big rock concert, to some degree, for publicity purposes?

GA: I feel secure in this position because my product sells very, very well and I have the security of a valid product behind me, something real, a solid market and a love from the public for my creations. This allows me to play a little — to be different sometimes, to be easy, approachable. This is a game I play, one I enjoy playing.

Celebrities came out in droves to Armani's "playground" the following evening, and Armani, in a tight dark T-shirt, greeted each and every one at the door. The armory had been transformed into a hedonistic scene: a beautifully swishy lounge where guests sat on big pillows on carpeted tiers in front of small, candle-lit tables crammed with martini glasses. Because tickets were at such a premium, I couldn't bring a guest and arrived with only my cameraman. For once, I wished I didn't have to hustle any sound bites — I wanted nothing more than to hang at the bar and chat with Condé Nast's editorial director, James Truman (we marveled at the estimated $2 million we heard Armani had spent on the evening); ogle John F. Kennedy Jr. and his sister Caroline; check out what Gwyneth Paltrow was wearing; and see Arnold Schwarzenegger in party mode. But I was obliged to get as much tape as possible with the stars. And all of them, from Lauren Bacall to Spike Lee, were only too happy to sing Armani's praises.

Finally, after being snubbed by Sarah Ferguson, the Duchess of York, I retreated to a tiny spot next to my Venezuelan supermodel friend, Patricia Velasquez, who was partying with a group of her Latin American pals. Patty had brought with her a Ziploc bag filled with some kind of exotic fruit similar to lichee nuts and was passing them around. We savored the sweet, juicy, grapelike flesh of the fruit as we bopped to the funky rhythms coming from the stage. Beautiful, well-dressed bodies were perched casually on pillows everywhere, drinking in the heady, sensual atmosphere and grooving to the music. We all felt privileged to have been invited to this exclusive, intimate soiree; to be privy to these wonderful command performances; to rub shoulders with so many famous people.

For a few minutes, it felt like we'd all died and gone to fashion heaven. Appropriately, it was the glamorous Giorgio Armani who'd taken us there.

Ford Has a Better Idea

You have to be involved in the fashion world for at least a decade before you really begin to see the way fashion reflects how we live our lives. I had spent the first ten years of *Fashion Television* going on about how

fashion is a barometer of society and a mirror of our times; even so, I couldn't get the whole picture until I learned to look at the clothes objectively and decipher the messages the designer was sending.

It also took me a decade to appreciate that many designers come and go, and some stay around for a long time, and a precious few really do have a social conscience. I'm not suggesting that these rare, brilliant individuals are trying to save the world — but they definitely want to hold a mirror up to our life and times.

To me, the most fascinating aspect of fashion has always been its preoccupation with self-expression and sex. And in that department, Gucci has shone these past few years. Tom Ford, the hot young Texan who helped revive Gucci's tired old image and send it skyrocketing into the category of super-chic and must-have, is one of the most astute and articulate designers around. Ford's intelligence is always evident in every garment the label produces, and not because Gucci is especially wearable (some of it is totally over the top). But you can always see where Ford is coming from when he puts out a collection: he's focused, and his messages are usually crystal clear.

"Face it, we're living in a violent society — that's why we wear so much black," Ford explained during fittings in a suite at the Chateau Marmont for his 1997 AIDS Project L.A. show. Ford, dressed in de rigueur black, was pumped, telling me about his aspirations to direct film — something I think he'd be very good at. His sharp intellect and keen eye would be perfect for the medium.

The suave and sophisticated Tom Ford redefined our idea of sexy dressing for modern times, and brilliantly revived the once ailing House of Gucci. (Courtesy Citytv)

Rows of patent stilettos with five-inch steel-spiked heels glistened below racks laden with edgy, dangerous garments: sleek black evening gowns accompanied by a variety of shiny black belts intended for wrapping around necks and upper arms. It was threatening, restricting, haunting. Ford had christened his new look "tough chic."

"Aren't you concerned this may be interpreted as a glamorization of violence?" I asked him.

"No, because we're looking at it with a 1997 eye. These images are beautiful to us now, not shocking. They're simply mirroring reality."

In the fall of '96, Ford had sent his models down a Milan runway looking sweaty and a little battered. According to the *New York Times*, the look suggested that the models had been forced to have sex in a steamy washroom stall before heading out into the cool nightclub once again. It was a stylization that many found disturbing, but it certainly didn't hurt Gucci's image or sales. The product was seen as sexy and out-there: kudos to the designer who'd shaken us out of our romantic complacency with this edgy take. Now Tom Ford, who'd emerged as the definitive designer for the late '90s, was continuing his hard-core theme. But by his fall '97 collection, he was advocating that people fight back and be tough.

Before. You can see the excitement in my eyes as Kevyn instructed me to lie down and get ready for his masterful makeover of me . . . (Photo: Kevyn Aucoin)

Lights, Camera, Makeover

New York, early summer 1997. It was about 12:30 a.m. and a hard rain made the Chelsea sidewalks glisten. Thunder clapped as I thanked my hosts and switched off my tape recorder.

"That was great," I gushed. "You guys have been so candid, I really appreciate it!"

Without missing a beat, Kevyn Aucoin piped up, "Okay. Let's do your makeup!"

In 1998, Louisiana native Kevyn Aucoin was the most celebrated makeup artist in the world, the favorite of movie stars, rock stars, and

During. Kevyn treats faces as though they are canvasses, and artfully brings out the best in all his subjects. I felt transformed . . .
(Photo: Eric Sakas)

legends from Liz Taylor and Barbra Streisand to Tina Turner and Madonna — both of whom took him on the road with them. His stellar connections, coupled with his profile as a staunch gay-rights activist, made him a perfect cover story for the gay community's *ICON* magazine. Because of my close relationship with Kevyn, I was commissioned to interview him and his then-boyfriend, Eric Sakas.

I first met Kevyn with RuPaul in the late 1980s, backstage at a Todd Oldham show. They both sought me out in that party-like atmosphere, gushing over what big fans they were. RuPaul was just starting to hang around the New York fashion scene, and Kevyn introduced himself to me as a makeup artist and contributing editor to *Allure*. He was a little goofy, extremely self-conscious, and painfully shy. I found him delightful and never suspected that I'd be hearing his name often and with great reverence in the seasons to come.

Curled up on Kevyn and Eric's vintage mission couch that rainy night, over a good bottle of wine, we talked about relationships, love, and marriage. Lipstick and mascara were the farthest things from my mind, but here I was, being offered a midnight makeover from the man who'd transformed Courtney Love and Lisa Marie Presley!

"The last person who had these brushes on her face was Julia Roberts," Kevyn told me. He instructed me to lie on the floor and pushed an old pillow under my head. It was an unconventional way to work, but I'd seen him do it before with his friend Andie MacDowell in her New York hotel room just before an awards show.

Eric brought in more weathered cosmetic bags while Kevyn plopped down, cross-legged, earnestly studying my features. I felt a little nervous and couldn't help smiling. He pulled out a pair of tweezers.

"Eric, do you mind putting some music on?" he asked.

Eric obliged, and Tori Amos, another one of Kevyn's friends and devoted clients, set the rhythm for the first round of plucking. Another crash of thunder rattled the apartment windows. Inside I was cozy and safe in the master's hands.

Kevyn isn't like a lot of other New York fashion people. Besides being very smart and funny, he is friendly, spiritual, and always sincere, and has a strong political conscience. He says he never wanted to be famous, just good at what he did. He's always been obsessed with beauty, mainly because he himself always felt ugly. His favorite pastime as a child was putting makeup on his sisters and then taking pictures of them. Tonight his Polaroid was standing by, ready to snap the new me. Kevyn adores women and wants to help them extract the inner beauty he feels they all possess. He says the confidence we gain from liking what we see in the mirror makes us feel more beautiful and gets us closer to our own personal truths.

Forty-five minutes later, I'd been brushed and blended into believing I was about to see the most beautiful me possible. He had gone for a classic look: no more black eyeliner and, most important, curled eyelashes and lots of carefully applied mascara, top and bottom. Finally, he held up the mirror. My hair was off my face for the first time. I was shocked — I'd never imagined I could look that good. Wow! Take a picture. Take several. This was one fashion fantasy I wanted to capture forever.

Back in my hotel room at 3 a.m., I studied my face intently in the bathroom mirror, lamenting that makeup remover would soon erase my newfound glamor. But the next morning, the image reflected still seemed new and improved. I brushed my hair off my face once more and decided to start wearing it that way. Kevyn had helped me see my own potential, changing my self-perception in a small but significant way. I'd never compare to a model or a movie star, but I felt better about myself than I had in a long time.

Sometimes, that's all we need — someone who believes in us for just one night. That and a fully loaded bag of makeup.

After a Fashion

Bye Bye Love

My husband Denny's morning radio show was axed in January '97, after almost two decades of dedication to the company. His sadness and frustration grew until by Christmas of that year it had come to a head. In terms of potential work, there had been one disappointment after another. For the first time in the eighteen years we'd been together, he was letting his guard down and admitting he was discontented.

I was desperately worried. This was "Mr. Together," the guy who was always telling me to be positive, be happy about my life, who scolded me whenever I expressed a negative thought. I begged him to tell me what was wrong.

One cold day in January '98, I'd just returned from a trip to St. John's, the first time in twenty years I'd been back to the Rock. It had been a cathartic experience: I kept reminding myself how much I'd grown and how far I'd come. Walking down Duckworth Street, climbing Signal

Hill, and running into old friends and acquaintances reminded me how simple life used to be. I had no idea how complicated it was about to get.

I'd never seen Denny as solemn as on that Friday afternoon when he closed our bedroom door and sat me down. He had told me over the phone that he was "ready to talk." The girls had a couple of friends over, and their screams and laughter as they ran through the house jarred with my anxiety about what I felt I was about to hear. My heart was beating like crazy.

"I guess you realize I've been very unhappy for some time now," he said.

"Yeah, honey. I know. I want to help you so much. It's the work thing, isn't it?"

"No, it's more than that. It's the relationship."

"The relationship?"

"Yeah. I don't want to be in the relationship anymore. I've decided I don't want to be married anymore. I want to leave."

My heart sank into my stomach. It was worse than when I'd found out my father was dying. It was the worst moment I'd ever lived.

"But surely you just need to get away for a while — go on a trip. I know, sweetie, things haven't been working out for you. Take some time, go away, think, reflect. You can work it out. We can work it out together. Oh my God — what are you telling me?" Every last bit of me was writhing with the most acute pain I'd ever experienced, screaming out that this was a bad dream and please, oh please, could I wake up because this couldn't possibly be happening.

But Denny looked resigned to his decision.

"I simply don't desire the relationship. I don't desire you. I'm not in love with you anymore."

Overwhelmed with nausea, I ran into the bathroom and leaned over the toilet. My stomach was heaving, but nothing came up. I looked in the mirror and was repulsed by what I saw: pale, pasty white skin, frightened eyes. Drawn, horrified, pathetic. No wonder he didn't desire me anymore. Still, I came back for more.

"There's someone else, isn't there?"

He shook his head. "No. Absolutely not. I wish there was someone else. Then it would make it easier for you to hate me. There's no one else."

"Don't I turn you on anymore?"

"You know you don't."

My world came crashing down. I heard the children playing outside our door. My God! What about the kids? We have these kids. It's not just Denny and I who are breaking apart here.

"The children. What about the children?"

"Oh, kids are resilient. They'll be fine."

It sounded so flippant. And then he started weeping.

If this is what he really wanted, why was he crying?

"Because it's all so sad," he said. "There's so much history there."

I couldn't believe that he was so adamant about throwing it all away.

He gave me exactly three weeks' notice. He wanted to move out as soon as possible — there was no sense hanging on. But I pleaded with him to let me catch my breath. I had to be there for the children. This was going to come as a terrible shock to them, too. We hardly ever fought — they, like me, were under the impression that life was rosy and love ruled. How would they relate to this? How was I going to manage?

Everyone was quick to offer advice, to try to make me see the light, eager to assist in any way they could. My friend Deenah turned me on to her psychologist, an attractive, smart woman who, ironically, had an office just down the hall from my kids' pediatrician. It totally flipped me out to go there sometimes, because I always flashed back to taking the kids for their check-ups when they were babies.

That had been such a proud and exciting time for us. We'd get them dressed up in their cute little outfits and bring them in to be weighed and examined and we'd be so happy when the doctor told us that they were fine and healthy and normal and growing nicely. And I used to walk down that corridor thinking how fortunate and blessed we were to have such beautiful babies.

Now, here I was a decade later, feeling so lonely and helpless and desperate about my life, walking down that same corridor. But this time, I'd have to walk past the offices where the cute little kids were waiting for their check-ups with their doting parents and head for the suite of a shrink — someone I thought I'd never have to see for help, because, you know, my life was so perfect and grand.

I naively thought that somehow I'd escape from life unscathed, because my parents had worked off so much bad karma in the war, they'd already paid dearly for our sins, too. Now I realize no one escapes from this life unscathed. We all have our unique baggage that helps define who we are and how we travel the road.

The first thing I wanted to do was quit my job. I was sure it was all the traveling and the pressure and being in the public eye and the fame and the obsession with my work that had driven Denny away from me. I started thinking I'd never be able to go back to the job I'd been doing. How would I ever be inspired to get dressed up, meet new people, and be charming and witty?

The whole notion of the fashion world seemed like a joke. What a shallow, stupid existence I'd been leading in terms of my career. What had I been thinking? I desperately wanted to forget it all and get a job at a bookstore. Then life could be unhurried and simple and sane. I felt I had to show Denny that it was never my career that I cared about: it was him, and the kids, and the cozy life we had together.

Didn't he realize that? Obviously not. He must have thought I'd become this monster, a blind workaholic who cared more about the collections than the cottage. God, that wasn't true. Not at all. But since Denny wasn't in love with me anymore, I must have changed in some horrible way. It didn't even occur to me that maybe Denny was the one who had changed — that the very things about me that used to turn him on now turned him off.

At any rate, I was sickened by who I thought I was in the light of these new revelations. And I never wanted to pick up a fashion magazine again.

Staying at home all day gave me insight into what his life had been like the past year: unemployed, sitting around with little to do. But now he had a mission. He had to sort out his stuff — a lifetime of stuff — and find himself a place to live.

I tried to work from home, writing my column for *Flare* magazine, making necessary calls, but mostly I just stared into space. Each day, I'd go to the supermarket to shop, determined to try and salvage the marriage any way I could. Every single night, I cooked a gourmet meal, all his favorite dishes from the past eighteen years. As sad as this period was, we had some of the greatest home-cooked dinners of our relationship, all by candlelight, all so nice and pleasant and civilized. I was trying to recapture the fantasy I'd been living, even though the bomb had dropped and the walls had already come crashing down.

Denny moved out on the eve of our twelfth wedding anniversary. It was a Friday. My friend Penny came over in the morning to take me for a drive in the country. I couldn't bear to see him leave the house with his things. Although it was early February, it was a gloriously bright, sunny day — almost warm. The kids had left for school; they too would be spared the pain of watching Denny walk out that door and out of our lives.

What would normally have been such a happy outing — a drive in the country on a sunny day with my best friend — was a tear-soaked nightmare. I kept thinking about Denny packing up his precious things; scouring the house for bits he'd need in the immediate days and weeks, scrambling to escape the life with me he must have so detested.

We drove by a country store, a kind of home furnishings shop filled with homemade jams and chutneys, cozy blankets, and other cottage *tchotchkes*. It was the type of shop Penny and I usually loved, so we stopped in for a visit. But the sight of all those wonderful things was unbearable to me. My comfy home was a lost dream to me now.

Penny slept over that night because she didn't want to leave me alone. The kids cried a lot at bedtime, trying to understand why Daddy didn't want to live with us anymore. It was me he was rejecting, not them, and I felt guilty for not being good or beautiful or exciting enough to have kept him content and happy.

Yet another sleepless night passed. The next morning, I went to my psychologist's husband, a psychiatrist, for a prescription for tranquilizers. My panic was growing, and I had to start getting some sleep.

So, my single life began. Some days I thought I was taking one tiny step forward; then the next day it was as if I was taking two steps back. The simplest things would trigger despair. Trips to the supermarket were torture; I'd walk down aisles filled with Denny's favorite foods and realize I had no need to buy them anymore. The prospect of cooking just for myself and the kids was totally unappealing. There was more pain and sadness when I saw other people filling their carts with all kinds of goodies; I was certain they all had nice, big families to cook for and romantic dinners to prepare — just like the ones I used to make. I never thought I'd ever find joy in preparing food again.

A week after he left, I removed my wedding band, that beautiful diamond ring he'd bought me on our honeymoon in Zermatt. It was just days after our wedding, on Valentine's Day, that he'd put it on my finger, replacing the temporary ring we'd used when we exchanged vows.

That evening, exactly twelve years after the most romantic night of my life, I threw my first little dinner party with a few of my single girl-friends. There were a couple of moments when I felt all right; that I'd be okay; that life goes on.

But most of the time I was in a dark place, depressed by the break-up. He called only once — to talk to the girls, of course. I asked him how he was doing and he said, "Not as good as you, obviously." He knew I had friends to help comfort me. He was all alone.

Absolutely nothing in my life has ever been as painful as learning that life is nowhere near as perfect as I thought. I suppose we all have our illusions, things we tell ourselves to help get us through our days and nights. But the very essence of mine — my belief that I was in an honest, pure, committed relationship with a partner I loved more than anyone or anything in the world and who loved me equally — proved to be a sham. I'd fooled myself into believing I had it all.

It wasn't until almost six months after Denny left that I learned of his involvement with a young woman who'd broken up with him a few months before he left me. That truth finally set me free, and my healing process could begin.

Denny has always been a very loving father, and because of our children, we'll always be connected. Sometimes that comforts me and sometimes it makes me crazy. In retrospect, I see that in some ways our relationship was less perfect than I had imagined. Yet I still love Denny as the guy I used to know, and often wonder just who he became.

Jeanne and the Martini, or, The Olive and I

With my depression, I'd lost a lot of weight and was feeling and looking weak. Everybody started telling me I had to work out, so I got turned on to an amazing trainer, a woman named Shelby Pilot, who was hip, tough, and focused.

My semi-weekly workout sessions became a kind of therapy for me: I got into them with a vengeance. Every time I thought I couldn't possibly do another repetition, Shelby assured me there were only a couple more to go, a few more seconds left. And when I'd done it, she'd say, "Good girl!" leaving me momentarily pleased with myself.

It was a great way to work out all my aggression, to show myself — and everyone else — that I could get through this exhausting stuff. I started to see my workouts as a metaphor for my life, and I reveled in the focus they demanded. Before long, I started to feel really good about my newfound physical strength, my body, and, most important, myself.

With my new body came a new confidence and a sudden feeling of sexiness. It had been over six months since I'd been held by a man. Needless to say, I missed the physical contact, to say nothing of the love. But the whole dating scene sounded like a nightmare to me. All my single friends told me it was grueling out there: cold, bleak, merciless. I couldn't believe I'd have to face this new reality.

I went on a mad shopping spree and bought about $500 worth of very expensive, very sexy lingerie. I also splurged on a Donna Karan little black dress. It was on sale but it still cost me far more than any dress I'd ever purchased.

My friends had been working hard to lift my spirits, but it was a date I wanted most: a simple dinner engagement with a straight man. I just wanted to dress up and sip martinis and see if I could even be coy and charming again with a strange man.

My friend Kate, who's about fifteen years my junior, was seeing an interesting fellow, a director about my age. She'd realized their relationship was to be merely platonic, and she thought I might like him, so she arranged a chic dinner date for the three of us.

It was a good excuse to wear my little black dress. It was also totally safe, since Katy would be there. I felt pretty good about the way I looked — the dress was fab, and Katy and the guy thought so too. It was fun sharing this cute, charming man as he strode down the street with us on either arm: Katy, the younger woman, and I the older — perfect complements, I thought.

As we cozied up at the dinner table and as I heard myself make conversation, I started to feel pretty capable, energized, witty. I was actually thinking this could be fun.

The giant olive at the bottom of my martini glass was soon staring me in the face. It was time to order another martini. I'd get the waiter's attention in just a minute — but first, down with the olive. Gingerly, I picked it out of the glass, admiring its extraordinary size and unusual hue. And I took a bite — right into the pit. Suddenly, something snapped. Crunched. Cracked. In horror, I realized it was my front tooth.

"Katy," I mumbled, my hand covering my mouth. She turned to me with her dazzling smile.

"What?"

"You're not going to believe this."

"What?"

The guy became intrigued: "Yeah, what is it?"

"I just broke my front tooth."

"No, get outta here!" Katy laughed. "Let's see."

I smiled to reveal the broken front tooth. My two dinner companions feigned calmness.

"Awwww, it's nothing. Honest," said Katy, a little too quickly.

"Can't hardly see it," said the guy.

I fumbled through my purse for a compact, scrambling to check out the damage for myself.

"You've got to be kidding!" I said, the moment I saw my image in the mirror. There looking back at me was a witch. A hillbilly. A hoser.

"I have to leave this instant!" I said, quickly shutting my mouth.

Maybe the martinis helped them, but somehow, the duo convinced me that a broken front tooth feels much creepier than it looks.

"Trust me, Jeanne. I'd tell you if it was that bad, and it isn't," Katy said.

"Absolutely," said the guy.

So we carried on: me on my quasi-first date, looking like Granny Clampett in Donna Karan. I tried being funny about it, but I doubt it worked. We ended up downtown at the loft of some old local rock star who remembered being interviewed by me in the old *New Music* days and who also tried to tell me that the gaping hole in the front of my smile was hardly noticeable at all.

Somehow, as the charming guy nuzzled Katy and the old rock star perpetually grabbed his seventeen-year-old girlfriend, I wondered if there was any hope for me at all.

Eventually, I realized that I'd have to make my own fun. I'd been sad for too long. It was time to enjoy life again with my beautiful daughters, who had been helplessly watching me cry every day for months.

Being able to share some of my pain with them had been a healthy thing for our relationship — unquestionably, it brought us closer. They'd been sympathetic and understanding. But I knew they were worried that life would never seem "normal" again and that I might never be happy again. I had to show them we could still have good times as a trio, so I arranged to take them to Martha's Vineyard for a week. First, though, I'd take a sojourn on my own — the first time in years I'd booked a holiday for myself, and the first time in years that I'd go to Europe strictly for pleasure. My wonderful Dublin friend, designer Louise Kennedy, had invited me to visit her many times. Finally, I took her up on the offer.

Stayin' Alive

County Laois, July 12. Without question, this is the most beautiful room I've ever stayed in, in the most beautiful house I've ever been in. "Capelard" is an exquisite sixty-room Georgian country mansion on 150 acres of gorgeous mountainside with an awesome view. The house is filled with antiques, and the richness and luxury are majestic. The house belongs to two guys, friends of Louise's, who deal in antique jewelry. Supermodels Naomi Campbell and Christy Turlington are two of their cherished clients.

In the afternoon a dozen people drop by for a superb lunch. Afterwards, when the rain stops, we walk around the rose gardens. There is a pet peacock named Charlie, who wanders about — I thought I was hallucinating when I first saw him through the kitchen window.

That evening, countless glasses of champagne later, we blast Motown music and dance around the opulent living room. This is bliss.

I love the times when Denny feels like a distant memory, when I can hardly recall his face. How great that this is my own, exciting, wonderful time that has absolutely nothing to do with him. There will be more times like this: I can have fun again — and in such style!

My room is golden in the morning. I stare through the rails of my

brass bed in awe of the gilt furniture and precious antiques. I draw a bath and think of all the lords and ladies whose lives were once surrounded by these beautiful things. Two tiny night tables beside the bed hold countless antique trinkets: flasks, belt buckles, pendants, boxes. Details are everywhere, like on a magnificently decorated movie set: the porcelain figurines are alive in my mind; a bowl of deep pink roses cheers my dressing table; and out the window are green lawns, lovely terraces, and flower-filled urns as far as the eye can see.

I look at my reflection in the silver-framed mirror. My face looks a little old, I admit. But I inhale the roses and remind myself that I'd have to have paid my dues to this degree to have the privilege of experiencing, and really appreciating, all of this.

St. Clerans, July 17. Merv Griffin bought director John Huston's old house near Galway and converted it into a twelve-bedroom hotel. St. Clerans is amazing: the colors are a little "cheery" California, but the opulence is impressive. I'm lying on a grand four-poster bed in Merv's own suite, in what used to be the director's bedroom.

I watch horses and one small colt running in the field outside my window. This is the house where Angelica Huston grew up, and it was *the*

Life is good at the Tea Room in the Clarence Hotel in Dublin, with my dear friend Louise Kennedy and her right-hand man, Paddy Bollard. Capelard (right) is one of Ireland's most beautiful country estates.

party house in Ireland when Huston lived here. Imagine those guests!

Earlier, Louise and I took a tiny plane to Inishmaan, one of the Aran Islands, and it was like going back in time: winding stone walls carve up the green and gorgeous island; thatched cottages are sprinkled

about; and goats, cows, and donkeys are everywhere. We had lunch at the home of Tarlach and Aine de Blacham, owners of the local knitting mill. Looking out from their dining-room window, I feel inspired to write for the first time in six months.

I'm confused sometimes at my range of emotions — how I can be so positive one minute and so sad the next. I suppose I always knew life couldn't be as sweet and perfect as it seemed, that one day some tragedy would touch my life and change my world forever. I should be happy that the children are okay, that I have my health . . . all that. And really, at the end of it all, I should be saying, "Yes! Thank God we're here and alive and healthy."

The Aran Islands were surreal — frozen in time. Dancing at Capelard, it was as though I'd rediscovered music and the joy of living. I realized then that life does go on.

Today, I'm well into life on my own, back on track, full steam ahead. But every so often I flash on the big picture and remember the terrible hole that's there. And there's no way of fixing it, really, and no way of ever filling it up again — not the way it used to be filled. So I just try to accept that and focus on the beautiful part of the picture. The emptiness I sometimes feel is based on the loss I experienced when Denny left — and that went far beyond losing a partner, a husband, a lover, and a friend. I lost my innocence when Denny left me.

Marc Jacobs

It's a quarter after midnight, and I'm sitting in an airport lounge in Tel Aviv, leafing through the February 2000 edition of *Vogue*, and suddenly there's a photo of Marc Jacobs — wind-blown, sneakered, in gritty black and white — being heralded as the "Prince of Cool." A couple of hundred pages into the magazine, I find a story about how the brilliantly talented boy from New Jersey came to rule the New York runways and then conquered not only Paris but also our whole sensibility about what makes fashion modern.

Unquestionably, the longer I stay in fashion, the more delight I take in remembering my first encounters with all these young geniuses. There's nothing more satisfying than witnessing the evolution of a celebrity or the birth of a fashion phenomenon.

It must have been early 1986. My friend Deenah Mollin was running a small Toronto fashion PR firm called Vizability, and her partner's husband had just decided to back a new young designer from New York whom, according to Deenah, "I just had to meet."

"He's amazing," she assured me. "And absolutely adorable — hair down to his elbows! He does the most fabulous sweaters — really whimsical. Great TV. You'll love him."

She told me this boy wonder's name and that he was coming into town to check out a factory and meet the Toronto media. And if I wanted, I could come out to the factory too, with a camera, to meet him and do a story on him.

"Jeanne, I'm telling you, this guy is going to be huge."

I convinced my producer that Deenah might be on to something and that even if she wasn't, the whole concept of following a young designer as he checks out his new manufacturing facilities might be cool. So on the appointed morning, my cameraman and I drove out to some barren industrial area in northwest Toronto to meet Jacobs. Deenah was right — Marc was absolutely adorable, extremely personable, and down to earth. I doubt that he'd ever been interviewed for TV before, and he acted a little nervous, but when he realized how informal we were, he relaxed and excitedly started showing me his small collection of colorful

Marc Jacobs was a hot young talent when I first met him at the Toronto factory that would be manufacturing his early line.

(Courtesy Citytv)

218

knitwear on a model Deenah had hired for the shoot.

Marc had worked at an upscale Manhattan boutique, Charivari, and had attended the Parsons School of Design. He had had some sweaters made as part of a student project and taken them into Charivari; the woman who owned the store had gone nuts when she saw them and decided to sell them there.

I wasn't surprised they were so well received. Marc's whimsical take on style was a breath of fresh air at a time when fashion had begun to take itself a little too seriously. I especially liked his sweater dress with

the big hands on it. Marc was bright and "with it," and most important, he really seemed to have a handle on what girls wanted and needed. He understood our lifestyle, our spirit, the mood of the time. Over the years, that's something that's always held true about him.

The next time I caught up with Marc, he was honing his media skills, meeting with the press at Toronto's chic Holt Renfrew. He was pushing a line of oversized sweaters, which were meant to be teamed with tights and little over-the-shoulder bags.

"What more does the modern girl need?" Jacobs asked earnestly.

Once again, I felt he was bang-on when it came to knowing us. He had graduated to the next level. Very media-savvy by now, he was well on his way to celebrity status as a designer. By the early '90s, Marc had landed himself a plum job as head women's wear designer for Perry Ellis. He'd most definitely arrived and we couldn't wait to see what he'd do for the venerable American label. I, for one, was expecting something at least a little gutsy, and Marc didn't disappoint.

In the fall of '92, we were incredulous when the Perry Ellis runway featured girls in grunge — a shocking approach to modern dressing, loaded with in-yer-face sloppy street attitude. Actually, it was refreshing as hell. But critics and retailers weren't ready for Marc's stark vision, and he was pretty much crucified. It was the beginning of the end for him at Perry Ellis. But deep down, I knew his edginess was a harbinger of things to come.

Back at the Perry Ellis showroom, Marc defended his position on modern fashion to me and explained how it was really about mixing it up, seeking out pieces, dressing for dinner and being comfortable and unique. It made perfect sense to me. And really, when you think about where fashion is today, Marc was a prophet.

Despite his sound philosophy and precious little pieces, Marc's vision didn't fly for Perry Ellis. Soon he was sacked. Eventually, he came back — on his own, with longtime business partner Robert Duffy. They swore to me up and down that the days of dealing with big-business fashion were over. From now on they would keep it small and pure and honest. They didn't care about dressing everybody, or making lots of money, or winning lots of support. They just wanted to do what they felt was right.

As we stood together out on a Soho fire escape outside his tiny new studio, I drank in every word Marc said. For me, Marc was fashion's purest voice — the hippest, most unpretentious designer I knew. And one of the smartest.

Fast forward to the spring of 1998. Marc Jacobs is the newly installed designer for the illustrious house of Louis Vuitton.

"But, Marc, what happened to keeping it small and simple and close to the heart?" I asked him backstage in Paris.

"I think I can still be true to myself, despite the pressure," he said.

And indeed, he has been. But Marc is different now, more intense, a little less generous with his time — out of necessity, no doubt. He always credited me for supporting him, for covering his collections and putting him on TV and giving him the necessary exposure. But there are bigger fish to fry these days. I can see the pressure backstage at shows, the intensity of it all. All the cool people are there: whether for his own collections in New York or the swishy Bernard Arnault crowd in Paris, the coolest people always make Marc's collections a priority.

His own shows in New York are invariably held in the evening, with all the best models and celebrities in attendance. Madonna sometimes comes in at the last minute, taking her conspicuous front-row seat. Marc has a history of getting all the best models, too. Naomi and Kate and Amber and Shalom and Linda were always there without fail, looking especially gorgeous and natural in his anti-fashion fashionable mode. Now it's always the hot young models of the moment who grace his catwalk. Backstage, it's always a scene, with lots of champagne, cigarettes, and schmoozing, and with Marc making the rounds and making sure everybody is in the right headspace to strut his stuff.

Tommy Boy

"Man, that's chutzpah!"

I was in front of a film camera in Tommy Hilfiger's 6th Avenue headquarters in New York. The showroom had been transformed into a mini-movie set, and Spike Lee was calling the shots.

I was in knee-high white leather boots (a gift from designer Jill

Stuart) and a nylon Tommy jacket that Andy Hilfiger, Tommy's brother, had given me — dressed to kill for my cameo in a special video being produced for the Council of Fashion Designers of America Awards show.

Tommy was being honored as Men's Wear Designer of the Year, and that was a big deal. Spike was asking me to reminisce about the first time I met Tommy, back in 1988. It was on the heels of his controversial ad campaign devised by in-yer-face New York ad whiz George Lois: "Move over Ralph, Calvin — Tommy Hilfiger's here."

And "First came Bill Blass . . . blah blah blah."

No one had ever heard of Tommy Hilfiger before. Yet here they were, telling us that one day this WASP kid from Connecticut would be in the same league as Calvin, Ralph, Bill, and the gang. A Saudi financier was pumping a lot of money into Tommy's business. But the whole thing seemed like a pipe dream.

Tommy had started his business while still in college, selling jeans out of the back of a VW van. The first time I met him, he struck me as super-friendly, all-American, squeaky clean, and extremely focused. He told me about regular camping trips he and his family used to take in Canada with his friend Bonnie Fuller, a Toronto native who's now at the helm of *Glamor* magazine. I remember envying Bonnie for having Tommy as a pal. He was so personable and easy-going compared to most of the other designers I'd met.

During our interview, I asked Tommy, "Do you honestly see yourself in the same league as Calvin Klein and Ralph Lauren?"

He looked me straight in the eye and after a moment of serious consideration, answered, "In time, yes."

Man, that's chutzpah! I thought. But in the fashion business, having a little chutzpah never hurt anyone.

Once the rhythm of Tommy's rise to fashion stardom had been established, I got a call from one of his people to ask if I'd like to be his guest at an upcoming CFDA awards dinner. I was pleased, but also wondered why he was asking. He even offered to send a limo to pick me up. Since I was working that night anyway and had to get there early to shoot people arriving, I accepted the invitation and told his office I'd see him at the dinner. He sat me right next to him, and was most gracious. He told me it would be really cool to see a channel devoted entirely to fashion.

Enigmatically, Tommy Hilfiger became a kind of folk hero to kids on inner-city streets. (Courtesy Citytv)

And who better to spearhead that than me? He had a real personal interest in this project.

"You should call my lawyer, Allan Grubman," he said. "He's incredibly well connected, very big in the music scene. Tell him I told you to call."

When Tommy's business went through the roof a couple of years later, I kicked myself for not at least trying to check out his tip.

Tommy met a lot of resistance from the industry in his early years. People were skeptical about him and his marketing techniques. He was brash, up-front, no-nonsense — something ultra-chic fashion snobs had no time for. But he was a solid businessman and had latched on to a brilliant strategy: taking the American Ralph Lauren dream and making it accessible to street kids. Suddenly homeboys and rappers — all the cool black urban kids — were embracing Tommy, loving both his logo and his clothes. It was bizarre that he'd captured the hearts of this inner-city sector, but hey, opposites attract. He became a kind of folk hero to these kids, too. Once, when I was walking down the street in New York with Tommy, a cool young black guy came up to him with a "high five." Tommy was wonderfully sweet to him.

Because Tommy understands the importance of cool associations, it made perfect sense for him to ask respected Afro-American filmmaker Spike Lee to direct his short promotional film for the CFDA Awards. I was honored to appear, but even more honored that I was being directed by the enigmatic Spike.

Spike is not very friendly or forthcoming. Once I told my story for him a couple of times, he just wrapped me. That was my big brush with filmmaking greatness. The only part of my story that wasn't left on the editing room floor was my "Man, that's chutzpah!" line.

And then there was a quick pan down to my fabulous white boots.

Bryan Adams captured a side of me that had never been brought out in a photo before. (Photo courtesy Bryan Adams)

Bryan's Babes

In the fall of '99, rock star Bryan Adams was launching his new photography book, *Made in Canada*, at *Flare* magazine's twentieth-anniversary bash, and I was hosting the event. I was finally starting to feel good about

myself after my break-up with Denny, and wanted to look hot, so I dressed in a sexy black camisole to go with my glitzy Misura pantsuit. The outfit seemed to have the desired effect, because when Denny came to pick up the kids before I left, his eyes popped at my decolletage. I felt embarrassed and vindicated all at once.

The evening ahead was to be a benefit for breast cancer; Bryan Adams had dedicated his book to the cause. His book was an eclectic collection of sensitive photographs of outstanding Canadian women. I was proud and amazed to have been chosen as one of his subjects.

He had taken the portrait in the summer of '98, while I was struggling with the depression that followed my marriage break-up. I wasn't really up to a photo shoot with one of the world's greatest rock musicians, but as a huge fan I couldn't miss the opportunity. So I showed up at the downtown Toronto studio at the appointed time and tried to think happy thoughts while the stylists worked their magic. Soon I was feeling kind of groovy: ready for my close-up, eager to see if a wildly talented musician could also be a wildly talented photographer. There was no doubt his work would be scrutinized.

No artist is ever truly content and Bryan Adams was obviously eager to push his own boundaries. He'd taken up photography with a passion, and early the previous year had proposed to his friend, Suzanne Boyd, editor-in-chief of *Flare*, the idea of regularly contributing portraits of women to the magazine. Boyd convinced Adams to take his commitment a step further and put together a book for the Canadian Breast Cancer Foundation. The first photo he took for the book was of supermodel Linda Evangelista. He captured her softly, subtly, without a trace of pomp or pretension. The project was off and running.

I was impressed with Bryan's sophisticated lighting, but surprised that he was going to shoot me with a Polaroid.

"I try to work in a medium that makes people see what's going on a little bit and get them comfortable and then work from there, because people like to see how they look," he said. "It's great if you can give them examples of how it's going."

The concept made sense, and I was delighted with the initial test shots. Now that I was comfortable with his work, I could get a little more comfortable with the situation. I'd known Bryan since the early '80s, when I first started interviewing him: a shy, wiry kid from Vancouver with the soul of a poet and a quiet, intense charm. Most women find him very sexy — even Princess Diana thought so. You sense that this guy really loves women, in the best possible way: with honesty, respect, compassion, and tenderness. It was a turn-on being in front of his lens, even though it wasn't a very beautiful time in my life.

Bryan must have sensed it. He made me feel sexy, but instead of trying to get me to look bright and bubbly, he went with my mood and brought out a side of me that had never been captured in a photo before.

Fifteen months later, the launch party for the book was held at Toronto's Royal Ontario Museum. Before the crowd arrived, Bryan gave me a private preview of his photographs. The work was stellar: an assembly of artists, journalists, athletes, and movers-and-shakers. Each black-and-white shot was a song unto itself, the gallery walls a symphony of beauty and achievement. There were pop stars like Celine Dion, Shania Twain, and Sarah McLachlan; models like Shalom Harlow and Chanel girl Estella Warren; and political and cultural figures like the Right Honourable Kim Campbell and the Honourable Hilary Weston. Even Margaret Trudeau was there. Adams's bold lens had captured their pride, glamor, and inner harmony.

As Bryan took me through the gallery, my camera rolled, doing duty for an upcoming *Star!TV* special on the book. Just as I was commenting to Bryan on the incredible scope of the work, in walked a graceful, diminutive woman in a long black outfit, a matching scarf around her head. She looked stylish and dramatic as she came toward us.

"Frances!" Bryan called out. It was Frances Hathaway, one of the world's best makeup artists, whom I'd worked with and always liked.

The Christmas before my world fell apart, she'd sent me a touching card on which she'd written: "Always cultivate a joyful spirit." I kept that card stuck in my bedroom mirror for months, and its message helped see me through my darkness.

"Frances, great to see you. It's been so long!" We hugged.

Then Bryan asked me if I'd seen Frances's photograph yet.

"No, not yet."

"It's right over there. Take a look."

It struck me like lightning. There was Frances, naked from the waist up, exposing a blatant mastectomy scar with an inspiring air of acceptance and serenity. I had no idea she had battled breast cancer.

"I'd never even met Bryan before the day he took my picture," explained Frances. "But when I found out what he was doing, I just had to be a part of it."

Bryan's portrait of Frances had helped put things in perspective for me: it was time to stop being so self-conscious and really start celebrating the beauty within.

The Designer as Diva

Few popular modern spectacles could ever compare with some of the runway shows that were staged in New York in the late '80s and early '90s. This was live, spontaneous theatre at its best. Of course, there were the costumes, each one a fantasy in modern living. But what really made the shows were those kick lines of stellar chorus girls (the models), who were adored and applauded for little more than their diversity and on-stage attitude — memorable girls like quirky Kristen McMenamy and sassy Tyra Banks alongside bona fide divas like Naomi and Linda. Driving the sensibility of these twenty-minute romps were leading men and women (the designers) who were seriously critiqued and ultimately revered for their performance behind the scenes. And if they didn't manage to generate an excitement bordering on frenzy from all their die-hard fans, they knew they hadn't done their job.

One of the most anticipated shows in New York each season came from a couple of young artistic souls who really knew how to dish out the glamor: Todd Oldham and Isaac Mizrahi. And they couldn't have been more different.

Todd was a casual sweetie from Texas, a friendly guy with tattooed toes who collected paint-by-number art, loved rock 'n' roll, and lived in blue jeans. His fantasy gals often took on cartoon proportions — saucy little bitches in wobbling stilettos who sparkled and wiggled in all the right places. Todd even had the balls to send out lovely drag queens in his early runway shows. And those dames really garnered their share of whistles and cheers.

Invariably, his shows always felt like a hedonistic smorgasbord — a sexy, delicious feast for hungry eyes that couldn't get enough candy.

Inspired, and in an effort to capture every last bit of the action, I started using a Hi-8 camera, shooting from the pit like so many other still photographers. We were the first ones to start shooting the shows that way. Now it's become commonplace. Back then, it was totally unconventional to use what was considered home video equipment in the field, but we thought it was perfect for the style of *Fashion Television*. It was exciting and edifying to be able to shoot up those skirts — I appreciated every centimeter of cellulite!

Todd's shows in particular were fabulous on Hi-8. His backstage was invariably an overcrowded party with dozens of crews running around after champagne-swilling models. You felt like you were in the center of the universe, and with my Hi-8 camera by my side, I felt as if I could capture every little nuance and not be at the mercy of my cameraman, who was off shooting his own take of the phenomenal scene.

Isaac's show was similar in spirit, but more constrained. Here, you felt you were witnessing important fashion statements, concepts that took themselves a little more seriously than the frivolity being dished out at Todd's. Oldham was easy-going; Mizrahi always struck me as slightly tormented — a true New York artiste struggling to get it right and, ultimately, be understood. He was always on, elegant in the best Italian shoes and black slacks, teamed with a perfect white or black T-shirt or crisp white shirt. Sometimes he wore a sports jacket backstage, depending on his mood. In the early days he always sported a navy bandana in his thick, wiry black hair, like a quirky badge of exotica. You knew he was the kind of guy who got off on Gershwin, Noel Coward, and intimate, chatty dinner parties. He seemed obsessed with modern, glamorous women with lots of money and good taste, and fixated on dressing them simply, dramatically, luxuriously.

"I don't necessarily hate sequins or feathers," he told me in '89, "but, honestly, my clothes to this point try to be dramatic in other ways, in more sculptural ways. Because that is what I see myself as, ultimately."

Liza Minnelli was one of Isaac's biggest supporters in those early years. In 1989 he designed a magnificent red dress for her that she wore to the Council of Fashion Designers of America Awards, where she presented him with the Perry Ellis Award for best new talent.

"You have to love this industry and love clothes and these objects and accessories more than anything else," Isaac told me in his Soho studio the next day. "You have to love the idea of creating more than you love the idea of a great deal of publicity, or becoming a star, or making a million dollars. You know, I'm not in it for any of those reasons."

I really believed him, but ironically his career in fashion evolved in ways that made you wonder. By the mid-'90s, the supermodel sizzle had been silenced and good sense had been splashed into the face of modern dressing. The reflections in the mirrors of fashion's funhouse suddenly came into focus, and reality reared its sober head. Designers were only as good as their last orders. At the end of the day, it was all about the clothes, not how well the models strutted them. More than ever, the pressure was on designers to come up with the goods and not only sell them, but sell their own sensibility, their own mystique.

Marketing master Calvin Klein got busy redefining youth culture for the late '90s, honing his ad campaigns till he made an exact science of controversy. Savvy Donna Karan prepared for the impending millennium by turning inward, exploring spirituality, and attempting to bring a Zen consciousness to her collections. Squeaky-clean Tommy Hilfiger adopted the guise of a working-class hero and began wooing homeboys and college types alike with his vision of all-American dressing. And Isaac Mizrahi started cultivating blatant stardom.

My tight relationship with Isaac won me an invitation to hang out with him and his buddy, Sandra Bernhard, for a day during the filming of his 1995 documentary, *Unzipped*. We were to meet at Isaac's Soho studio, then trip around the local streets and shops with Douglas Keeve, who was the film's director as well as Isaac's boyfriend. When my cameraman and I arrived, Isaac was busy auditioning models for his upcoming show, assessing their looks and studying their gaits. I went upstairs to a makeshift back-room recording studio, where Sandra was singing her heart out — giving Douglas a very soulful rendition of the theme from *The Mary Tyler Moore Show*. The '70s sitcom's starring character was evidently Isaac's muse that season.

Later, we all went outside. Isaac and Sandra were leading the pack, ahead

Isaac Mizrahi and Sandra Bernhard in Soho, during the filming of *Unzipped*. I envied their special friendship. (Courtesy Citytv)

of Douglas with his mini-crew and me with my cameraman. I had my trusty Hi-8 camera with me and darted alongside the stellar duo in my platform sneakers, keeping up with their brisk pace and neurotic, angst-ridden intellectual musings, which were hysterically funny.

"Basics," whined Bernhard. "I need some basics!"

At first I thought she was referring to things like a relationship, a steady gig — those staples that ground you. But they were talking clothes. Isaac was saying she had enough basics, and was pushing for items that made statements; Sandy insisted that what she really needed were things like simple black T-shirts.

I envied their friendship — they were on the same wavelength, a couple of Jewish, artsy misfits whose stars were rising.

Of all the designers I've met, Issac has always been one of the most engaging. I saw him as a Renaissance man, always helping us better appreciate the importance of style in our lives, elevating the role of fashion designer to some kind of social therapist.

"What really does influence me when I'm designing is my own life," he once told me, his cigarette smoke curling above the clothes racks. "Most days, I wake up and I'm literally in the same clothes from 7:30 in the morning until midnight and I have to look right in all these contexts: board meetings, lunches, cocktail parties. If I were a woman, I'd probably be picking kids up in a carpool, too. I can't imagine how else to be designing a collection than by really trying to solve these daily problems. That's what's so exciting, because that is what I'm good at — problem solving."

Eventually, I think, Isaac's image may have become more important than the clothes he was putting out. By 1999, he'd put his career as a fashion designer to rest, partly because of soft business, but perhaps really because he felt he'd gone as far as he could in that arena. The huge success of *Unzipped* had turned him into a cultural icon. And that became a career in itself.

"We've become like pop stars in a funny way," he reflected in '96. "I mean, I'm not like Madonna or anything, but I can't leave my house without constantly getting noticed or without being asked for my autograph. When I saw what kind of response there was to me as a person with *Unzipped*, I just wanted to totally open up and really show my insides. It inspired me, not to be more of a celebrity, but to be more of an artist. So that's why I want to get involved in all these other projects."

Last time I heard, Isaac was working on a screenplay for some Hollywood studio.

Some may argue that all the attention designers have been getting these last few years is unwarranted, that their status as cultural icons is undeserved. After all, what could a bunch of dressmakers really teach us about the human spirit? But we all need images of glamor and poetry and style in our lives. If designers deliver on that front, I applaud them.

"So, did you get what you needed?" Isaac asked earnestly as one of our last interviews drew to a close.

"Yeah, thanks. A pleasure, Isaac, as always." I assured him.

"Okay, hon, gotta run. I've got another taping." He dragged his hand through that wild hair. A quick hug and kiss and he was off in a flash to a waiting limo downstairs.

The next night, he breezed into a crowded party for Karl Lagerfeld at the opening of the big New York Chanel boutique, Sandra at his side. There was a buzz, but he didn't hang around enough to really schmooze. Besides working on all his fabulous creative projects, Isaac was busy being a star. And that's precisely why we loved him.

I'd be remiss if I didn't tell you what happened a couple of years later, just after Isaac bowed out of fashion design. He was asked by American *Vogue* to ramble on about what he thought of all the fashion we were seeing on TV. When it came time to talk about me and my work, he said it was hard to be objective, since he considered me a friend.

I didn't quite know what to think about that, though it was nice that he considered me a friend. But when Charles Ghandee, the interviewer, asked him about the way I dress, Isaac said, "Well, she tries."

Maybe I was being oversensitive, but I took that as a slam. I've never considered myself a serious fashion plate, but if Isaac really was a friend, as he claimed, he could have been a little less catty. I was hurt, and immediately phoned Sandra. She was incredulous. She assured me that Isaac adored me and would never say anything mean like that — it must have been taken out of context.

I tried to let it roll off my back, but honestly felt that maybe all fashion people were phony creeps after all. I'd supported Issac all these years, and now that he didn't need me for my coverage anymore, he was free to diss me.

About a week later, I got a frantic call from Isaac, who'd heard from Sandra that I was upset with what had been written in *Vogue*.

"Oh sweetie, you know I worship you. I think you're a goddess. I'd never say anything against you. I thought what I said to that interviewer was a tribute, not a slam. I guess I'll have to reread it — they must have taken me out of context. So next time you're in New York, call me and let's have dinner. Promise? I can't wait to tell you what I'm up to."

I thanked him for calling and hung up, wondering if I'd ever call him again.

Gentleman Ralph

The first time I had a date to interview Ralph Lauren, he stood me up.

Since the early days of *Fashion Television*, we'd been trying relentlessly to nab the classic American designer for more than the usual two-minute sound bite at the end of his runway show. But Ralph was always elusive — camera-shy, some felt — and reluctant to take part in situations where he wasn't in total control.

Finally, in 1993, he agreed to a sit-down chat. We were elated. My cameraman and I grabbed the earliest flight out of Toronto for New York and headed straight for his Madison Avenue headquarters. But when we got to his impressive oak-paneled offices, we were told he wasn't feeling well and had to call our interview off. Defeated, we made the tired trip back to Toronto, another fantasy squashed.

Seven years later, Ralph finally agreed to meet with me in advance of his fall 2000 show. Fittings were going on, but he'd take time out for our camera. We wanted to capture the color of Ralph at work, but moments before our interview was to start, Ralph had the room cleared out. So there we were, amid the lifeless racks of luxury clothing, Ralph looking wonderfully tanned and fit in a tight black sweater, hip khaki cargo pants, and bright orange running shoes, and me in my most reverent mode. At long last, I was face to face with the master of modern American

Ralph Lauren let us drop by his studio when he and his team were preparing for his fall 2000 show. I was honored that he'd share such precious time with me and my camera. (Courtesy Citytv)

glamor, without an army of competing crews waiting for their two minutes of glory.

Ralph traced his love of style back to the sixth grade.

"I'm the youngest of a family of four," he recalled. "I grew up in the Bronx, not in this great social thing. My father was an artist, and life wasn't that easy, but it was still that great. I played basketball in the schoolyards of New York, so I loved sport. I also wanted to look cool when I went out on a date so I started early, borrowing my big brother's clothes. The love of style sometimes comes from wanting something you don't have, or wanting your big brother's clothes. Basically I had a sense of style that had nothing to do with fashion. I didn't even know what a fashion designer was, but I knew what a movie star was. I knew who Paul Newman was and Marlon Brando and Cary Grant and Fred Astaire. When you're growing up, that's your entry into the world outside.

"And you get a lot of inspiration from stars, as people do today."

Ralph told me he was amazed that his particular sensibility and aesthetic had permeated the hearts and minds of the world to such an extent. "It's amazing to know that people in China are wearing your clothes. It's amazing to put on the TV and all of a sudden see kids wearing your T-shirts or the president of France on the front page wearing a polo player on a button-down shirt. I mean, he's the president of France! It's thrilling because it's exciting to see you got your message across and there's a wide world out there that's getting your message. When I was growing up, I was a great Cary Grant fan. I used to say, 'I'm wearing a Cary Grant look.' Or, 'Don't I look like Cary Grant today?' And someone said, 'Ralph, would you send some ties — I was making ties when I started out — would you send some ties to Cary Grant?' So I sent some ties and they got to Cary Grant and one day he called me.

"And he said, 'I don't go into stores but I've been wearing your ties that someone brought me and I love your ties.' And then I said, 'Well, Cary, great talking to you. If you're ever in New York, I'd love to meet you.' So a couple of months later, he came to my office in this beautiful Polo coat and he said, 'I want you to know I always wear your ties.' And he took one of my old ties out of his pocket and showed me this silver tie that I had called a Cary Grant tie. And then we actually became friends.

"The same thing happened with Audrey Hepburn, whom I

admired and got to know," he went on. "She called me one day and we met. She told me she had been wearing a lot of my things, too. It's amazing because you admire certain people and you don't know if they know you even exist. And all of a sudden, they're calling you and loving your things. So they inspired you and all of a sudden they're getting it right back from you."

Ralph Lauren has become a fashion classic in his own right. He was one of the first in America to invent that kind of persona and that kind of image. He had the vision that it was possible to execute classicism as a fashion designer.

"You don't have plans — you just go ahead and do what you think you love and I just kept doing it. And I kept trying to be pure about my thoughts and trying to be true to who I was. My goal every year is to try and be a better Ralph and still be aware of the world and not live in an ivory tower. There always has to be a message there, when people see my clothes. The goal is to keep your identity, but still be subtle. For me, it's always been about taste and style. It's not walking into a room and saying, 'Oh my God, that's drop dead!' That's not what I'm about. The collection is about a whole world, about a message, so you get a story — it's like a movie. When I design, I'm making a movie."

The movie theme keeps creeping back in Ralph's conversations. So why hasn't he ever tried designing for film?

"Well, first of all, no one's asked me. But seriously, it's not that easy to do. The frivolousness of thinking you can do something — well, maybe you can do it if you really believe in it. But I put so much energy into what I do know. I love what I'm doing and you're here doing this interview with me, so in some way, I'm the star in your world. And I'm happy to be there. I took a different route. In the end, it really is about consistency and hard work and loving what you do. And that's why I'm still here."

Ralph's smooth, gracious manner left me feeling that this diminutive, silver-haired man was one of the classiest guys in fashion.

And at the end of our interview he said something to me so flattering, I'll cherish it always. It was one of the greatest compliments an interview subject has ever paid me.

"I know we're not the same age, but I really feel as though we grew up together," he said. "I know we've only spoken briefly over the years but I feel as though you really know me by the questions you asked."

Zebra Is the New Leopard

Zebra is the new leopard.

If this concept makes any sense to you, you've been following fashion too closely for too long. I learned this about myself only recently, during a New York Collections Week, when I detected an absence of my beloved leopard prints on the runway. In their place was zebra: black and white and bolder than ever, looking as brash and '70s as an Austin Powers ad. It was lamentable — but understandable — that leopard had finally fallen by the wayside as the jungle print of the moment. For several seasons now, the wild, spotted look had represented a certain funkiness and freedom for us: as an accessories accent, it always did the trick. But the fashion gods practically made it extinct for spring 2000 (though it would make a return by the fall . . .). In its place: dynamic, unpredictable zebra, a metaphor for definitive, unbridled action in the millennium ahead.

The fact that my tired brain would even give way to such inconsequential musings during a standard runway show has me worried. Fashion has been my professional life for nearly sixteen years. I've witnessed the rise of mega-hype along with the rise of the supermodel and tsk-tsked their subsequent demise. But all of us leading this rarified existence are getting slightly bored now, waiting for the next big thing. Fashion, as we once knew it, is over.

In her book, *The End of Fashion, Wall Street Journal* reporter Teri Agins blamed it on mass-marketing geniuses — or villains — like Tommy Hilfiger, who branded style to death until what emerged was so watered down and accessible that it lost its cachet.

In the wake of fashion's death, some things are beginning to appear utterly nonsensical, hilarious, and often a little scary to me. Things that I once just accepted I now begin to question. I constantly find myself marveling at the insanity of that *Ab Fab* sensibility that's inherent in the scene.

238

I'd just ordered a skinny latte outside the Fashion Week tents at New York's Bryant Park when the lanky guy behind the counter started looking at me funny.

"Hey, aren't you Donna Karan?"

"Are you serious?" I asked.

He was, and wouldn't believe me when I insisted I wasn't. Okay, so we're both forty-something, brunette, and have weird noses. But otherwise, we look nothing alike. Maybe it was my oversized Armani sunglasses, six-inch Stefan Kelian platforms, Gucci purse, and well-worn Louis Vuitton document case, and the fact that I was wearing leather pants in 80 degree weather, that did it.

I'd unwittingly become a bona fide "fashion person," at least in terms of attire: a *fashionista* caricature, so larger than life that the poor coffee guy just assumed I must be America's most famous female designer.

This was an obvious indication for me that fashion has had it. The coffee guy's mistake struck me as hilarious at first, then a little scary. I couldn't decide whether it was a compliment, or an insult.

That afternoon I went to a Randolph Duke show. He sat me front row center, beside the two biggest stars in the room, Miss USA and Miss Universe, on the prowl for a little glitz to wear to all those functions they have to attend. Evidently, the death of fashion has translated into slim celebrity pickin's at most shows. Except for Donatella Versace (she snagged Rupert Everett and Madonna) and Helmut Lang (he got Hugh Grant), who still make it their business to haul in two or three biggies each time out, the celeb thing at shows is pretty much over.

I made small talk with the beauty queens as we waited for the show to start, and learned it was the first major fashion show for both of them. Before things got underway, they both decided they had to use the toilet, got up, and left. Moments later, a frazzled PR lady wearing a headset ran up to me in a panic.

"Where are they — Miss Universe and Miss USA?" she asked frantically.

"Gone to the washroom," I said.

"Well that's it. They're going to miss the show! We have to start right now."

What irony that these two quasi-celebrities would be missing their first big show, I thought. But just as the lights were about to go down, the lovely duo returned, relieved in more ways than one that they hadn't missed a thing.

The episode left me amused at the notion that people as beautiful and perfect as Miss Universe and Miss USA would ever have to pee at all, especially right before their first big fashion show. The fact that I'd become so immersed in what these babes were up to proved there wasn't too much else going on — and that's scary.

Dying for fashion is an especially scary prospect. So when it was announced that several afternoon shows had been cancelled in anticipation of Hurricane Floyd's arrival, there was a round of applause from anxious editors. Most also assumed that the evening's show by Alexander McQueen would be cancelled, too. As much of a pot-stirring rebel as he is, nobody expected him to endanger our lives by making us schlep out to Pier 55, where his presentation was to be staged. But a recorded message at his publicist's office assured us McQueen's show would go on, no matter what. After all, it was costing him a million dollars to stage — besides, I knew he would be reveling in the fact that he would be inconveniencing all those snooty fashion types.

Prepared to die, about a thousand of us fashion fiends trekked bravely over to the waterfront. And as the rain pounded down, we witnessed McQueen's magic. His runway, a shallow pool of water through which models traipsed, shoes and all, suddenly transformed itself into a bed of giant nails. Above, a veiled woman in black robes, seated in the lotus position, glided by, high above the danger. It was a mystical circus act: a dramatic display of theatrical artistry, a runway presentation elevated into a memorable event.

But in my new and improved state of awareness, the spectacle became a metaphor for the responsibility of a fashion reporter today, now that fashion is pretty much over: stay cool, calm, detached, and above it all. There's no longer a way to ground yourself in this perilous arena. You've got to rise above the dangerous inanity of the scene, this place of mistaken identities and inconveniently full bladders — a world that's robbed us of our rationality and has me actually convinced that zebra is the new leopard.

Fashionably Ever After

This has been the story of a starry-eyed girl who loved to dress up and dream more than anyone she ever knew. Her family encouraged her fantasies and taught her to believe that anything was possible, if you really worked hard and never gave up. The girl worked relentlessly, convinced that if she stayed on track all kinds of wonderful things would happen to her. And they did.

But sad things happened to her, too. There was even a time when she forgot who she was and became so unhappy that she thought she couldn't possibly go on dreaming and dressing up and working so hard anymore. She cried every day, ten times a day, and lost her appetite for life.

But her tears eventually dried, and her appetite for life slowly returned. Eventually, she remembered who she really was once again and why she needed to go on dreaming and working.

And dressing up.

Index